Reading Tolkien in Chinese

Perspectives on Fantasy

Series Editors
Brian Attebery (Idaho State University, USA)
Dimitra Fimi (University of Glasgow, UK)
Matthew Sangster (University of Glasgow, UK)

The first academic series with an exclusive critical focus on Fantasy, *Perspectives on Fantasy* publishes cutting-edge research on literature and culture that brings sophisticated discussion to a broad community of debate, including scholars, students, and non-specialists.

Inspired by Fantasy's deep cultural roots, powerful aesthetic potential, and reach across a broad range of media – from literature, film and television to art, animation and gaming – *Perspectives on Fantasy* provides a forum for theorising and historicising Fantasy via rigorous and original critical and theoretical approaches. Works in the series will cover major creators, significant works, key modes and forms, histories and traditions, the genre's particular affordances, and the ways in which Fantasy's resources have been drawn on, expanded and reconfigured by authors, readers, viewers, directors, designers, players, and artists. With a deliberately broad scope, the series aims to publish dynamic studies that embrace Fantasy as a global, diverse, and inclusive phenomenon while also addressing oversights and exclusions. Along with canonical Anglophone authors and texts, the series will provide a space to address Fantasy creators and works rooted in African, Asian, South American, Middle Eastern, and indigenous cultures, as well as translations and transnational mediations.

The series will be alive to Fantasy's flourishing fan cultures, studying how audiences engage critically and affectively and considering the ease with which participants in Fantasy communities move from being readers and watchers to players, writers, and artists.

Editorial board members
Catherine Butler (Cardiff University, UK)
Paweł Frelik, (University of Warsaw, Poland)
Rachel Haywood Ferreira (Iowa State University, USA)
Robert Maslen (University of Glasgow, UK)
Ebony Elizabeth Thomas (University of Pennsylvania, USA)
Anna Vaninskaya (University of Edinburgh, UK)
Rhys Williams (University of Glasgow, UK)
Helen Young (Deakin University, Australia)

Titles in this Series

Queering Faith in Fantasy Literature: Fantastic Incarnations and the Deconstruction of Theology, Taylor Driggers

William Hope Hodgson and the Rise of the Weird: Possibilities of the Dark, Timothy S. Murphy *Imagining the Celtic Past in Modern Fantasy* edited by Dimitra Fimi and Alistair J. P. Sims

Mapping Middle-earth: Environmental and Political Narratives in J.R.R. Tolkien's Cartographies by Anahit Behrooz

Forthcoming Titles

Justice and the Power of Wonder in 21st-Century Fairy Tales, Cristina Bacchilega and Pauline Greenhill

Fantasy and the Politics of Subversion: Speculative Writing in Colonial India, Mayurika Chakravorty

Femslash Fanfiction: Analysing Queer Time in Swan Queen Fan Narratives, Alice Kelly

Reading Tolkien in Chinese

Religion, Fantasy, and Translation

Eric Reinders

BLOOMSBURY ACADEMIC
LONDON • NEW YORK • OXFORD • NEW DELHI • SYDNEY

BLOOMSBURY ACADEMIC
Bloomsbury Publishing Plc, 50 Bedford Square, London, WC1B 3DP, UK
Bloomsbury Publishing Inc, 1359 Broadway, New York, NY 10018, USA
Bloomsbury Publishing Ireland, 29 Earlsfort Terrace, Dublin 2, D02 AY28, Ireland

BLOOMSBURY, BLOOMSBURY ACADEMIC and the Diana logo are trademarks
of Bloomsbury Publishing Plc

First published in Great Britain 2024
Paperback edition published in 2025

Copyright © Eric Reinders, 2024

Eric Reinders has asserted his right under the Copyright, Designs and Patents Act,
1988, to be identified as Author of this work.

For legal purposes the Acknowledgements on xi constitute an extension
of this copyright page.

Series design by Rebecca Heselton
Cover design by Rebecca Heselton

All rights reserved. No part of this publication may be: i) reproduced or transmitted in any form, electronic or mechanical, including photocopying, recording or by means of any information storage or retrieval system without prior permission in writing from the publishers; or ii) used or reproduced in any way for the training, development or operation of artificial intelligence (AI) technologies, including generative AI technologies. The rights holders expressly reserve this publication from the text and data mining exception as per Article 4(3) of the Digital Single Market Directive (EU) 2019/790.

Bloomsbury Publishing Plc does not have any control over, or responsibility for, any third-party websites referred to or in this book. All internet addresses given in this book were correct at the time of going to press. The author and publisher regret any inconvenience caused if addresses have changed or sites have ceased to exist, but can accept no responsibility for any such changes.

A catalogue record for this book is available from the British Library.

A catalog record for this book is available from the Library of Congress.

ISBN: HB: 978-1-3503-7464-5
PB: 978-1-3503-7468-3
ePDF: 978-1-3503-7465-2
eBook: 978-1-3503-7466-9

Series: Perspectives on Fantasy

Typeset by RefineCatch Limited, Bungay, Suffolk

For product safety related questions contact productsafety@bloomsbury.com.

To find out more about our authors and books visit www.bloomsbury.com
and sign up for our newsletters.

For Vivian

Contents

Acknowledgements		xi
Notes on Citation		xii
Abbreviations		xiii

Part 1 Religion, Fantasy, and Translation

1	Religion and Fantasy—What's the Difference?	3
2	Translation, an Elven Craft	13
3	Tolkien in Chinese: Books and Titles	25
4	Genre across Cultures, and in Middle-earth	39

Part 2 Reading Tolkien in Chinese

5	Gods and Heathens	55
6	Elves and "Men"	69
7	Race	86
8	Hell and Other Theories	100
9	White Shores and Beyond	113
10	Fate and Doom	125
11	Language	138
12	Magical Language	149
13	And Back Again	160

Bibliography	163
Index	175

Acknowledgements

My thanks to Deng Jiawan for generously sharing her thoughts on her work.

I am grateful to Emory University's Department of Religion, under two chairs: Gary Laderman and María Carrión. And our exemplary staff: Toni Avery, Candice George, Emiaya Curry, and Andy Boyles. Emory College of Arts and Sciences funded a trip to Taiwan with a Program to Enhance Research and Scholarship grant. The Emory Confucius Institute sponsored the presentation of a part of my research. I attest that financial support has not influenced anything I have written.

My gratitude also goes to: Chung Yu-ling of National Taiwan University of Science and Technology, and to Ya-chun Liu of the University of Leeds, for conversations on literature and translation in Taiwan. To Chen Tingting of Anhui University, for her assessment of stylistic qualities of the translations. To Dimitra Fimi for sage advice. To Robin Anne Reid, for helping me reconceive a rather miscellaneous chapter into one focused on race. To Brian Attebery, editor of the *Journal for the Fantastic in the Arts*, and the anonymous reviewers of my tentative first publication in this area. To the three reviewers of my proposal to Bloomsbury, for constructive and helpful advice. And to Lucy Brown and Aanchal Vij at Bloomsbury.

Many friends and colleagues: Cai Rong, Wendy Farley, Bill Gilders, Li Hong, Deborah Monroy, Maria Franca Sibau, Thee Smith, Yu Li, Mike Walsh. My companions in the translation theory reading group hosted by the Bill and Carol Fox Center for Humanistic Inquiry: Lisa Dillman, Angela Porcarelli, Jon Masters, Julia Bullock, Peter Höyng, Jenny Wang Medina, Li Hong, Cheryl Crowley. My research assistant, Victoria Shen.

A number of academic organizations were helpful. The Tolkien Society, for two seminars, on "Tolkien and Diversity" (July 2021) and "Translating and Illustrating Tolkien" (November 2021), ably hosted by the Tolkien Society Education Secretary, Will Sherwood. The organizers and many participants of the International Conference on the Fantastic in the Arts (ICFA) facilitated my early attempts to articulate what interested me about Tolkien in Chinese. I also benefitted from a meeting of the American Literary Translators Association. Thanks to the organizers and participants of the 2016 conference "Translation and Religion: Interrogating Concepts, Methods and Practices" at the University of Edinburgh. Thanks to William Fliss, archivist at the John P. Raynor, S.J. Library of Marquette University. Thanks too to Chad and Steve, Fans for Christ.

As much as I learn about the works of Tolkien, I have repeatedly been humbled and enlivened by the fannish scholars and scholarly fans who post to the forums of the One Ring.net. For example: N. E. Brigand, Pryderi, dernwyn, CuriousG, Dreamdeer, squire, Aunt Dora Baggins, Elthir, Lissuin, Ataahua, Otaku-sempai, acheron, and Cirashala. When we hear so much about internet trolls and online abuse, it's worth acknowledging an online space of good humor, erudition, and generosity.

Notes on Citation

The Return of the King is, in different translations, *Wangzhe Huilai*, or *Wangzhe Zailin*, or *Wangzhe Wudi*. For the sake of clarity, I will refer parenthetically to the Chinese texts using the translators (Deng, Zhu, or Wu) or the publishing house (Yilin), and then the *original English name* of the book in abbreviated form, plus page number. Hence: (Deng *RK*: 25) instead of (Deng, *Wangzhe Huilai*, 25). This departs from conventional usage, but moving briskly among multiple translations, it would otherwise be difficult to keep track of which book I'm quoting. Similarly, when back-translating from Chinese I will rarely reproduce the various Chinese pronunciations of proper names, as it would be hard to catch that Jialadeli-er, also known as Gailadeli-er, or Kailancui-er—is Galadriel.

I follow citation conventions of the journal *Tolkien Studies* ("Conventions and Abbreviations"). Due to the large number of editions, I will cite the original texts of *The Lord of the Rings* by book, chapter, and page, and *The Hobbit* by chapter and page. For example, *Fellowship* book two, chapter 4, page 318, would be: (*FR*, II, iv, 318). However, I will not use this method on the translations, as these generally follow references to the English original, and of which there are far fewer editions in any case.

In the original and most translations, in *The Return of the King*, when the main story ends and the text continues into the Appendixes, the page numbers continue in sequence, with two exceptions. Zhu's translation gives the Appendixes a different set of numbers, running in the *opposite* direction (starting with page 1 on the last page of the book). Hence, a citation such as (Zhu *RK*: 50) is ambiguous—there are two page 50s in the book. Citations to Zhu's translation of the Appendixes must be specified as such: (Zhu *RK* Appendix: 50). The same is the case for the supplementary matter at the end of Deng's 2002 translation of *The Silmarillion*.

I have inserted Chinese characters only for key terms and to avoid ambiguity, and in traditional or simplified form depending on the text I am quoting.

Abbreviations

FR	The Fellowship of the Rings
H	The Hobbit
Húrin	The Children of Húrin
JW	Journey to the West (Xiyouji)
LOTR	The Lord of the Rings
OED	Oxford English Dictionary
OFS	On Fairy-stories
RK	The Return of the King
S	The Silmarillion
TT	The Two Towers
UT	Unfinished Tales of Númenor and Middle-earth

Part One

Religion, Fantasy, and Translation

1

Religion and Fantasy—What's the Difference?

The annual fantasy/science fiction convention known as Dragon-con is for me a religious event. It's partly just being around 80,000 people having fun, which does rather alter one's consciousness. It's partly the pervasive presence of religions in the mix—Kali in the parade, Jesus in the lobby. But mainly, it's the *pretending*. Large numbers of people show up in costume. They start acting "in character," and people play along. No one says, "Are you *really* Darth Vader?" (Gosetti-Ferencei 2018: 43; Hale 2014). No one calls the bluff. We're all in on the joke. We simultaneously behave as if that woman *is and isn't* Galadriel. It is a collaborative, communal performance of the double-vision inherent to cosplay, and indeed inherent to all fiction. As Jennifer Anna Gosetti-Ferencei remarks, "play and fiction allow split reference and attention to the real and to the possible"—though I would add, to the impossible as well (2018: 71, also 89–90).

Translation is also a kind of fantasy, an *is and isn't* at the same time—the Source Language word is, and yet never is, the Target Language word used to translate it. Especially among languages that are historically unrelated, said Friedrich Schleiermacher, "not a single word in one language will correspond perfectly to a word in another" (2021: 46). Umberto Eco called the perfect correspondence of two words "an impossible dream" (2001: ix). And yet, we can seriously pretend (or have faith) that two different things are the same. We easily forget they're not the same.

To play with the metaphors: translation is language acting in character, language doing cosplay. Mark Polizzotti uses a more sinister metaphor: "In some ways, translation and spying are natural bedfellows: both involve double allegiances, parallel modes of expression, the ability to observe and interpret; to jump, like a seasoned performer, from one role to another" (2018: 33). Translation is one language spying on another?

This double vision or dual allegiance is often called the willing suspension of disbelief, a phrase coined by S. T. Coleridge. William Wordsworth specialized in "realistic" observations of natural phenomena which nonetheless produce a sublime effect; and Coleridge is famous for his supernatural fantasy which even so tells us some kind of truth. Coleridge wrote: "my endeavours should be directed to persons and characters supernatural, or at least romantic; yet so as to transfer from our inward nature a human interest and a semblance of truth sufficient to procure for these shadows of imagination that willing suspension of disbelief for the moment, which constitutes poetic faith" (2004: 490). The word "faith" is certainly telling here, signaling a central concern of the Romantics: the intersections of the the imagination and the sacred.

We basically *don't* believe that the woman in the lobby is Galadriel, but we momentarily "suspend" our skepticism. Tolkien, however, considered Coleridge's famous phrase too circuitous, and wanted to call it a certain kind of *believing*. The double negative was too convoluted for the immediacy of what happens when we lose ourselves in a story. He called it enchantment, a spell, the elven craft. He writes of being *inside* a story. To describe the experience of reading fantasy, he uses the language of the fantasy world itself—magic, spells, entering a new world, becoming someone else. Tolkien's comments on Faerie drift ambiguously over several meanings, including both a magical realm and our human imagination of (and desire for) that realm (Milburn 2010: 55).

I suggest the vocabulary of all three categories—religion, fantasy, translation—may be used fruitfully on each of the three, and on their intersections. In her poetic meditation on translation, *This Little Art*, Kate Briggs similarly connects the three themes of religion, fantasy, and translation:

> this is what reading offers us: occasions for inappropriate, improbable identification. For powerful reality-suspending identification with a character, a writer, an idea, an experience, a fantasy. Fantasies that apparently have nothing to do with me—isn't this, in its way, the power of fantasy?—that do not appear to directly concern or pertain to me. But that catch me up nonetheless. Like a complicated miracle. Like the everyday complicated miracle of reading books written by other people—especially, perhaps, books in translation. (2017: 171)

Similarly, Polizzotti notes "the nervous-making reality is that all communication rests on a suspension of disbelief" (2018: 32). All reading, all moments of communication, have something death-defying about them. Briggs' book on translation, a novelistic portrait of the semiotic chaos that a translator goes through, constantly wavers in the double vision of translation: she notes how easily we say we've read a book without remembering that it was *in translation* (2017: 43–44; see also Venuti 1986; Kadiu 2019). We might observe it at the start ("translated from the Chinese by …"), but once we're "in" the story, we forget it. There are moments when we experience a hiccup such as a translator's footnote, and then we remember it's a translation, but then slide right back into not thinking about it. Why would we, when the story is so inviting? Translators and academics may be interested in translation, but readers are in it for the story.

Coleridge noted the same thing in a slightly different sense: he observed the obvious point that a play is an imitation of reality, not an accurate copy, but notes "the impassive Slumber of our Sense of Probability when we hear an Actor announce himself a Greek, Roman, Venetian or Persian in good Mother English" (2004: 337). Or when we read Frodo speaking Chinese. Or, in fact, *English*. True, "impassive Slumber of our Sense of Probability" rolls off the tongue somewhat less than the "willing suspension of disbelief," but it refers to the same phenomenon, whether regarding the fantastic in poetry, the art of the actor, the craft of the cosplayer, the illusions of translation, or the counter-empirical claims of religion. I put my Sense of Probability to sleep at page one. In some religious traditions in which it is called "faith," suspending disbelief is a supreme virtue.

Religion, Fantasy, and Truth

A man rises from the dead, and we call it fantasy; a man rises from the dead and we call it religion. What's the difference? Both kinds of stories have marvels, the normally impossible, but religious stories are different, due to their insistence, their urgency, and the high stakes (such as your immortal soul). A reader who claims to believe *The Lord of the Rings* to be literally true is suspected of irony, performance, or mental illness; one who claims the Bible is literally true has the support of a very large segment of Christians, and enjoys various kinds of legal protection of their "freedom of belief." Religious and fantastic stories have different social positions, rhetorical registers, and genre expectations. But the key difference seems to be truth. A religious story is presented as true. Certainly, when Jesus tells the story of the prodigal son, no one believes it to be true—it's a parable—but the fact that *he said it* is presented as true. And it is assumed there is some truth "behind" the story. Even for Christian believers who do not subscribe to a literalist reading, the Gospels must still be true—*somehow*. What kind of "true" is this? In what sense, *somehow*?

Ursula K. Le Guin writes,

> Fantasy is true, of course. It isn't factual, but it is true. Children know that. Adults know it too, and that is precisely why many of them are afraid of fantasy. They know that its truth challenges, even threatens, all that is phony, unnecessary, and trivial in the life they have let themselves be forced into living. They are afraid of dragons, because they are afraid of freedom. (1979: 44)

This view of adulthood strikes me as polemical hyperbole—are adults who don't like fantasy literature really *afraid* of it? (Tolkien makes a similar implication when he says that people belittle fairy stories because of "disquiet and consequent dislike" (*OFS* 60).) Have they been *forced* into a phony life? (Was she channeling Holden Caulfield?) But the question here is still: what is this "truth" that is not "factual"? We all understand what she's saying: through a fiction involving the normally impossible, a writer may say things fundamental about ourselves which might be inaccessible in a realist novel or in non-fiction. And the very experience of imagining an unreal thing also gives us something we can't find elsewhere. If there is a conspicuous divergence from empirical factuality, there may yet be insight, vividness, and clarity. Le Guin does not oppose fantasy's truth to falsity, but to the phony, unnecessary, and trivial.

Le Guin warns against the automatic assumption that if a story has a dragon in it, it's not worth reading. What then is the truth of a dragon? Or an elf? Or a god? For the purposes of this exercise, I am suspending any judgment on whether these terms refer to real things or purely fictional objects. I differ with Tolkien: a suspension of disbelief also requires a suspension of belief. Tolkien *wanted* to believe (in his God, and also in Faerie). Deep down it would never be enough for him merely to temporarily *not disbelieve* in God. So, I set aside the question of "belief" in the religious sense. In any case, belief may not be nearly as important as used to be thought—certainly no one in Religious Studies today wants to reduce "religion" to "belief."

Some might be affronted if I talk about religion as fantasy, because it sounds like I'm saying, religion (or more annoyingly, *your* religion) is not true. Yet no less pious an authority than Tolkien wrote: "The Gospels contain a fairy-story, or a story of a larger kind which embraces all the essence of fairy-stories" (*OFS*: 77–78). Of course, he added that the Gospel is the *best* fairy story, because in addition to being a good story, it is true—by which he meant: it actually happened. In the best fairy stories, he wrote, there is a deepening sense of inevitable doom, but then "the sudden, joyous 'turn'" (*OFS*: 75). All would seem to be lost—the blameless hero is even *dead*—and then he rises from the dead in a moment of "sudden and miraculous grace: never to be counted on to recur" (*OFS*: 75). The Happy Ending of a good story mimics the Happy Ending of the Christian story (at least if you're on the side of the angels). "The Christian joy, the *Gloria*, is of the same kind … But this story is supreme; and it is true. Art has been verified" (*OFS*: 78). Ultimately, for Tolkien, truth must be more than mere affect (Coutras 2016: 31). I don't share the theology but that's an interesting way of thinking about religion and fantasy. If Tolkien thought fantasies may be little bits of God, I would add, gods may be big bits of fantasy.

He was not the first to make the connection between fiction and divine creation. George MacDonald, for example, wrote that imagination is "that faculty in man which is likest to the prime operation of the power of God" (1893: 2). And: "The imagination of man is made in the image of the imagination of God" (ibid., 3). Tolkien's theories here derive in part from MacDonald, or from the tradition of understanding imagination as divine. Going further back might take us, for example, into the literature of philosophizing about the Sublime, that emotionally overpowering sensation, closely related to horror, so central to the Gothic and the Romantic (Castle 1966: xxii; also Brady 2012: 43–45).

The conceptual impetus for this book was the possibility of a cross-cultural comparison of imaginations—a comparison not of ideas about "imagination," but of what is imagined, or even the experience of imagining. It is impossible to specify the content of "imagination itself." Still, we certainly have access to the inherited *formulae* of imagination, and there of course we find difference and similarity, distinct patterns, discernable *shapes* of the vast *et cetera*. Religion and fantasy both posit superhuman powers which, being non-empirical and non-denotable, feel suggestive of something profound—as John McRae once wrote (of Chan mythology), "it's not true, and therefore it's more important" (2003: xix).

Miracles and Fairies

"Science fiction began to separate from fantasy when science began to deliver on the promises made by alchemists and magicians" (Attebery 1992: 106). Science, as a materialist and empiricist mode of thinking, emerged as consciously independent of any church, gained momentum and explanatory power, and accumulated an impressive record of achieving tangible results, so that "religion" shrank—it either retrenched itself in opposition to "science," with a heightened emphasis on "faith" (here meaning more than just "trust," but conceived of as the virtue of believing in something *without empirical evidence*); or it withdrew its jurisdiction, no longer claiming that lightning bolts were direct acts of God, no longer claiming the world was created in six days. For some, the Bible's contradiction with empirical science was reason enough to reject the whole thing. For those who accepted science but wished to remain in some sense Christian, a negotiation was needed—and the first item on the agenda was the miraculous.

Starting (at least) with Enlightenment thinkers such as Spinoza, Voltaire, and Hume, the dominant trend in scholarly interpretation of the Bible has been to treat miracles as impossible. Spinoza made the argument that a God who made the "laws of Nature" could not then break His own rules. Hume associated belief in miracles with fiction, superstition, and low social class (Alkier and Moffitt 2013: 317). If a miracle was not possible, then by definition it must belong to delusion, or *fiction*. Alkier and Moffitt outline various attempts to explain biblical miracles, including the views that these stories come from a more primitive stage of humanity, or that the real events were simply misunderstood. Exorcisms *might* be factual as long as they are understood as a pre-modern form of psychotherapy, but no one can *really* walk on water. Most importantly, these events come to be read as stories which code Truth deeper than the mere (and now rejected) factuality of the words. This "demythologizing" approach is associated with Rudolf Bultmann, and later with John Macquarrie, who understood miracles as "true legend" (Alkier and Moffitt 2013: 332). Macquarrie writes,

> although existential interpretation of a story does not in itself deny the factual content of the story, it certainly does put that content 'in brackets', so to speak. The objective reference becomes bracketed in the sense that interest has shifted away from it to the existential significance. The question of fact is no longer being raised. (1960: 19)

In critical scholarship on the Bible and more generally in any "scientific" thinking about religion, miracles were the first to go. For many, by definition miracles could not be taken literally, and thus were either rejected entirely (along with the rest of the Bible perhaps), or reinterpreted in various ways which attempted to excuse the authors of lying and which attempted to preserve some value to the stories. Miracles became parables.

There is always a widespread desire for and belief in the scientifically impossible, yet today that appetite is as likely to be satisfied by Tarot, astrology, New Age spirituality, conspiracy theories, alien abduction stories, guardian angels, a warm fuzzy animism, and most of all by *fiction*, as by any form of Christianity. The desire to experience the normally impossible never went away, but the rise of science as an ideology and its mirror-image fundamentalism seem to have rearranged where that desire manifested. One might say that the fictionalizing of the miraculous encouraged the miraculizing of fiction.

It is worth juxtaposing this relocation of the miraculous with the thinning of the fairies. In Carole Silver's *Strange and Secret Peoples: Fairies and Victorian Consciousness* (1999), we see a variety of phenomena blamed for the disappearance of fairies: urbanization, standardized education (185); "cheap newspapers" (193); pollution, industry (200–203, 209); "rationalism" (200); "electrification" (203); "science" (185, 204); and a dominant mood of disbelief in anything (199–203). These changes challenged belief in the literal truth of the Christian Bible as much as belief in fairies, but fairies were also persecuted by Christianity (185, 197–199). Biblical miracles and fairies were both explained (away) in rationalistic terms, but fairies were also driven out by a more dominant religion.

But not without a fight. We see an analogy with the literalist defense of miracles in the efforts to scientifically prove the real existence of fairies, which met with no greater success. Silver writes, "the tendency to render the elfin peoples material and/or scientific inadvertently diminished their importance" (1999: 185; see also Purkiss 2000: 284–293). If one saw through the Cottingley photographs (of fairies, or paper cutouts), the lesson was that fairies don't exist and anyone who believed in them was a fool; yet even if one accepted the photographs, the fairies in them are barely there: children's butterflies, pathetically diminished from the menacing folk of old, and not very mysterious after all. Popular fiction itself was blamed for the decline in authentic (i.e., folkloric) belief (Silver 1999: 186). For example, Andrew Lang complaining about the proliferation of fairies in fiction, because the creative elaborations of authors such as Lewis Carroll and J. M. Barrie had overwhelmed or compromised the traditional folklore (Silver 1999: 188). Similarly, novelists and film-makers have flooded the market of miracles. It's getting so that rising from the dead isn't really all that impressive any more.

Onto the story of modern disbelief in miracles and fairies, a narrative of the rise of fantasy and science fiction may be superimposed. If the literal truth of the miraculous was to remain in Christianity, it could only survive either by occupying a space of half-belief (a delicate philosophical what-if—a faith in faith itself), or in the besieged castle of fundamentalism, not coincidentally the form of Christianity most hostile to fantasy fiction. The magical imagination of the normally impossible (which used to reside in religion) took refuge in both fantasy and science fiction. Fantasy is a discourse which preserves the sacramentalism, the mystic potency, the sense of infinite possibility and meaning, without the burden of having to actually believe it to be true. Fantasy's relation to reality is ironic and metaphorical, more of a playful riddle (Roberts 2013: 5–6; Attebery 2014: 21). By contrast, science fiction is a discourse which attempts to express those same aspects of wonder while using the language of science to obscure its contradiction with reality.

Hence, "scepticism about the possibility of supernatural influence on the world (as what was understood as supernatural fell to scientific explanation) opened a space for a playful approach to the fantastic" (Mendlesohn and James 2009: 15). The miraculous and the fairies thinned—or rather, evicted by science and feeling no longer welcome in religion, they snuck out to find new homes in other places, and above all settled in the welcoming home of children's literature and later fantasy fiction, to be treated as guests rather than embarrassments, and no longer forced to shoulder the ill-fitting mantle of literal truth.

Flies in the Ointment

Amidst my annual pilgrimage to Dragon-con's festival of the miraculous, I find two groups rather dissonant. First is a group called Fans for Christ, and second, its apparent opposite, the Skeptics Track.

Fans for Christ existed from 2003 to 2016; an "offshoot" called The Bridge is currently represented at Dragon-con. Related groups include Geeks Under Grace, Costumers for Christ, Geeky Guys for God, and other experiments in alliteration. Before the ministry ended, I interviewed some Fans for Christ at Dragon-con, and they reported a variety of concerns: not being mocked by all the cool kids there, and feeling alienated by some of the more demonic or bacchanalian imagery at the event. One, named Chad, described an almost schizophrenic situation. When people at Dragon-con see their FFC table, he said, "a lot of people are relieved that they can find a place where they can not feel like they have to hide one side or the other of themselves, hide their Christian side around their more geeky friends, hide their geeky side from their church friends." He noted "the prejudice that comes from the average person in the church."

And when I asked about the well-publicized protests and warnings about Harry Potter, for example, coming from certain voices within American Evangelical culture, another Fan for Christ, Steve, remarked, "you're not going to learn how to do magic from any of these things any more than watching *ER* or *Grey's Anatomy* is going to teach you how to do surgery." Good point. These are people I would generally categorize as mainstream evangelical, and they are aware of the potential dissonance of fantasy and their religious beliefs, yet have found ways to reconcile these tensions. They might well join Tolkien in recognizing the similarities between the Gospel and certain fantasy stories, but like Tolkien retain the crucial difference: the Gospel's irreducible truth. Yet, Chad's remark about hiding his enjoyment of fantasy from his church friends signals a tension which others have sought not to resolve but to exacerbate.

Fundamentalism began as a late nineteenth-century reaction against Modernist theology, biblical criticism, certain types of science, and non-religious culture in general. It focused on a set of "fundamentals" including the infallibility of scripture and the historical factuality of the miracles of Jesus. Extending from the specific case, the term has come to mean a conservative literalism in the reading of scripture, and more broadly any kind of dogmatic insistence on the absolute truth of a text—though obviously not of all texts. When a story is placed into the category of scripture, it separates itself from general storytelling: "because many accept it as the divine Word, by a cognitive disconnect it becomes removed from notions of variant phrasings and external cultures" (Polizzotti 2018: 26). Scripture is a distinct genre, one which presents itself as not merely the product of a particular human context, but in its essence, outside of time and place. It's *always* true.

Literalism in interpretation sometimes produces belief in the magical potency of words. The translator Deng Jiawan was amused to tell me of a church pastor in Taiwan who banned his congregation from watching *The Lord of the Rings* simply because of the word *mo* 魔 (magic, but also demonic) in the series title, *mojie* 魔戒 ("magic ring"). Literalism is based on a naïve and "magical" understanding of language, the notion that there is a one-to-one correspondence of the word to the thing—hence the word *mo* is itself magical/demonic. In fact, as a believer in the potency of words, Tolkien also shied away from too explicitly describing evil, for fear the words themselves would be a conduit of Evil (Petty 2011: 57). Sauron and the balrog are evoked rather than described.

In any rigidly literalistic reading there are only two kinds of propositions: true and false; and all true statements are true in the same way. I call this the monologic of truth.

Whatever ingenious devices are used to make this tribal chronicle from the Iron Age speak to me personally today, this kind of reading presents itself as quite simple, and deliberately unsophisticated. The evangelical claim is: we read the Bible without interpretation. And of course that's not possible. All reading is interpretive, and in their particular case, their texts come to them already highly interpreted. Thinking you're reading without interpretation is an interpretation. At best, it's aspirational. It signals a desire to receive God's word without human mediation.

So, naturally, fundamentalists sometimes find fiction rather difficult. Fiction is language with great power to change our minds while being obviously untrue. I am reminded of John Calvin's objection to theater—not to bad theater which is obviously unreal but to good theater, which successfully deceives us. But on the other hand, Tolkien discusses the question of whether children are really *deceived* by fairy stories. When children ask, "is it true?" Tolkien says, this question arises from the child's desire to classify the story (*OFS*: 53). I'm all for giving children credit, but is this explanation plausible? Surely sometimes children really do believe, at least in some of the stories (Gosetti-Ferenci 2018: 90, 92). In defense of fairy stories, Tolkien sets aside the possibility of a child being deceived, while literalist readings set aside the possibility of a child *not* being deceived.

Dragon-con celebrates all things unreal, yet the Skeptics Track is a full program of around 27 sessions over four days, devoted to debunking delusions. In 2017, the events included panels promoting "critical thinking," "skepticism," "atheism, "applying science to the paranormal," "scientific and skeptical outreach," and "how to effectively deal with faith-based claims." The Skeptics Track primarily critiques dogmatic religion, as if all Christians were fundamentalists. But science also operates on a monologic of truth. The willing suspension of disbelief has a kind of opposite, the destructive aggression of disbelief: here's the magician pulling a rabbit from his hat, and someone thinks it a moral imperative to point out the hidden compartment. A "new strain of 'aggressive reason' took hold in Europe at the end of the 17th century" (Davies 2019: 20) and following in this tradition, someone "breaks" the spell, "shatters" the illusion. The rhetoric of scientific truth-telling is often about breaking, unmasking, exposing, penetrating, and dissecting.

Allegory

One very common way of reading a truth in a text one knows to be non-factual is by way of allegory. Tolkien rather famously resisted the urge to interpret his works allegorically, perhaps because C. S. Lewis and others had made their allegories too obvious, or because he did not want to be seen as writing in the genre of scripture. Adam Roberts for example concedes, "We need to take Tolkien's cordial dislike seriously" (2013: 12). And he explains: "Taking the characters of any story 'allegorically' is to subordinate their individuality to some larger scheme, a notion repellent to Tolkien on religious and ideological as well as artistic grounds" (ibid., 12; see also Ashford 2018: 26). And yet, when Tolkien and Lewis are invariably cited (for example, by evangelicals at Dragon-con) as *Christian* writers of fantasy, inevitably some form of reading is "allegorical" at least in the sense of understanding one story in terms of another. What needs to be avoided is simplistic formulae such as "Aslan is really Jesus" or "the Ring is Satan," but it strikes me as futile to expect readers not to see one story as like another, and then to make systematic comparisons. A good deal of Tolkien studies scholarship explores the comparison to the Bible. I asked Deng Jiawan whether the fact that she is a Christian mattered to her translation of Tolkien's works, and her answer immediately went to biblical symbolism:

> I feel it was relevant. For example, a very simple thing was, every time they had some trouble, it was always the eagles that came to save them.... It's in *The Hobbit*, and then it's in *Lord of the Rings*. It's also in *The Silmarillion*. And in *The Children of Húrin*... So, the concept of the eagles saving them, this idea or concept, this is in the Bible. So, in other words, Tolkien used a lot of this kind of thing. If you are familiar with the Bible, as soon as you read ... the stories of Middle Earth, immediately there's the Biblical background—immediately. (Deng 2017)

She isn't saying "eagles = Holy Spirit," but the recurrent trope of being saved takes on special significance which she feels might be lost on someone unaware of the Christian Gospel, whereas for her the significance is "immediately" present in her reading. Tolkien's widely known Catholicism predisposes some readers to see the trope and think of it as analogous to Christian salvation. Deng views the entire oeuvre in biblical terms:

> Middle Earth's structure and the Bible's structure are the same. For example, he wrote a creation, a Fall, and a return. So, the Old Testament is Creation and Fall, and after various kinds of losses, the New Testament is the return of the King. That King is Jesus. So the structure of his Middle Earth is like this. (Deng 2017)

Allegory is only one of many hermeneutic strategies. There is no clear limit to or rule about what "outside" elements a reader might bring to their reading of a text. It might include seeing Aragorn as Jesus. It might even include whatever happens to be occurring outside as you pause in reading and look out through your window (Briggs 2017: 53). The resources we all bring, to feel the nuances of a text, are always eclectic and promiscuous, whether we interpret them as the intention of the author or quirks of our own minds. As Ludwig Wittgenstein wrote, on the chaos of what we bring to reading: "The book is full of life—not like a man, but like an ant-heap" (1980: 62).

Conclusions

The goal of this chapter was to lay out some of the intersections between religion and fantasy, especially regarding the suspension of disbelief. Despite being obviously made up, fantasy is "true" in Le Guin's terms—or in Tolkien's terms, stories to be "believed" (not merely not-disbelieved). This hermeneutics is basically the same as that of religious faith, except where scripture is taken literally, as in the case of fundamentalist reading. In reading fantasy and in modernist Christianity, affect is more important than affirmation of the truth of a set of propositions. Diverging from an assumption of scripture as factual, the liberal Christian mode of reading miracles sets aside factuality to find a much more important truth; this is also a description of reading fantasy fiction, which however no one ever claims as factual.

I have noted that translation also involves a kind of faith or magic, what Briggs calls the "everyday complicated miracle of reading" (2017: 171). Since this is a study of Tolkien in translation, the next chapter deals with translation in more depth. Rather than treating the original text as an absolute standard and focusing only on what is "lost," I want to reverse or suspend the hierarchy of original and translations, in order to read the translations as stories in their own right. Doing so is, I believe, consistent with contemporary Translation Studies theory, and also with Tolkien's own writings on storytelling.

2

Translation, an Elven Craft

"Versions of the Same Story"

Tolkien wrote his essay "On Fairy-stories" at a time when he felt structuralist anthropologists and folklorists were disassembling stories and evaluating them only in terms of their shared elements, and thereby diminishing the creative specificity of each storytelling. Structuralist understandings of narrative seemed to fragment stories into pieces, as if the sequences and individual variations didn't matter, while at the same time reducing all the variations into some ur-story or single system. The tradition of analysis epitomized by James George Frazer's *The Golden Bough* (1890–1915) and Joseph Campbell's *The Hero with a Thousand Faces* (1949) similarly makes every story more or less the same story. Certainly Campbell and others in that vein acknowledge the uniqueness of each individual story, but the overall approach always prioritizes the "monomyth." Yet, the "monomyth" tells us almost nothing. If you have a template that "fits" literally every single story, you've created a generalization so abstract that it describes no story in particular (Attebery 2014: 108).

An exclusive emphasis on the shared elements, Tolkien argued, produces a distortion of all the stories. The particular details matter (*OFS* 39–41). To evoke the mingling, promiscuous nature of stories, he used the metaphor of people adding and recombining ingredients of a soup in a vast cauldron. No storyteller has absolute originality, but newness is always possible. Each retelling attempts to set the stage anew, playing with the tension between the reader's expectations and the author's innovation. In Brian Attebery's terms, a dialectic between fantasy as *mode* (pure imagination) and fantasy as *formula* generates fantasy as *genre* (1992: 2–4). On this point—on insisting on the uniqueness of each telling of a story—I side with Tolkien. Each retelling is its own domain.

So, from one point of view, with the original text by Tolkien and three Chinese translations, we still have only one story; from another perspective, we have four. We could plausibly say, we have four "versions" of the "same story," but my approach is still to say: we have four stories. A story is much more than just plot. While there is an obvious relation between the original texts and the various translations, the whole point of this book is to take the differences seriously. To treat them as one story would be to impose a kind of categorical domestication on the translations, which Lawrence Venuti has criticized as "illusionism" (2005: 182). Despite appearances, the original text and the translations considered here are not "the same story." Even the most "faithful" translation is a new telling; to be considered "as iteration, as repetition-with-a-difference, a mode of textual proliferation rather than a mode by which semantic content is transferred" (Emmerich 2017: 161; see also Hutcheon 2012: 16).

Translation as a pure mode is something ineffable, like Walter Benjamin's mystical theology of "pure language" (1996: 257; Eco 2001: 10). We can't access "pure translation" as such, because it is an abstraction relying on the illusion of a "meaning" which is not in any particular language. The match of any two words is always imperfect, the overlap always only partial: this is the case within a language as much as between languages, though the "between" here invites us to think in terms of transactions and migration and transference, of a "meaning" which has somehow left one language and not yet landed in another. Yet, as Wittgenstein wrote, "When I think in language, there aren't 'meanings' going through my mind in addition to the verbal expressions: the language is itself the vehicle of thought" (1958: 107).

Pretend that the first time you are reading the story is in the Chinese—or even, imagine that Tolkien translated it from Chinese, or *wrote* it in Chinese. Looking at a translation, comparing it to the original but also allowing its own new vision, gives one a unique experience, a mirror image. To use the Dickensian/Chestertonian metaphor Tolkien picked from the soup, the same text is now seen from *another side*, like the words "Coffee Room" on a window in a train station, seen from the inside. What is this "Mooreeffoc?" One of the gods of Pegana? Or a city Marco Polo passed through, or a spice, or a password, or a dragon? "The word Mooreeffoc may cause you suddenly to realize that England is an utterly alien land" (*OFS*: 68). By the merest change of perspective, a banality is transformed into a spell, a fragment of the "elvish craft" (*OFS*: 61), a trigger for "imagined wonder" (*OFS*: 35). A translation is surely Mooreeffoc writ large, or rather—small: applied word-by-word to the fine grain of the sub-created world, whereby we realize that Middle-earth is also an alien land—*once again* alien, as if we are reading it for the first time, free from "the drab blur of triteness or familiarity—from possessiveness" (*OFS*: 67). I would never call Tolkien's works trite, but they have become familiar—especially to those most enthusiastic about them. After multiple rereadings of the books we might eventually become so familiar with Lothlórien that its name is, so to speak, etched in glass at Bletchley train station. The texts need to be re-foreignized. By means of a translation we move from one side of the glass to the other. Having turned a Coffee Room into Mooreeffoc, we might wonder what this newly and doubly unknown place Néirolhtol might be like. As Wittgenstein said using a similar metaphor, "Language is a labyrinth of paths. You approach from *one* side and know your way about; you approach the same place from another side and no longer know your way about" (1958: 82).

Looking at something mundane and perceiving something far greater is surely one of the strongest potencies of fantasy; as Gosetti-Ferencei wrote, "imagination may be involved in our perception of reality by registering its halo of potentiality and in the projection of a unified world that provides context for such perception" (2018: 71). Anything we see in the real world can be given such a "halo," even such ordinary things as "stone, and wood, and iron; tree and grass; house and fire; bread and wine" (*OFS*: 69). And when a story has lost its magical radiance from overuse, a translation can bestow a fresh nimbus. As Tolkien wrote,

Creative fantasy, because it is mainly trying to do something else (make something new), may open your hoard and let all the locked things fly away like cage-birds. The gems all turn into flowers or flames, and you will be warned that all you had (or knew) was dangerous and potent, not really effectively chained, free and wild, no more yours than they were you. (*OFS*: 68)

In considering familiarity as a kind of cognitive possessiveness or "intellectual greed" (MacDonald 1893: 322) from which we should free ourselves, in emphasizing the great "recovery" of cleansing one's perceptions to see the world anew in all its potency and beauty, Tolkien sounds rather Buddhist. The world becomes a magical or sacred place—even a coffee room can have a halo—through the free play of our imagination, and the slightest change of perspective on the most familiar thing is a catalyst of that transformation. I would like to think of translation in these terms—as a magical or even sacred alchemy.

Wittgenstein wrote, "to imagine a language means to imagine a form of life" (1958: 8). The task of any fantasy writer is to make us imagine a different form of life using a language which is, despite its occasional foreignisms, still ours (or close enough). For Tolkien, to make that form of life convincingly different from our own world meant excluding explicit Christian references, though the stories are rooted in a Christian sensibility. Because Middle-earth is an entirely invented world, anachronism, especially at the level of word choice, must be avoided. No Queen Victoria, no Bletchley, no French Impressionism. The description of Gandalf's dragon rocket passing over Bilbo's party "like an express train" (*FR*, I, i, 27) is jarring, and Dimitra Fimi notes other possible anachronisms in the material culture of the Shire: tobacco, potatoes, umbrellas, camping kettles, matches, clocks, pocket handkerchiefs, fireworks (2009: 185; see also Turner 2006: 171). The sense of anachronism may be because we tend to picture the Shire as medieval or pre-industrial, or because we ask too many hard questions of political economy. Tolkien admitted umbrellas was a mistake (Hammond and Scull 2005: 72). But above all, Fimi and others consider the express train as "the most extreme anachronism" (2009: 185). Nonetheless, Tolkien sustains the writer's conceit that Bilbo is not in fact English. And (as Coleridge had noted) we have no objection to reading *in English* words which could never have been spoken in English. Nor Chinese. A translation, such as Tolkien's work rendered into Chinese, inevitably evokes yet another form of life, with another set of exclusions. A Chinese translator has to exclude Hadrian's Wall but also the Great Wall.

In fact, one translator, Deng Jiawan, gives us exactly what Tolkien said: an express train (*tekuai che* 特快车) (Deng *FR*: 34). The Yilin Press translator makes no mention of any express train, but uses the expression *longfeng chidianche* 龙风驰电掣, dragon-wind swift as lightning flash (Yilin *FR*: 31). And Zhu Xueheng uses the onomatopoeic *honglong* 轰隆, a rumbling giant sound, which happens to include three vehicles (three 車 in one 轟) (Zhu *FR*: 57). Deng's commitment to fidelity leads her to reproduce this minor blunder, but the other two make Middle-earth slightly *less* anachronistic in Chinese. But not consistently: a reference to an "engine" in *The Hobbit* (I, 20) survives as "train" (*huoche* 火车) (Yilin *H*: 16, Wu *H*: 27), and "steam engine" (*zhengqilu* 蒸氣爐) (Zhu *H*: 24), making the Chinese slightly *more* anachronistic.

The priority of the original over the translation seems to be immutable. Chronological and otherwise logical sequences establish the relationship as hierarchical. "The dividing line between original and translation has been one of the assumed constants of translation theory and commentary" (Polizzotti 2018: 8). Traditionally, the line between them had been less clear, but "Around the early seventeenth century, however, attitudes began to change. Not only did the distinction between original and translation harden, but the sacred authority of the original was established" (ibid., 9). This change was partly because of the printing press, and a stronger sense of authorship and copyright (ibid., 9; see also Hutcheon 2012: 3–4). The commodification and mass-production of fiction encouraged the sanctity of the original work.

Inverting that hierarchy may well be "transgressive" (Bassnett 2007: 368; see also Gander 2013: 115). But a translation can be better than the original. And if a translation is poor, not to worry—soon there will be another one. There will only ever be one original, but new translations are always possible. Of course, maybe there never was just *one* original (Emmerich 2017: 102–7). Not only because of textual variants, but because the reading of a published work even in its original language by a native reader is already never a simple and singular matter. The original is not "a defined, monolithic whole that can never be replicated adequately, but rather a zone of energy" (Polizzotti 2018: 8). The blur between three distinct translations is not at the edges but literally in every word. In every letter. Translation is thus an absolute demonstration of the lack of closure of a text.

Untranslatability and Loss

One common manifestation of linguistic chauvinism is the assertion that certain words can never be known outside of their own language. We often hear people say that a certain word is "untranslatable," more so in popular than academic discourse (Moore 2004; Rheingold 2000). Motives for this assertion may include nationalism, orientalism, or elitism (Raw 2017: 496). Certainly cultural difference makes some concepts more complicated than others. But either all words are untranslatable, or none of them. "The Moon," for example, is universally denotable. But what the Moon *means* (its connotations) differs widely by language and culture. Rather than identifying a certain set of words as uniquely untranslatable, it would be better to say that there is always untranslatability in all words, even those which name the most easily denoted objects. Untranslatability can be claimed of any reading or listening. There is always a loss of context, even if I'm reading a novel written in English from my own time period, my own "culture," my own gender, my own class, and so on. How much like myself does a novel have to be before there's no loss of context? There is always "the unsolved mystery of how we come to know what someone else means" (Bellos 2011: 4). I never fully understand what I am myself saying. Recalling Briggs' remark about reading as a "miracle" (2017: 171), and Le Guin's distinction between factuality and truth (1979: 44), translation represents a similar miraculous bridging of the chasm between the "factuality" (of the printed words in the source text) and the "truth" (of what they mean), which is then again knowable by the second factuality of the target language.

Along with a claim of "untranslatability," we often hear the phrase, "lost in translation," where the emphasis is on the regrettable failure of a translation to evoke some particular sense in the original text. On this point, I see near total divergence between popular and academic usage. At conferences such as the American Literary Translators Association, one hears the phrase "lost in translation" immediately followed by a curt dismissal of the concept—yet, academics continue to *need* to dismiss it because it is so firmly present in popular consciousness. It is in the middle of the single most famous quotation in English on the topic of translation.

The phrase comes from Robert Frost's widely cited (but apparently unpublished) remark, "I could define poetry this way: it is that which is lost out of both prose and verse in translation. It is also what is lost in interpretation." Frost implies that though the *words* may be translated, the "poetry" cannot. A translated poem is therefore like Frankenstein's monster: it walks and talks but has no soul. It looks like a poem but it has no "poetry"—and there is no recognition that the new object may have its own "poetry." Setting aside inept translation or misunderstanding, but still following Frost, loss of "poetry" is the inevitable result of some quality in the original that simply *cannot* be translated. That quality might be defined as the *specificity* of word choice, especially within a native reader's heightened awareness of the extended field of connotation. Confronted with such a situation, people often say that a certain word is "untranslatable." Indeed, in the "Translator's preface" to the Yilin edition of *The Fellowship of the Ring*, Guo Shaobo remarks, "Ancient people said, poetry has no perfect explanation. That's not wrong. Really, translation is also like this. Often for the sake of the superficial (*pimao* 皮毛, skin-hair) you get rid of the spirit (*jingshen* 精神)" (Yilin *FR*: 8; see also Venuti 2019: 109–118).

Among all languages, Chinese has often been singled out as English's quintessential other, perhaps most famously by Ernest Fenollosa's *The Chinese Written Character as a Medium for Poetry* (1919), which treats English as sadly impoverished by its distance from the "primitive sap" of linguistic creativity which Chinese still retains (1936: 28). Fenollosa treats every translation from Chinese to English as a loss. Or one might take *Nineteen Ways of Looking at Wang Wei* (1987) by Eliot Weinberger, in which a series of translations of a single four-line Chinese poem are treated with a certain sense of futility: even while he praises certain of the translations as good poems in themselves, Weinberger seems resigned to the inevitable *failure* of any translation to capture an essential *Chineseness* of the original. I can't decide if this is profound or banal. He seems to ignore the simple fact that we now have nineteen *new* poems.

Since we are thinking about religion and translation, there is an analogy here. Is the untranslatable related to the ineffable? In response to various approaches considered to be reductionist, some defenders of religion (or Religious Studies) have sometimes claimed a certain *sui generis* or irreducible element of religion that sociologists, historians, and anthropologists cannot quite grasp. Schleiermacher asserted that because religion was fundamentally non-rational, any rationalistic explanation of the interior feeling of the absolute dependence on God is bound to fail. Rudolf Otto famously remarked that readers who have not themselves had "a moment of deeply-felt religious experience" should cease reading after a few pages of his *The Idea of the Holy* (1923: 8). Mircea Eliade was particularly hostile to any attempt to understand the "essence" of religion on any terms other than his narrowly conceived form of religion. Consistent with the Romanticism of this interpretive tradition, Eliade considered art and poetry in much the same way: "Works of art, like 'religious data,' have a mode of being that is particular to themselves; they *exist on their own plane of reference*, in their particular universe" (1969: 6). If works of art and literature, like "the sacred," are irreducible, they can never be "translated" into social conditions, psychological states, mere "history," or even into another language. Or, if translated, only at the loss of their "poetry"—namely, the sacred. Recall that Frost added, "It is also what is lost in interpretation." Whether we agree with this or not, we in Religious Studies are heir to a tradition of interpretation which regards all non-religious understandings of religion as, to use Fenollosa's metaphor, forms of anemia (1919: 28). Positing a special quality which resists "translation" into another explanatory discourse might be compared to a proprietorial or turf-guarding attitude of native speakers who insist on something *your* language will never understand.

Scholarship on translations of Tolkien has been hampered by an outdated tendency to focus entirely on semantic loss, treating the source text as an absolute standard and relentlessly pointing out failures of the translators. Or when a translation is praised, it is because of its "fidelity" to the original. Reverence towards Tolkien does not help. Each translation or retelling deserves its own interpretation and not only as a flawed substitute for the original. The move from original text to translation is not exclusively a loss, but also a gain, or better: a change. Yet, how can we get at the nature of the change?

Comparing English and Chinese

It seems absurd (and certainly impolite) to claim one language is "better" than another. When that supposedly superior language happens to be one's own native language, we naturally suspect mere chauvinism. Yet, each language has its own unique nature, its idioms and games, particular things it can do better—or at least, differently. Surely it may still be worth asking: what can English do better than Chinese? And what can Chinese do better than English? Is it just a matter of predisposition, or is there some empirical way to answer those questions? It would be misguided to start with the great pinnacles of each language, such as by asking which is better, the poems of Wordsworth or of Wang Wei. We have to start at a much more basic level, with innate features of the languages, or with individual words. This section will serve as the grounds for the discussion of differences throughout part two of this book.

Here, I present a brief sketch of only the written aspects. Written English is alphabetic, Chinese is logographic. Chinese sounds can be represented in Romanized form known as *pinyin*. In their written forms, English puts space between each word, where Chinese does not. When I translate from Chinese, one of my first tasks is to mentally insert those spaces, going from 在地底洞穴中住著一名哈比人 (which looks to me like inaholeinthegroundtherelivedahobbit) to 在　地底洞穴　中　住著　一名　哈比人. Chinese is monosyllabic *in a sense*, but as this example shows, "words" tend to be clusters—hence the distinction between "character" (*zi* 字) and "word" or "term" (*ci* 詞). Characters are combined with others to form words, but each character itself does not change; this is in contrast to English where many elements can be changed or added to each syllable. Verbs are inflected in English—to indicate tense, case, voice, or number. Chinese is uninflected. Rather than changing the word itself (morphology), Chinese relies on its relation to other words in the sentence (syntax). The syntaxes themselves are different. "I am reading in the library" becomes "I in the library am reading." (And conversely, 我在圖書館讀書 becomes 我讀書在圖書館.) A complication in translating Tolkien is his frequent "Germanic" syntax, in which the verb comes at the end: "Not idly do the leaves of Lórien fall" (*TT,* III, ii, 414; and cf. Deng *TT*: 19; Yilin *TT*: 17; Zhu *TT*: 32). Such constructions are often more natural in Chinese than in English, and therefore might not communicate the intended Saga-like formality. Zhu's translation for example, runs literally: "Lórien's leaves absolutely don't with no reason fall" (Zhu *TT*: 32), a word order which is natural and idiomatic in modern Chinese.

Complex English sentences, this one for example, with multiple subordinate clauses in which the subject of the sentence may be far removed from the verb or the direct object, or in which subordinate clauses are nested within subordinate clauses, tend to be difficult to translate. I asked Deng Jiawan to translate the above sentence. 复杂的英语句子，例如有多个从句的句子，句子的主语可能远离动词或直接宾语，或者从句嵌套在从句中，往往很难翻译. She preserved the long, rambling quality of the sentence, but for clarity's sake she chose to reiterate the subject: "Complex English sentences, for example *sentences* with a lot of subordinate clauses, *the sentence's* subject might be distant from the verb or the direct object, or subordinate clauses are nested in subordinate clauses, are often very difficult to translate" (cf. Baker 1992: 192). Taking "Yea, I am Tuor, son of Huor, son of Galdor, son of Hador" (*UT* 21) and rendering it as: "Right, I am Huor's son Tuor, and Huor is Galdor's son, Galdor is Hador's son" (Shi and Deng *UT*: 34) is a perfect example of the tendency to restate the subject of each subordinate clause. English is considered subject-prominent. The frequency of the insertion of grammatical subjects into English-influenced Chinese was noted at least since the May 4th Movement of 1919 (Chan 2020: 56). In reading Deng's translation of "On Fairy-stories," I noticed Tolkien throws in phrases like "I think," or "in other words," more or less anywhere in the sentence; Deng was inclined to get "I think" out of the way quickly, at the start of the sentence. Conversely, when translating a complex Chinese sentence I often feel inclined to change commas into periods or semi-colons, for otherwise the translated sentence will read like a cascade of several overlapping thoughts.

The passive voice is used more commonly in English, whereas Chinese generally avoids it. The passive voice in Chinese tends to be used for negative events. A Chinese translation from English will probably have more use of the passive voice than most native Chinese texts (Chan 2020: 56). *Italics* and **bold** are both possible in modern Chinese, but Capitalization is not. Chinese does not have definite or indefinite articles ("the" and "a"). I will say more about capitalization and "the" in Chapter 11.

The translations for the Taiwan market are traditional in format: the books read right to left, and the lines are vertical. In common with norms in China, all the other translations are left to right, and horizontal. It is hard to say what difference this makes.

Similarly, whereas the original continues the numbering through all three volumes of *The Lord of the Rings* (so that, for example, volume two begins with page 403 in the Houghton Mifflin edition), all three Chinese editions restart the numbering in each volume.

Traditionally, Chinese texts were unpunctuated or given minimal punctuation, using the *dian* 點/点：。or "dot" to mark phrasing pauses, which when translated is neither quite a comma nor a period. However, the norm now is modern, more or less Western punctuation. It is not exactly the same set of punctuation marks: in Zhu's texts, quotation marks are 「and 」 (except of course vertically aligned); Chinese also has an enumeration comma 、 as opposed to , used for lists—in English we use either our measly one comma (,) or "and."

Chinese uses count nouns much more than English, not only those which have close English equivalents such as "one **piece** of paper" = *yi* **zhang** *zhi* 一張紙; but some which don't: "it was void." (*S* 78) becomes "it was **an expanse of** nothingness [*yi pian xuwu* 一片虚无]." (Yilin *S*: 73). When Galadriel says of Gandalf, "a grey mist is about him," (*FR*, II, vii, 346) the Yilin edition uses *tuan* 团, a count noun for round masses: "There is a **round mass** of grey leaden mist enveloping him" (Yilin *FR*: 433). These count nouns add some nuances—such as that the mist is round or blob-like, or the emptiness is a single, vast expanse, both of which give us a more spatial image. Speaking of the terrible power of the Darkness, we read it had the power to "strangle the very will" (*S*: 81). (Naturally we *assume* "strangle" might well involve killing, but the Chinese in all three versions names that, using *jiaosi* 绞死 strangle-to-death.) But where Yilin, and Deng's later version, translate "will" straightforwardly (*yizhi* 意志) (Yilin *S*: 76, Deng *S* 2015: 107), Deng's earlier version uses a count noun: "strangle-kill every *gu* 股 of the will" (Deng *S* 2002: 103). As a count noun, *gu* 股 is used for things that are long and narrow such as threads and streams of water, and for moments of sensory manifestations in space, such as *bursts* of energy, *streams* of hot air, *whiffs* of fragrance. So, now we feel that the "will" which the Darkness can strangle to death is a long thread or a puff of air—Darkness strangles every particular *ejaculation* of will, every *tendril* of intention, rather than the will in general—which in comparison now feels a bit abstract.

English does have something like *chengyu* 成語, set phrases which reference or abbreviate some longer saying or story; we make biblical references, for example. Or we single out one element from a larger situation: You're asleep; the man who lives upstairs comes home drunk; he takes off one shoe—clunk!—and wakes you up. And now you can't relax enough to get back to sleep because you are "waiting for the other shoe to drop." But Chinese can be credited with an unusually rich vocabulary of these set phrases. Some of them are so embedded in the stories for which they are the punchlines that they evoke a form of life too specifically *ours* to be possible in Middle-earth. For example, the *chengyu wanbiguiZhao* 完璧歸趙 ("return the jade to Zhao" = return something to its rightful owner) ought not to be possible in Middle-earth because of its specific reference to the ancient state of Zhao, and the originating story involving historical figures from the *Records of the Grand Historian* (the *Shiji*). Deng commented, "When we use *chengyu* [in a translation], we particularly pay attention to the situation; this *chengyu* of China, does it have a historical background or not? If it has a Chinese historical background, we certainly don't want to use it. If it's just an ordinary *chengyu* from daily life, that's fine" (Deng 2017). Yet, if we agree with Wittgenstein, that even a *chengyu* without explicit historical references still implies a "form of life," this distinction is not always obvious. Furthermore, there are many phrases which are not strictly speaking *chengyu*, but are certainly set phrases, mostly four characters in length. I discuss the tendency towards four-character phrases in the next chapter.

An example of a beautiful *chengyu* relates to Celeborn and Galadriel: "no sign of age was upon them, unless it were in the depths of their eyes" (*FR*, II, vii, 345). The Yilin edition has: "The years and months had not left any mark on their bodies, there was only the profound gaze that revealed an unlimited sense of blue mulberry" (Yilin *FR*: 432). These last two words are *cangsang*, short for *canghai sangtian* 沧海桑田, the deep blue sea becomes a mulberry field. Yilin elaborates the original line with a phrase implying an awareness of the great changes that time brings about, i.e., when the sea turns into dry land—seeing *that* in Galadriel's eyes is a powerful image—especially since we know she lived through the great geological rearrangements which changed the map of Arda, the Atlantis-like submerging of Beleriand in the First Age and Númenor in the Second.

Boromir says to Frodo, about entering Sauron's territory: "it is folly to go without force into his domain" (*FR*, II, viii, 360). Yilin: "entering his domain with bare fist and empty hand (赤拳空手 *chiquan kongshou*) without doubt is a flying moth throwing itself into a fire (飞蛾扑火 *fei-e puhuo*)" (Yilin *FR*: 450; cf. Deng *FR*: 461–462; Zhu *FR*: 570). "With bare fist and empty hand" certainly means unarmed—though it might not quite mean "without force," especially as *kongshou* (empty hand), better known by its Japanese pronunciation *karate*, would be sure to evoke martial arts in China, especially in the context of an adventure novel. A moth throwing itself into a fire evokes the futility and stupidity of "folly" but also the self-destructive fascination associated with the Ring—and a consuming fixation on reaching a fire-mountain (*huoshan*), along with a foreshadowing of Frodo (or as it turns out, Gollum) falling into it and burning up.

Another case of a distinctively Chinese effect is how its script is capable of subtle visual puns not really available in English. When Boromir recites his prophetic verse, he says, "For Isildur's Bane shall waken" (*FR*, II, ii, 240). Derived from words which mean "killer," bane is a thing of bad luck, an object which brings one's death. The Chinese terms for such things involve stars, hence constellations, and hence what is "in the stars" or one's fate. ("Astrology" is one's star-fate (星命 *xingming*).) Deng has: "Isildur's conquering star (*kexing* 克星) will revive (*suxing* 苏醒)" (Deng *FR*: 308). Yilin has: "Isildur's ill-luck star (*zaixing* 灾星) will wake (*xing* 醒)" (Yilin *FR* 299). The star image is strong, not just because *zaixing* and *kexing* are literally star of ill-fortune and star which conquers, but also because in Chinese "star" and "wake" are homophonous, and the phonetic component (in this case on the right half of the character) of the verb *xing* 醒 (wake) is the character *xing* 星 (star), so there's a nice poetic echo there in the Chinese. Do native speakers actually see this? It could be the sort of thing that foreigners see, because we are more focused on how to write each word as we learn it. In a poem we're more likely to notice it because we expect such subtlety in poems. But when reading Chinese becomes easy and natural, this sort of effect may pass unnoticed. In prose it might be subliminal.

Even with tone-marks, but certainly without them, Romanization makes Chinese look simplistic, having a shockingly tiny phonetic range compared to English. Namely, around 409 syllables; if each of those has four tones (which is not actually the case), that would make a theoretical total of 1,636 single syllables. That seems like a lot—especially as in fact, single-syllable words are quite rare, and two- or three- or four-word combinations are the norm. There are (theoretically) over 2.5 million two-character combinations possible—the actual number in reality is much smaller of course. But still, that seems like a lot—plenty enough to be getting along with. On the other hand, compare that to the virtually indeterminate number of possible single-syllables in English, with its accumulation of consonants around a vowel-nucleus (not possible in Chinese): a, ac, act, acts, racts, tracts, stracts—all one syllable. English comes across as infinitely mutating, while Chinese appears linguistically impoverished *if we only read pinyin*. But as soon as we look at the Chinese *script*, that illusion of impoverishment vanishes. From the perspective of the Chinese script, English now seems more like a line of computer code, a dull string of simple letters lacking nuance or variety. A mere twenty-six, with just the five vowels accounting for about 38 percent of the letters on an average page. About three-quarters of this paragraph is ten letters.

When we begin to sing the praises of the Chinese script, there is a danger of intoxication. There is a history of Westerners such as Ernest Fenollosa and Ezra Pound waxing rhapsodic over the great mystery of Chinese characters, with their interesting constructions, combining elements to make new ideas. Fenollosa read *ming* 明: "Thus you write literally, 'the sun and moon of the cup' for 'the cup's brightness'" (1936: 22). This kind of character interpretation might be useful for remembering how to write characters, but almost always relies on bogus or fanciful etymology. We should beware of this kind of faux-etymological literalism. The character *ming* 明 ("bright") is indeed composed of sun 日 and moon 月, but it doesn't *mean* sun-and-moon (see Gander 2013: 112).

Back-Translation

There is ultimately no way around the fact that any translation represents a radical leap; yet clearly some translations are "closer" to the original words than others. An *absolutely* literal translation is an absurdity; but there is such a thing as a *relatively* literal translation. Even though no scholar makes a claim of *absolute* commensurability, everyone assumes *relative* commensurability—otherwise translation would be impossible. Even the slight shifts in perspective between more literal and less literal translations can yield something. This book relies on back-translation, a mediating language emphasizing formal equivalence. It is an intentional "translator's English" (Nida 2000: 133). It is more or less grammatical, yet the phrasing may be convoluted because the goal is to imitate what the Chinese is saying, and how it is saying it. In fact, most acts of translation go through this middle phase, as the translator tries to stay true to that literal understanding but also to move closer to the intention or effect of the line, or in any case closer to something publishable.

A highly literalistic (unidiomatic, hard to follow) translation may be more "accurate" in some ways and less so in others. Naïve concepts of accuracy have long been discarded in Translation Studies. Scholars in Translation Studies as well as Adaptation Studies continually distance themselves from the specter haunting their work: fidelity (Johnson 2017: 87–95; Hutcheon 2012: 6–7; Emig 2018: 28). Unlike most scholarship on Tolkien in translation, such as Mark T. Hooker's *Tolkien through Russian Eyes* (2003: 8), I am not concerned with measuring each translation against the original, though I am very interested in the differences. A literalistic translation accompanied by additional commentary highlights the mechanics of the sentence and its word-choices. It tends to foreignize rather than domesticate. An awkward literalistic translation of an elegant original certainly represents a loss. A more polished translation takes the mechanisms and isolated words through a translator's imagination and cultural competency to arrive at a line which (it is hoped, or gambled) evokes more accurately the intention or effect or "truth" of the original. This book relies on the space between formal and dynamic translations, between a more literal (source-text-oriented) translation and a more polished (target-text-oriented) translation.

However, I should note a regrettable history of overly literal translation of Chinese, a history which includes light entertainment, orientalist stereotypes, and egregious racism. Think of pidgin English as composed by Bret Harte and Mark Twain, Charlie Chan movies (though not the novels, to be fair), Chinglish memes, and "Confucius say" (not "said"). And the pervasive use of what is called the "Chop Suey letterform." More than any other language, "Chinese" has signified for Anglophone cultures peculiarity and inscrutability. So, I am aware of the need to be clear about my technique here. An overly literal translation of a Chinese sentence into English produces something partly incoherent, and vice versa. Obviously neither language is *in itself* incoherent. Haun Saussy wrote, "Translation, then, creates asymmetries and incommensurabilities while allowing us to think of these as intrinsic to the objects of study, not to the process" (1999: 112). The process produces effects which we may carelessly attribute to the language being translated—and we must resist this inclination.

Conclusions

When comparing the original text to a translation, the sense of inaccuracy and loss of meaning are sometimes unavoidable, but that sense of loss should not obscure the new world which has been brought into being by this new set of words, in this other language. For Chinese readers, reading only the translations, the world in which Gandalf speaks Chinese is the real Middle-earth. This book is an attempt to evoke those different Middle-earths to an English readership. My approach is fundamentally Humanistic—literary and philosophical, qualitative rather than quantitative, and certainly not sociological or "scientific."

Translation does at least some of what Tolkien meant by his point about Mooreeffoc—the fresh perception of a familiar thing. We usually think of translation as making the foreign familiar (because we are usually consuming foreign works translated into our own tongue). But contemplating translations from one's own familiar language re-foreignizes the old story.

A good, finished translation is more organic than mechanical. But my process here attempts to reveal the mechanics by translating the Chinese into English in a relatively literalistic way, and by adding commentary. Even in cases where one feels a very strong concordance of a word in one language and in another, as soon as we move from denotation to connotation, the meanings of the two words more clearly diverge. Here, we have the thought that translation is impossible, or at least always accompanied by a sense of loss. Just as there is no such thing as a story that is no story in particular, there is always an irreducible element ("poetry," metaphorically) in any particular version of a story and in any language. Yet rather than taking the original as absolute and considering translations in terms of loss, I prefer to think of loss and gain, or better yet, to set aside any such zero-sum calculation. I prefer to resist the "cognitive possessiveness" and embrace the gamble. Chinese is not my native language, and inevitably some of what I say is idiosyncratic, impressionistic or exploratory. I am sure I have missed many opportunities. I hope this study is provocative, but it is certainly not definitive. Perhaps this study will inspire Chinese native speakers to write more on Tolkien in translation.

The next chapter will take up these thoughts on translation and address a set of key terms, starting with the book titles, while introducing the translators and publication histories.

3

Tolkien in Chinese

Books and Titles

The Yilin Press Edition

I bought my first set of Tolkien translations in a bookstore near Beijing University. The books were on sale sealed with shrink-wrap, to discourage extended in-store reading by children, which is a common practice in China. Removing the wrapper of *The Hobbit*, out fell two identical loose book covers, unrelated to *The Hobbit*, obviously included so that the reader could hold them in place over the book's real covers and appear to be reading a very serious book, not some frivolous fantasy novel. In this case, naughty girls and boys would appear to be reading a school textbook called *Marxism: Principles for the Study of Political Economy* 马克思主义：政治经济学原理. Would the old Tory laugh or cry to find himself sandwiched between Karl Marx and the Chinese Communist Party?

And why a textbook on Marxism? I imagine that conversation:

How about a maths textbook?
No, maths is too important. We want a subject guaranteed not to interest *anyone*.
    Something parents *pretend* is important but would be more likely to flee from . . .
Let's see . . . Ah! Eureka!"

This 2001 edition was translated by several people, rushed out to capitalize on the *Lord of the Rings* films—it is worth noting that the first generation of readers in China read the works in the shadow of the films. In accordance with Chinese scholarly and fan usage, I will refer to these books by the publishing company, Yilin Press (译林出版社), and to the other translations by the translators' names. Rapid translation and publication of popular fiction is the norm in China since the 1980s, along with collaboration by multiple translators. Yilin is particularly known for its agile responses to market trends and its dynamic publicity operations. My general impression of this translation is that it is the simplest, as if the translators were working within a firm notion that these were children's books. I might recommend this translation to a Chinese child. It is the easiest for me to read. There are some errors and missed opportunities, and for the most part Chinese scholars tend to praise Zhu and Deng over the Yilin translations (Li and Yi 2010: 217; Gao 2011: 135; Wang 2020: 181), yet there are points to praise: Li and Yi argue that Yilin's translations of poetry are better than Zhu's, for example (2010: 218).

The Yilin edition reframes the entire opus in a new way. In the original English, *The Hobbit* was published first, in 1937, and *The Lord of the Rings* later, in 1954–1955, as a set of three volumes, and *The Silmarillion*, though submitted in some form for publication as early as 1937, appeared in print only posthumously, after much revision, in 1977. Yilin, on the other hand, presents all five—*Silmarillion, Hobbot, LOTR*, in that order—as a single set called *Mojie* (魔戒), which (for the time being) let us translate as "Magic Ring." In English, virtually no one reads *The Silmarillion* first—they read it last, if at all—now imagine *starting* with it. *The Silmarillion* is named as the "beginning" and *The Hobbit* as the "prequel" to a work called *Mojie*, which seems to be *The Lord of the Rings* but also refers to all five books. This was hardly Tolkien's plan, though "The Magic Ring" was apparently his first draft title for *LOTR*. Marquette University has the original manuscript, dating from 1938, and on the first page it says, "~~The Magic Ring~~ The Lord of the Rings" (McIlwaine 2018: 331). I will return to this key term, *mojie*, below.

The Yilin Press (Nanjing, 2001) set is as follows:

Mojie qiyuan: Jingling baozuan 魔戒起源：精灵宝钻 ("The Beginning of The Magic Ring: The Elves' Jewels") [i.e., *The Silmarillion*]. Trans. Li Yao 李尧.

Mojie qianzhuan: Huobite ren 魔戒前传：霍比特人 ("The Prequel to The Magic Ring: Hobbit person/people"). Trans. Li Yao.

Mojie: Mojie zaixian 魔戒：魔戒再现 ("The Magic Ring: The Magic Ring Re-appears.") [i.e., *The Fellowship of the Rings*]. Trans. Ding Di 丁棣. The three *LOTR* volumes are also credited to Guo Shaobo 郭少波, *jiaoding* 校订 (proofreading and revisions).

Mojie: Shuangta qibing 魔戒：双塔奇兵 ("The Magic Ring: The Surprise Attack of the Twin Towers.") [i.e., *The Two Towers*]. Trans. Yao Jinrong 姚锦镕.

Mojie: Wangzhe wudi 魔戒：王者无敌 "The Magic Ring: The King is Triumphant." (Or, "Invincible"—literally, "has no (more) enemies.") [i.e., *The Return of the King*]. Trans. Tang Dingjiu 汤定九.

"The Two Towers" is turned into *shuangta*, "twin towers" which is also the colloquial name of the New York World Trade Center (*Niuyue shijie maoyi zhongxin*). *Shuang* 雙 / 双 is definitely twin (or dual, double) rather than merely "two." To say "two towers" in Chinese would be *liangzuota* 两座塔 requiring the insertion of the count word *zuo*, losing much of its rhetorical crispness, and (especially without "The" or capital letters) implying not so much *The* Two Towers as "a couple of towers." In English, Two Towers is not Twin Towers, but in Chinese both are *shuangta*, increasing the possibility of dissonance, especially after September 2001. There is some debate about what the title refers to (Roberts 2013: 131–133). The two towers most likely referred to, Orthanc in Isengard and Barad-dûr in Mordor, are not really "twins," since they are far apart, different in design, and ruled separately. They are temporarily in alliance during the story, and the Chinese title accentuates their allegiance by twinning them.

If you did not already know, you might see the cover of Tolkien's first novel and wonder what the title refers to. "Hobbit" seems to be a proper noun of some kind. Of course, by the second page of the story we have our answer, but the Chinese tells you right on the cover: *Huobite ren* (or in Taiwan, *Habi ren*—China and Taiwan have slightly different processes of transliteration; see Cai 2015). A hobbit is a *ren*: a person—or people.

Guo Shaobo's "Translator's preface" begins with a description of an advance screening of part of *Fellowship* in 2001, in Cannes. "When the projection was over, the clapping sound was like thunder. This was the location of the 'Magic Ring' film's mountain first appearing from the clouds (*yunshan chulu* 云山初露)" (Yilin *FR*: 1), an idiom for the first sight of a great thing. As if to confirm that the film was the stimulus, only after discussing the film's budget, release plans, and financial success does he turn to the question of a Chinese translation. "Perhaps it was coincidence, but only after the past half century did Mainland Chinese readers finally see a Chinese 'Magic Ring'" (Yilin *FR*: 1). Coincidence? Hardly. But this preface was not the place to note the history of the Party's cultural control, or its marginalization of fantasy literature, or its tight control of translation (Wang 2016: 48–73).

The Preface continues with six pages of standard information about Tolkien, but then returns to the translation. Guo notes the linguistic richness of the text, the old-fashioned spellings and invented languages. He writes, "the author was a notable linguist, and the crucible fire of his linguistics work was pure" (Yilin *FR*: 7). He then describes some of the challenges of translating these texts:

> The author's unique narrating style and style of argument often make people fall into a period of bewitchment: is what the author says real, or made up out of thin air (*pingkong xugou* 凭空虚构)? Of course, if readers of English go to look at the original text, because of having the same cultural feeling (*wenhuagan* 文化感) and historical feeling as the author, then these linguistic phenomena, in which what seems right is wrong (*sishi erfei* 似是而非) and what seems wrong is right, are like a maze, stirring up their intense curiosity and desire to explore. Their own ethnicity's cultural knowledge and historical knowledge are a great help to understand the real truth of the work; but if we translate these maze-like words into another language, the charm which stirs one is suddenly gone. So to tell the truth, we really felt uncertain about when to translate plainly and when to be implicit. If we translate plainly, the reader will understand, but what they read and understand is the translated text, and the original text's meaning is completely absent; and if implicitly, it is like the reader has fallen into five miles of fog, not knowing what is said. To sum up, no matter what kind of situation, [Chinese] readers have no way to use their accumulated knowledge and cultural feeling, hence I'm afraid the only method is to add an explanation. (Yilin *FR*: 8)

Much the same could be said of any translation, but Tolkien's works have a particular added complexity arising from his depth as a philologist, and from the mixture of real and invented philology. In fact, most native speakers of English will miss much of the historical resonance of the works, and it takes a fellow philologist like Tom Shippey to reveal what was embedded deep in the language. Guo candidly admits the tension of foreignizing and domesticating translation, and also of modern versus archaic diction. As it turned out though, the Yilin edition does not provide many footnotes or stealth glosses (explanations in the text itself). Rather, the tendency was towards clear domestication, especially in comparison to the other translations (Li Hong-man 2010: 21).

This study focuses on the three main sets of translations: the set I have just introduced published by the Yilin company by several translators, in simplified characters for the China market; next, I discuss a set translated by Zhu Xueheng 朱學恆 (Lucifer Chu) in Taiwan, in traditional characters and for the Taiwan market; and then, works translated by the Taiwan-based translator Deng Jiawan 邓嘉宛/鄧嘉宛 (Joy Teng), in both simplified and traditional characters depending on the market. There are more. The bibliography includes a representative sample of other translations.

Translations by Zhu Xueheng

Zhu's translation was a labor of love, and the quality is high. He claims to have learned English by playing video games. Chung Yu-ling and others have noted how Zhu's background in gaming affected his vocabulary, and I too noticed some of that: When Frodo puts the Ring on his finger on Amon Hen, the narrator says that Sauron's gaze searched for Frodo: "Very soon it would nail him down" (*FR*, II, x, 392). Deng uses *dingzhu* 钉住 literally "nail down." (Deng *FR*: 503.) Yilin says the gaze would "cover (*zhao* 罩, envelop) him" (Yilin *FR*: 489). But Zhu uses the expression: "it would lock onto (*suoding* 鎖定) this target (*mubiao* 目標)" (Zhu *FR*: 616; see Chung 2013: 129; Hsu 2008; Li and Yi 2010). Overall though, Zhu's broad cultural competency with fantasy literature is a positive asset (Gao 2011: 134–135).

Zhu is a very creative entrepreneur. He was proactive in persuading the Linking company to accept his proposal (Chung 2013: 104). However, after his *Lord of the Rings* came out in 2001, there was a lively online debate about the quality of the translation. Zhu was criticized for omitting words, misinterpreting, and watering down Tolkien.

> To counter such a harsh review, Zhu initiated a public event, encouraging people to revise his translation at the end of 2002. Joy Teng was appointed the proper person to revise *The Lord of the Rings* by Zhu. Here, Zhu showed a genuine fan's desire for a better translation. But this event ended up with the publisher refusing to reissue Teng's revised version of *The Lord of the Rings*. (Chung 2013: 105)

This refusal was for reasons related to marketing and cost. Eventually, however, Linking published the Zhu translation revised by Deng Jiawan. In this book, I am using this revised translation which dates from 2012.

Zhu's translator's introduction starts with his characteristically blunt style: "As for those readers who only seek to enjoy 20th-century epics, such people certainly don't need to read this essay. Because, 'Magic Ring' was considered a good story, and then considered a great work. No one needs to prove all this by means of exaggerated words, beautiful descriptions or surprising numbers" (Zhu *FR*: 7). He notes the well-known story of Tolkien writing "In a hole in the ground there lived a hobbit," then: "Starting from this split second, the world divides. . . . there are only two kinds of people left in this world, those who have read 'Magic Ring' and those who have not" (Zhu *FR*: 7).

The Zhu Xueheng translations (Linking, 2012) are as follows:

Habiren 哈比人 ("Hobbit person/people"). The cover includes the line *mojie chuanqi de qidian* 魔戒傳奇的起點 "The starting point of the legend of the magic ring." There is also a phrase applied to all four of Zhu's translations, "*Tuo-erjin zuopinji* 托爾金作品集 "Collected works of Tolkien."

Mojie xianshen 魔戒現身 ("The Magic Ring Appears"). The title of this volume is preceded by the phrase, *mojie shoubuqu* 魔戒首部曲, "the first book of Magic Ring." The next two volumes have their respective labels, "second" and "third."

Shuangcheng qimou 雙城奇謀 ("The Ingenious Plan of the Twin Walled-Cities").

Wangzhe zailin 王者再臨 ("The King Again Approaches").

For "Two Towers," Zhu chose *shuangcheng* instead of *shuangta*. Although *ta* (tower) seems more accurate than *cheng* (walled city, castle), in some ways *cheng* is the better choice, because *ta* has a rather lightweight connotation. Buddhist temples have *ta*, and we call them pagodas. Orthanc is not a pagoda. Admittedly, neither is Isengard a walled city, but *cheng* has a stronger sense, the city wall itself or the walled city as a whole, an image of mighty fortifications and a large population. It is, however, more horizontal than a tower.

Zhu is no longer working in the field of Tolkien translation. In 2002, using profits from his *Mojie* translations, Zhu founded the Fantasy Culture and Arts Foundation 奇幻文化藝術基金會. Zhu is a "geek god" (*zhaishen*), maintaining an active presence on television, radio, and social media. He runs a chatty YouTube and Facebook series on current events in Taiwan, gaming culture, food, studying English, and his cats. He writes humorous motivational, pro-science, and topical books. His books include *The New World Has No Gods* 新的世界沒有神 *Xinde shijie meiyoushen* (Gaiya wenhua 蓋亞文化, 2009); *About Geek: There is No Turning Back!* 一入宅門深似海 *Yiru zhaimen shensihai*, more literally: "once you enter the way of the geek it's deep like the sea" (Gaiya wenhua, 2012); and *The Power of Dream: We Don't Live Twice!* 夢想無懼！ *Mengxiang wuju* ("Dream without fear") (Gaiya wenhua, 2015).

Translations by Deng Jiawan (Joy Teng)

Zhu has never translated *The Silmarillion*. The traditional-character *Silmarillion* available in Taiwan is by Deng Jiawan:

Jingling baozuan 精靈寶鑽 (The Elves' Jewels) (Linking, 2002).

The cover bears both *zhongtudalu de shenhua yu chuanqi* 中土大陸的神話與傳奇 and the English equivalent, "The myths and legends of Middle-earth." Later, Wenjing press published Deng's simplified-character translation *Jingling baozuan* 精灵宝钻 (The Elves' Jewels, 2015). The differences between the 2002 and 2015 editions justify treating them as two distinct translations.

Deng's *The Lord of the Rings* is not available in Taiwan, though some bookstores in Taiwan have begun to stock simplified-character books, and of course anyone can order Deng's *Lord of the Rings* online. (Judging from the Baidu Tieba Tolkien site, fans in China have access to publications from Taiwan. Since 2011, for example, Zhu's translations have been available in China in simplified characters, from Yilin Press.) Deng's translations of those core texts, for the China market, in simplified characters, were published by Wenjing 文景 (Horizon) with ISBN licensing from Shanghai People's Press 上海人民出版社. The overall title for the three volumes of *The Lord of the Rings* is the familiar *Mojie*, with "Part one" and so on. Deng translated the bulk of the text; Du Yunci 杜蕴慈 translated the poems; and Shi Zhongge 石中歌 (who also goes by Ecthelion) translated the introduction and appendixes. I asked Deng why they had divided up the task in this way. Involving three translators may have saved a little time, but it seems to have been primarily done in the spirit of friendly collaboration. Wenjing signed a contract with HarperCollins in February 2012, and wanted the new translation out in time to benefit from the release of the first *Hobbit* film in December that year. After some negotiation, Deng proposed working with these two other *mojiemi* 魔戒迷 (fans 'lost' in *Mojie*) (Deng 2017).

They are as follows (all Wenjing, 2013):

Mojie tongmeng 魔戒同盟 ("Alliance/Fellowship of the Magic Ring")
Shuangta shutu 双塔殊途 ("Twin Towers Different Routes")
Wangzhe Huilai 王者归来 ("The King Returns")

For the second volume, *shutu* (殊途) is part of a common phrase, *shutu tonggui* (殊途同归) "converge by different roads," or "come to the same point via different paths." It implies Orthanc and Barad-dûr coming from different starting points, and reaching a shared political goal. Perhaps it might also suggest the two paths taken: Frodo and Sam towards Mordor, and Merry and Pippin towards Isengard.

Deng and her friends have become the central figures in the ongoing translation of Tolkien's works. Also translated by Deng for the Taiwan market are *Hulin de zinü* 胡林的子女 (*The Children of Húrin*) (Linking, 2008); and with her collaborators Shi Zhongge and Du Yunci, *Beilun yu Luxi-en* 貝倫與露西恩 (*Beren and Lúthien*) (Linking, 2020). Most recently, in simplified characters for the China market, Wenjing has published *Unfinished Tales of Númenor and Middle-Earth*. *Numennuo-er yu zhongzhou zhi weiwan de chuanshuo* 努门诺尔与中洲之未完的传说 (Unfinished Legends of Númenor and Middle-earth), translated by Shi Zhongge and Deng Jiawan (2017). And *The Fall of Gondolin: Gangduolin de xianluo* 刚多林的陷落, translated by Deng Jiawan, Shi Zhongge, and Du Yunci (2020). Deng is currently translating John Garth's *The Worlds of J. R. R. Tolkien: The Places that Inspired Middle-earth* (2020). Deng has even translated Tolkien's dense essay "On Fairy-stories," an incredible challenge with little hope of commensurate financial reward.

In later chapters I discuss specific passages, and we will see how each translation deals with the original text in different ways. Sometimes there will be a clear sense that one of the translations has missed a point, or hit on a beautiful resonance, but I am not primarily concerned with any general comparison. Nonetheless, I may say that Deng's translations seem to be of an exceptionally high caliber. She is extremely attentive to the original text, often translating an idiom in close to literal Chinese, at points where the other translators go for a more general paraphrase. Wen Yixin argues for a consistent foreignization throughout Deng's translations (Wen 2021).

Literal fidelity to the original is not automatically a virtue, yet as I see it, Deng finds ways to stay closest to Tolkien's text while retaining elegance, a view shared by Wang Jin (2020).

There is an additional translation of *The Hobbit*. *Huobite ren* 霍比特人 (Hobbit person/people), translated by Wu Gang 吴刚 (Shanghai People's Publishing House 2013). Judging by word choice, and occasionally whole paragraphs almost word for word, Wu relied heavily on Zhu's translation. I assume there was a perceived market need for a simplified-character translation of *The Hobbit*, given that the Yilin edition was from 2001 and in some ways a lesser translation. Overall, Zhu's superior but traditional-character translation clearly served as the model, though Wu may have domesticated the text more (Mao 2020: 89).

Some of the earliest translations, in Taiwan, have not been examined in this study for a mixture of reasons. I was not able to acquire them all, being long out of print. These include a *Hobbit* in 1996; a *Hobbit* and *LOTR* published as a single series in 1997–1998, in fifteen volumes; and a 1998 *LOTR*. All of these were superseded by the translations of Zhu Xueheng.

Publishers of Translations

Chinese translation of Western fiction began in earnest in the late nineteenth century, as a means of visualizing cultural reform, and to meet popular demand for entertainment. There was a steady flow of Western works in Chinese until the 1950s, when the stream dwindled, and then virtually dried up during the Cultural Revolution (1966–1976). From the 1950s to the late 1970s, all publication explicitly served the state. The only Western works made available tended to be ones which could be understood as revealing the miseries of capitalism: Tolstoy, Dickens, Hugo. Publication was limited to a few houses, and there was no real profit motive involved. While other Western works (Camus, Sartre, Solzhenitzyn, Salinger, Kerouac) were translated, they were never on sale in bookstores, but restricted as "internal publishing" (*neibu faxing* 内部发行). These White Cover Books circulated only among elites, or illegally (Wang 2016: 67–71).

Bonnie S. McDougall's memoir of working for the Foreign Language Press in the 1980s reveals the rigidity and simplicity of the translation work most influenced by Party control, nationalism, and the continuing atmosphere of the Cultural Revolution: "The concept of translatability, which has occupied much attention in Western translation theory, was not raised as an issue by the editorial or translation staff. The apparent belief that meanings in written texts are fixed and that translations of written texts are likewise matters of simple equivalence seems to suit the authoritarian nature of the modern Chinese state" (2011: 11). She gives examples of literalistic Chinese-to-English translation (ibid., 78–79). There was general misunderstanding about literary translation: "On the simplest level, it held that if one translation was correct, then other translations were not. It may also have appeared in the belief that translation imposes a fixed meaning of a literary text that may or may not be ambiguous in its original form" (ibid., 125). Her book is filled with examples of this monologic, literalism, and hostility to ambiguity.

Very soon after Mao died in 1976, publishers began to cultivate the market for Western fiction, both of a "classic" or "serious" nature, and for a popular market. Many new publishing houses were formed, with a steady increase of published titles through to a peak in the late 1980s. Publishers went from a relatively random selection process to becoming more attuned to international bestsellers and film adaptations. Yilin Press was one of the more innovative of the new companies.

The magazine *Yilin* ("forest of translations") was founded in 1979, attached to the Jiangsu People's Publishing House (*Jiangsu renmin chubanshe*), based in Nanjing. In 1988, the Yilin Press was formed. The established presses "tended to adopt an elitist and often academic approach" (Kong 2005: 127), whereas Yilin was more commercial. The editorial guidelines announced interest in current and popular works. "This statement about welcoming foreign popular fiction, although innocuous today, was very bold for its time, when cultural elitism and political puritanism were still tightly enforced" (Kong 2005: 128; see also Qi 2012: 152–153). Their high-profile publication of *Ulysses* in 1994 broke new ground. Yilin and others departed from the very staid and minimal cover design then normal for serious literature. Yilin's *Mojie* series is a typical case, rapidly produced to capitalize on hit films, with colorful covers and a marketing campaign. The covers, at least of the hardback editions I purchased, featured illustrations by Greg and Tim Hildebrandt, showing scenes from the books, except for *The Silmarillion* and *The Hobbit* which anachronistically show members of the Fellowship.

Wenjing (Beijing Century Wenjing Culture and Media Co. Ltd., *Beijing shiji wenjing wenhua chuanbo youxianzeren gongsi* 北京世纪文景文化传播有限责任公司) was founded in 2002. The books list as publisher both Wenjing and Shanghai Peoples Publishing House. Basically, Wenjing does all the work, but Shanghai People's Publishing House sells them the ISBN, because not all publishers have a government license to issue ISBN numbers. Both of these are subdivisions of Shanghai Century Publishing Co 上海世纪出版集团 (*Shanghai shiji chuban jituan*), founded in 1978.

The translations by Zhu Xueheng, and those by Deng Jiawan for the Taiwan market, are published by Linking (聯經 *lianjing*). Founded by Wang Tiyu (1913–1996) on May 4th (a date intentionally evoking the May 4th Movement), 1974, Linking is now one of the most established mainstream publishers in Taiwan. They publish a full spectrum of books including translations of the *Alice* stories and the novels of Christopher Paolini, P. D. James, and Isabel Allende. Their primary rival in Taiwan is Crown (*Huangguan* 皇冠), founded in 1954, which publishes the *Harry Potter* series. Linking's publisher and editorial director Linden Lin said: "Taiwan publishers' open-mindedness is without equal. We are open to foreign authors, new themes, and different perspectives. Not surprisingly, translations account for nearly 28% of all new titles produced annually, and they include most world languages" (Tan 2011). In addition to publishing foreign works in Taiwan, they publish Taiwanese works in English and in simplified Chinese characters.

China and Taiwan have very different publishing cultures. Yet, even in Taiwan, it was only in the 1990s that *The Lord of the Rings*, a major Western novel published in the 1950s, was translated, a little ahead of China but not by much—and less obviously a result of the films. This long delay may be a manifestation of cultural repression under martial law from 1949 to 1987, and the broad "liberalization" of culture after 1987.

Deng commented on aspects of the difference from the translator's point of view. In Taiwan, relatively unrestricted internet (or earlier, BBS) access allowed for rapid consulting with interested parties in Chinese or other languages. Even today when internet access in China is somewhat less restricted, she said, there remained an insular habit in China which discourages translators from wide international consultation (Deng 2017).

The Films

The first of the New Line films was released in China in April 2002. They were major box office successes, though the release of *The Two Towers* was severely hampered by the SARS epidemic. The current study deals with translations of Tolkien's books, but here I will compare the titles at least—the title of a work being a crucial framing device. In China, the overall title, as seen on posters for example, is *zhihuanwang* 指环王 "king of the ring." It's not clear to me why this variant was used instead of *mojie*, magic ring, which was used on the covers of the books, and also widely in reference to the films. In Taiwan and Hong Kong, *mojie* was used. The individual films are, officially:

Hujie shizhe 护戒使者 "the Envoys/emissaries who Protect the Ring." In Taiwan, the film titles followed Zhu's translation (see above).
Shuangta qibing 双塔奇兵 "the Surprise Attack of the Twin Towers."
Wangzhe wudi 王者无敌 "The King Is Triumphant/Invincible."

However, in the pirated DVDs I bought at a Beijing street market, the titles of the films are translated slightly differently. The overall series is called *Mojie*, but the three films are now called:

1. *Mojie xianshen* 魔戒现身, "The Magic Ring Reveals Itself."
2. On the packaging, the same as the Yilin edition, *Shuangta qibing*. But in the film itself: *Shuangcheng qimou* 双城奇谋, "The Clever Plan of the Twin Walled-Cities."
3. *Guowang guilai* 国王归来 "The King Returns."

I should note that the pirated DVDs I acquired feature an inept mixture of dubbing and subtitles, so that Frodo goes back and forth between Elijah Wood's English (with Chinese subtitles), and an uncredited Chinese actor's voice. Also, the menu options do not work. You get what you pay for.

The Hobbit, as all fans know, was stretched into three long films:

Huobite ren: yiwai zhi you 霍比特人：意外之游 (Hobbit person: Unexpected Journey/Wandering) [*The Hobbit: An Unexpected Journey*]. Global release in late 2012, early 2013 in China. In Taiwan: "Hobbit" uses a variant transliteration: *Habiren* instead of *Huobiteren*. And in Taiwan this film is: *Yiwai lücheng* 意外旅程 which also means unexpected journey. Where *you* means journey, travel, roam; *lücheng* is journey, route, itinerary—the latter having more sense of intention.

Huobite ren: Shimaoge zhi zhan 霍比特人：史矛革之战 (Hobbit Person: The Battle of Smaug) [*The Hobbit: The Desolation of Smaug*]. Late 2013; early 2014 in China. In Taiwan: *Habiren: Huanggu elong* 哈比人：荒谷惡龍 (Hobbit Person: Desolate Valley Evil Dragon).

Huobite ren: Wujun zhi zhan 霍比特人：五军之战 (Hobbit Person: The Battle of Five Armies) [*The Hobbit: The Battle of Five Armies*]. Late 2014; early 2015 in China. In Taiwan: the same except for the transliteration of "Hobbit."

The titles in China are mostly very close to literal translations of the English film titles. The film titles bear little connection to the book or its chapter titles, although the first chapter of the book is of course "An Unexpected Party." The main divergence is the second film, as released outside of China, with its inventive new title, the Evil Dragon of the Desolate Valley.

I also found a pirated DVD of the fan-produced short film, *The Hunt for Gollum* (2009). This film, made in Britain on a miniscule budget, shows Aragorn and Gandalf seeking out and finding Gollum. The film begins with a legal disclaimer, that this is a non-profit film, with no affiliation with the Tolkien estate, New Line Cinema, or any other stake-holders. "This work is produced solely for the personal, uncompensated enjoyment of ourselves and other Tolkien fans." This statement is not translated into Chinese. As so often happens, the Chinese title in the film and on the packaging is different. In the film itself, the title is given as *Souxun gulu*, 搜寻咕噜, "the search for Gollum." But on the packaging and on the DVD menu: *Gulu taonanji* 咕嚕逃難記 (in traditional characters, even though purchased in Beijing), "A Record of Gollum Fleeing from Disaster," and the subtitle describes it as: *Zhihuanwang waizhuan.* 指環王外傳. The first phrase, *Zhihuanwang*, is "King of the Ring," and *waizhuan* ("outer biography") means unofficial or unauthorized biography or even secret history. *Waizhuan* is a venerable genre in China, often implying a version closer to the truth precisely because it's not official. In contrast with the morally didactic official histories, *waizhuan* are more interesting because they include gossip or negative views of the heroes. We would recognize *The Hunt for Gollum* as unauthorized fan fiction, but the category *waizhuan* combines this marginal legal status of the film with the promise of some revelation of previous suppressed information.

So far we have seen many variations of the titles. Just for *Fellowship*, we have five variations. Even in the naming of the stories and in their marketing design, we begin to see a different world. Cumulatively, by merit of the many retellings, Tolkien in Chinese begins to appear as far more complex and diversified than a single series of books. True, very few people would ever sit down with all of the versions of the books plus the films, but nonetheless the Chinese Tolkien offers a diversity missing from the finite canon of the originals.

Four-Character Titles

Traditional Chinese literature features relatively standardized title styles, at least compared to the often idiosyncratic English book titles. China seems to have a stronger sense of naming conventions, which tend to make the contents or genre expectations clearer. To take some examples culled from a recent visit to Taiwan: Yelena Black's *Dance of Shadows* is *mogui zhiwu* 魔鬼之舞, the dance of demons (Linking, 2013), a phrase which indicates more explicitly the genre. After all, a book named *Dance of Shadows* might be a John le Carré spy thriller. *Frankenstein* is *kexue guairen* 科學怪人, "science monster," which could hardly be less explicit. *The Mummy* (2017) is the relatively generic *shengui chuanqi* 神鬼傳奇, "legend of gods and ghosts." *Inception* is *daomeng kongjian* 盜夢空間, "stealing dreams in empty space." *Transformers* is *bianxing jingang* 變形金剛, "form-changing vajra" (= vajrasattva—a category of adamantine beings in Buddhism). *Resident Evil* is *shenghua weiji* 生化危機, "biochemistry crisis." *His Dark Materials* loses the "His" to become the four-character *Heian wuzhi* (dark material). All these are four-character phrases. Chinese titles are not always four characters: *Miss Peregrine's Peculiar Children* is the five-syllable *guaiqi gueryuan* 怪奇孤兒院, "the strange orphanage," and there are of course other examples (see Lin 2002: 165–166; Li Hong-man 2010: 21–22).

Even chapter titles are frequently converted to four-character phrases. For example, in *The Lord of the Rings*, the English chapter titles show a common pattern of "The . . . of . . . ." Hence, "the Passing of the Grey Company," or "The Muster of Rohan." But not all: "Mount Doom," "Homeward Bound," or "Many Partings." Certainly there is no consistency at all regarding number of syllables or stressed syllables. But every single chapter title in the Yilin edition of *LOTR* is a four-character phrase. "Minas Tirith" (four syllables in English, but six in Chinese) is changed to *Gangduo ducheng* 冈多都城, "the capital city of Gondor." "The Passing of the Grey Company" becomes *youxia qishi* 游侠骑士, "the knight-errant riders." Both Zhu and Deng follow the original titles more closely, without trying to compress the meanings into four characters. Even so, of the sixty-two chapter titles, Zhu has eighteen in four-character phrases (29%) and Deng has twenty-six (42%). So, for Zhu and Deng, "Minas Tirith" becomes *Minasitilisi*, a transliteration in six characters. "The Passing of the Grey Company" becomes for Zhu, *huiyiren chuxian* 灰衣人出現 "the grey-clothed people appear." And for Deng, *huiyi jinlü de zhengcheng* 灰衣劲旅的征程, "grey-clothed crack force's journey." Oddly, the Yilin edition of *The Hobbit* and *The Silmarillion* have varying chapter title lengths—perhaps another instance of the inconsistency resulting from multiple translators with a tight deadline.

The naming of the story genre in the title is common in China. Not all Chinese novels include genre clues in their names, but many do (Lin 2002: 166). If we consider some of the classic novels: *Xiyouji* is a *Record* of a westward journey. *Shuihu zhuan* is *Biographies* of (bandits on) the Water Margin. *Hongloumeng* is The *Dream* of the Red Chamber, in which "Dream" tells us what kind of story it is, even if it is not literally about a dream; and the book has an alternate title: *Shitouji*, the *Record* of the Stone. *Sanguo yanyi* is the *historical novel* or *romance* of the Three Kingdoms. *The Scholars* is *rulin waishi*, the *unofficial history* of the 'forest' of literati. In the twentieth century this trend almost vanishes, and indeed when Lu Xun started his *True Story of Ah-Q* (阿Q正傳, 1921–1922) with an apparently irrelevant discussion of the story's genre category, his fussy prevarication is part of the satire. Some standard English translations include the genre identifiers (*Dream of the Red Chamber*, *Romance of the Three Kingdoms*), while others don't (*Journey to the West, Outlaws of the Marsh, The Scholars*). Except for *Numennuo-er yu zhongzhou zhi weiwan de chuanshuo* (Unfinished *Legends* of Númenor and Middle-earth); Wanxiang's 1996 *Xiaoairen lixianji* ("The *Record* of the Adventure of the Small Dwarves"), and one of the titles of the non-canonical *Gulu taonanji* ("A *Record* of Gollum Fleeing from Disaster"), the translators seem to have conformed to modern rather than traditional naming conventions.

Mojie 魔戒

The widely accepted general title for at least *The Lord of the Rings* and possibly *The Hobbit* and *The Silmarillion* or for the entire legendarium is *mojie*. While this may be rendered as "magic ring," it is more complicated than that. In conventional terms, *jie* means "ring" among other things (such as "precept," "guard against," and "exhort"). The other term for ring is *zhihuan*, "finger-surround." In the English title, *Rings* is plural, because the One Ring is "lord" of all the other rings; whereas in the Chinese translations *mojie* refers only to the One Ring, hence the singular "magic ring." Usually when the original says "the Ring" or "the One Ring," it is translated as *mojie*. For comparison, Galadriel's "Ring" of Adamant is merely *jie* in Yilin and Deng, but oddly, *mojie* in Zhu (*FR* II, vii, 356; Yilin *FR* 445; Deng *FR* 456; Zhu *FR* 564). *Mo* is very interesting, especially if we compare it to "magic." In different combinations, *mo* can be either menacing or fun.

In various dictionaries I have consulted, we find the following glosses for *mo* in English: 1. evil spirit, demon, fiend, devil; 2. magic, occult, mystic. This basic division of usage persists in the various two-character combinations. On the bad side are terms such as: *modao* (*mo*-path: domain of the devil, sorcery, evil ways); *mofa* (*mo*-method: sorcery, witchcraft); *moguai* (monsters); *mogui* (demon, monster); *moku* (den of iniquity); *mowang* (king of demons); *moying* (shadow of a demon, spectre of evil); and *mozhang* (devil's clutches). The character *mo* 魔 consists of the phonetic element 麻 (*ma*, hemp, sesame, rough) which tells us the word is pronounced *mo* or *ma*, and the character *gui* 鬼, meaning ghost or monster, and by extension something sinister, clever, or "wicked." (There is also an obscure Buddhist use of *mojie*, which means a precept undertaken for bad motives such as personal gain or fame.)

Mo is an abbreviation of *Moluo* 魔羅, better known in its original Sanskrit form of Mara, the embodiment of evil or temptation in Buddhism. Along with his intimidating army and his alluring daughters, Mara appears before the Buddha in an attempt to stop him from achieving enlightenment; and he appears shortly before the Buddha's death. Or *Mo* can be plural, as the class of beings under Mara. The term "demon" is slightly misleading, because Mara resides in one of the celestial realms ("heavens"); He is the king of the Mara-heaven, the 6th heaven of *kammaloka*, the desire-realm. Another being, Yama, presides over the hells, though he does not fit the mold of Satan either. Yet Mara is the principle enemy of the Buddha and all things good. In the scriptures, Mara is not equivalent to Satan, though in popular usage one finds some similarity. The use of *Mo* is extensive in all the Chinese translations of Tolkien's works. *Mowang*, "king of demons," is used to refer to Morgoth, the first and most powerful of the deities created by the uber-deity Ilúvatar. Among those that Morgoth corrupted include: "the Valaraukar, the scourges of fire that in Middle-earth were called the Balrogs, demons of fire" (S: 23). To translate this line, the Yilin edition uses *mo* twice: "Valaraukar—'fire demons' (*huomo* 火魔). In Middle Earth, they were called Balrogs—'frightening demons' (*kepa de mogui* 可怕的魔鬼)" (Yilin S: 23).

In other fantasy, the word *mo* is commonly used for a range of meanings related to demons, devils, and monsters. In Bram Stoker's *Dracula*, "his eyes blazed with a sort of demoniac fury" ([1897] 1981: 26). For "demoniac," both Liu Tiehu's and Ye Anhei's translations give "like a *mogui* 魔鬼" (Stoker, trans. Liu 2007: 34; Stoker, trans. Ye 2013: 40). In Liu Xiaohua's translation of China Miéville's *Perdido Street Station*, the term "daemons" is *e-mo* 惡魔 (evil *mo*); the terrifying slake-moths are *mo-e* 魔蛾, *mo*-moths. We should not impose more strict consistency than the usage implies—and after all, it's not as if we all know what "demon" means. At times I have been tempted to translate *mogui* as "boogie-man."

So that's all pretty horrible. But in contrast, there is *moshu* 魔術 (arts of *mo* = magic, conjuring, slight of hand), *mogun* 魔棍 or *mozhang* 魔杖 (magic wand); and also, *mofang* 魔方 (*fang* = square or cube; hence, Rubik's Cube). In translating Hogwarts School of Witchcraft and Wizardry, Pen Qianwen first transliterates the word "Hogwarts," and then translates the rest as: magic and wizard academy (*mofa yu wushu xueyuan* 魔法與巫術學院) (Rowling, trans. Peng 2000: 19). The word *mo* is used in translations of "magic word" (*mozhou* 魔咒, *mo*-spell, 18). In Fu Hao's translations of W. B. Yeats, he uses *mo* to translate faery: "faery vats" are *motong* 魔桶, *mo*-vats (2000: 36–37). But also demons and devils (ibid., 73, 149, both *mogui*). Mei Lüjin's translation of Christina Rossetti's "The Goblin Market" is *xiaoyao moshi* 小妖魔市, the *mo*-market of the little *yaos* (2015: 169). I will return to *mo*, *yao*, and other categories of boogie-men in Chapter 5.

The negative connotations of *mo* far outnumber the benign ones, and this is certainly the case in the translations of Tolkien. Whereas *mofa* (the *method* of *mo*) translates as witchcraft, *moshu* (the *art* of *mo*) translates as magic, as in magic shows and conjuring. So *mo* does capture Tolkien's sense of the Ring better than the potentially trivial-sounding "magic ring." And yet *mo* does not give away the game in the way that a title like "demonic ring" would. *Mo* preserves the ambiguity of something that might be intriguing but ultimately trivial (to Bilbo in *The Hobbit*, for example), while strongly hinting at the ring's sinister malevolence. In comparison, "magic ring" sounds like something you got in a Christmas cracker. Apparently, Tolkien began with the idea of the ring as a trivial item, a plot device, and gradually increased the sense of the demonic.

When I pointed out the ambiguity of *mojie*, Deng remarked, "I agree with you. In Chinese, I haven't yet thought of a better word" (2017). She explored the terminology with reference to genre:

> But there's a different tradition, you know China has lots of *wuxia xiaoshuo* 武俠小說 (knight-errant or adventure novels). In *wuxia* novels there's often an ordinary person, he goes into the mountains, and he encounters a 'master,' and studies a lot of *gongfu* 功夫 (Kung-fu). Or he goes into the mountains and encounters a *xianren* 仙人 (immortal or transcended being), so he studies some [using the English

word:] 'magic.' After he returns, he can use this [English:] 'magic' to do some special things. About this, in Chinese we use the term *fashu* 法術. So it turns out, when we are translating, I don't remember if I used these two characters *fashu*, but most of the time I use *mofa*. Because *mofa* and *fashu*, in fact their content is the same, both transcending nature. *Fashu* and *mofa* both transcend nature. But if I use *fashu*, the feeling is a bit more ancient, if I use *mofa* it's a little more of a Western feeling. (2017)

In all of this, of course it seems absurd to ask what a *mo* really is. What a demon really is. And whether a *mo* "is" a demon. More to the point, what if we think of the whole of Tolkien's work as a single story, about a ring which is characterized by an ambiguity, wavering between comedy and horror, between trivial and Evil, between a trick and damnation?

Conclusions

Tolkien's works have been translated many times, and in many languages more than once. In the case of *The Lord of the Rings*, we are considering three, all produced within a period of less than twenty years. However, they differ by the location of the translator and the intended market, with the interesting quirk of a Taiwan-based translator working for the China market. Talk of editions (*ban* 版) is part of Chinese fan discourse in a way vastly more significant than comparisons of the initial English-language Allen and Unwin edition and subsequent editions, whose differences (of spelling, pagination, or font) are trivial compared to the word-by-word differences of the Yilinban, Zhuban, and Dengban.

The framing of the works sometimes differs from English editions, both in the sense of presenting the five core books as a series titled *Mojie*, and for example by naming the *Silmarillion* as "the beginning" and *The Hobbit* as a "prequel." A book's title is probably the first piece of text to be read. Chinese naming conventions include the four-character tendency and the naming of the genre in the title. Genre is also a form of framing. The next chapter turns then to genre—in other words the question of what kind of stories these are.

4

Genre across Cultures, and in Middle-earth

The Anachronism of All Categories

This chapter problematizes the idea that Tolkien's work is "fantasy" in an Anglophone context, and then in translation. Given that "fantasy" in a Western word, we may ask how the concept was translated, how it interacted with indigenous genre terms, and how new Chinese terms have been coined to chart something like the terrain of "fantasy literature." What if *The Lord of the Rings* is not, after all, a work of "fantasy literature"? And, dealing as we are with stories in which the nature of stories is repeatedly questioned, what do the stories themselves say about genre—in the original and in the translations?

There has been much scholarship on the question of defining "fantasy" as a genre. If we posit an essentialist or "scientific" definition, the search for "fantasy" in any given society becomes like the search for a certain mineral in an excavation: it's either there or it isn't, and one's subjectivity is irrelevant. Yet, this aura of objectivity always obscures the cultural contingency of the terms—of Science itself—so that we may be deluding ourselves, hegemonically imposing an interpretation while imagining it to be no interpretation at all.

Essentialist definitions of "fantasy" tend to gravitate around some element which *conspicuously and deliberately differs from some assumed sense of reality*—what I call the normally impossible, in which "normally" indicates that each society or age, or even each person, has different ideas about what is real. As long as reality is a moving target, any definition of fantasy can only function in reference to a particular cultural context. Hence, in defining the modern sense of fantasy as genre fiction, rather than using a categorical or essentialist definition, Attebery posits fuzzy sets, with certain quintessential examples at the center. This approach focuses on actual (empirically verifiable) usage of a word in a given context rather than any purely "scientific" classification. What, he asks, is the quintessential example of Anglophone fantasy, the example virtually everyone gives when asked what fantasy is? Answer: *The Lord of the Rings* (Attebery 1992: 13–14; also Attebery 2014: 33). With *LOTR*, "a new coherence was given to the genre" (Attebery 1992: 14). There is a circularity in defining *The Lord of the Rings* as "fantasy" since the genre "fantasy" was and still is defined by *The Lord of the Rings*. Still, if we accept "things like *The Lord of the Rings*" as an empirical definition of fantasy fiction, we are still left with the problem of defining in what sense, *like*? Neither an essentialist nor a fuzzy-sets definition can operate in isolation. Indeed,

Attebery also approaches the question by defining fantasy as genre as a mediating concept between fantasy as "mode" (imagination itself, which may reasonably be considered a human universal) and fantasy as "formula" (the "dragons and wizards" of fantasy, always embedded in particular cultural contexts) (1992: 2–4). With this approach, we might look for fantasy-as-genre as a dialectic between the human capacity to imagine, and the inherited catalogue of fantastic things which have already been imagined.

There has been a similar problem in Religious Studies. If we say that all societies and all time periods have had something called "religion," we have to account for certain facts: the word was not always available as a label in the societies we are speaking of; it effects a serious distortion when applied to pre-modern and non-Western contexts; translations of the word may obscure significant differences in meaning; and its meaning has changed over time. Can a historically contingent, culturally specific term be used to identify a supposed human universal, without a distortion which risks transforming diversity into homogeneity? Rather than proceeding as if there has always and everywhere been an essential thing called religion (as a mode) which modern scholars can discover, Jonathan Z. Smith says we should accept the fluid inventedness of the idea, which has creatively called "religion" into being out of a formulaic repertoire (1998: 281–282). The problem is that we constantly confuse religion as a "mode" with religion as a "formula," thereby falsely assuming that we can describe human universals using conceptual tools which only make sense within our own culture (at best). Much of the history of Religious Studies in the twentieth century was an effort to shake off the formula, and also a skepticism about whether anything can be said about religion as a mode—just as it may be impossible to specify the content of "imagination itself." Yet, it would also be an error to think of religion or fantasy as only formula.

Compared to "religion," the use of "fantasy" (as a literary genre) is very recent—it emerges in the mid-twentieth century. Williamson argues that "fantasy" was not a self-conscious genre until the 1960s, whereupon it was retrojected onto what he calls "pregenre fantasy"—namely the now-familiar "lineage" or "canon" which includes William Morris, J. M. Barrie, Robert E. Howard, and indeed Tolkien (Williamson 2015: 13). A similar term is "taproot texts," suggesting a living continuity moving beneath the visible surface of culture (Clute 1997: 921; Attebery 2014: 22). Prior to "fantasy" as a distinct genre category, what has come to be called fantasy was labeled as children's literature, fairy-tale, romance, saga, or science fiction. Or just "literature." Certainly it's worth noting that authors of the past could not have labeled their own work "fantasy literature" or "science fiction" until the terms themselves came into circulation. But does that mean that their work was *not* fantasy—or better, is there not some value in thinking of them as fantasy? We might also think in terms of "pregenre religion," features of a culture which can retroactively be considered religion. This is about anachronism, but also about cultural difference. What happens when we label a text from another culture using our own labels? How do the Chinese and English terms affect our reading?

In this chapter, I will address these questions in two ways. First, there are questions of the history of genre in China. How have modern genre classifications entered

Chinese usage? What indigenous genre terms seem analogous to fantasy? How does a reading or framing of Tolkien change when we approach the works in Chinese genre terms? How does the history of fantasy as a genre in Chinese compare to science fiction?

Second, I ask what *Mojie* itself can tell us about its own genre. Tolkien's works are very concerned with genre, to the extent that characters in the story actually debate genre questions. They use a range of terms: legends, "old-wives' tales," bogey-stories, dreams, marvels, ballads, songs, tales, and stories. Frodo and Sam engage in an extended discussion of "adventures." When these conversations are translated, how do the Chinese terms change the debates? This section signals a shift in this study, from theoretical or thematic questions, to the mode of analysis used in the rest of the book: asking questions directly of the original text and its translations.

Fantasy and China

It is worth risking some very brief and necessarily impressionistic generalizations about the literary histories of English and Chinese pregenre and genre fantasy. We can trace a steady trickle of original compositions in English, which we might evoke with reference to notable pregenre examples: *The Faerie Queen, A Mid-summer's Night Dream, A Christmas Carol, Peter Pan* ... and then, *The Lord of the Rings*—followed by a great flood of fantasy writing, simultaneous with the establishment of the category itself. Deng noted a similar sudden impact of *Mojie* in Taiwan, regarding the influence of the films on the emergence of a bibliographic category:

> many people originally didn't know that *qihuan wenxue* 奇幻文學—*qihuan wenxue* is 'fantasy'—and science fiction were not the same. *Star Wars* is science fiction. So, in the 1980s, 1990s, everyone knew, there's one category which is science fiction, but no one knew there was a category of fantasy—until the film *Mojie* was shown, and then suddenly everyone knew there was such a thing as fantasy. (2017; see also Mao 2020: 88)

Just as the *LOTR* books established fantasy fiction in English, the *LOTR* films seem to have had the same effect in China and Taiwan, though we should also factor in the *Harry Potter* films, starting with a rapid translation and publication of the first three books in 2000, and the Chinese release of the first film in early 2002 (Qi 2012: 153–154, 170; also Mao 2020: 88). And, to a lesser extent, George R. R. Martin's books, starting in 2001 in Taiwan and 2005 in China. Yu-Ling Chung writes,

> The genre of fantasy did not exist in Taiwan until bestsellers such as *The Lord of the Rings* and the *Harry Potter* series caught the attention of the local market through translation. Before this sudden increase of translated fantasy books in 1998, translators did not know how to term fantasy literature. Therefore, they just translated fantasy works according to local publishers' classification of the books, such as children's literature or adult romance. (2013: 129; see also Mao 2020: 88)

Chinese pregenre fantasy, on the other hand, is much older than in English, by simple merit of the fact that "English" came into existence much later than "Chinese." Chinese texts of a thousand years ago need some training to read but are considerably more accessible to modern readers than, say, *Beowulf* is to us today. There are "weird tales" (*zhiguai* 志怪) collections from before the Tang (7th–9th centuries CE), often with a Buddhist morality but clearly also as a form of entertainment. "The magnitude of *zhiguai* production in traditional China simply cannot be exaggerated. This whole tradition, rooted in various forms of pre-Han 漢 literature, continued uninterrupted until the end of the Qing 清" (Chan 1998: 2). There was an uptick in the Ming with many published collections, and with the publication of *Xiyouji* (*Journey to the West*), a lavishly fantastic novel and one of the culturally hallowed classics of Chinese fiction. A common literary device in *zhiguai* fiction is the memorate, "a firsthand account of an experience, usually a supernatural or paranormal one, that links the teller to a traditional belief or legend" (Attebery 2014: 35). This claim to have personally witnessed a marvel (or to have heard it from someone who did) should be recognized part of the genre, rather than some kind of documentary realism.

Chan writes, "until the end of the Qing," which brings us into the complicated twentieth century, during much of which social realism was the dominant mood. Indigenous genres featuring the normally impossible such as *zhiguai* and *wuxia* 武俠 fiction were too closely associated with religion, superstition, and feudalism. Neither Chinese modernism nor Communist rule have been kind to the fanciful imagination. Chan remarks, "most *zhiguai* collections invite interest only as documents from which information about religious beliefs in certain localities can be culled" (Chan 1998: 3). There was already a strong tradition of Chinese writers gathering folk tales and compiling them, usually with some rewriting in the interests of literary refinement or ideological correction. However, especially from 1918 through the 1930s, some urban elites grew more interested in "folklore" (*minsu* 民俗, a coinage from Japan), and *tonghua* (children's stories). Under Communist control, folklore continued to be gathered and heavily processed to conform to political programs, or repressed if that was not possible. One of the first Chinese art films to gain international attention, *Yellow Earth* (*Huangtudi* 黃土地, 1984) concerns a Red Army soldier sent to live among poor peasants to rewrite their folk songs and tales. As documents of folklore, *zhiguai* may be studied, but as a living genre, they struggled in the social realist and anti-religious atmosphere of twentieth-century China.

In recent years there has emerged an increasingly detailed history of Chinese science fiction in the twentieth century, but there is far less of any comparable history of fantasy in modern China—not least because the concept of China having such a thing as "fantasy literature" (*qihuan wenxue* 奇幻文學 and other terms) was not common until the early twenty-first century. There are of course studies of *zhiguai*, miracle tales, ghosts stories, hagiographies, and other pre-genre fantasy in China, but when we move into the twentieth century the story seems to peter out.

Or does it? The impression that there was no indigenous Chinese fantasy in the twentieth century at all is due to a widespread bias against genre or popular fiction in elite and academic cultures. However, as soon as one suspends the modernist and class-based snobbery over what counts as "serious" and "real literature," we find a fairly robust tradition of something like fantasy, mainly oriented around the category *xia* 俠, translated as adventurer or knight-errant. The term *xia* is modified in several ways. First, there is *wuxia*, martial or martial-arts hero (Chung 2013: 56–58). The genre can be traced back most prominently to *Shuihuzhuan* 水滸傳 (*The Water Margin*, 14th century), a tale of 108 bandits, of novel length but highly episodic. In the 1920s, writes Wu Fuhui, *wuxia* was "an independent literary genre" (2020: 339). Modern *wuxia* novels were written from the 1950s, most notably by Jin Yong and Liang Yusheng of Hong Kong and Gu Long of Taiwan. Note that the three most famous *wuxia* novelists wrote outside of China, though there were also efforts in Taiwan to repress the genre (Chung 2013: 58). These stories feature a relatively light touch of the normally impossible, having to do with Daoist energy cultivation, uncanny swords, strange poisons and cures, secret kung fu techniques, and the mysterious workings of karma. There is a related genre, *xianxia* 仙俠, combining *xian* (immortals, sylphs) with *xia*, which features a more "high fantasy" level of magic, usually in a Daoist context, involving a quest for cultivation of transcendent powers, and typically with a higher level of romance than in *wuxia*. An example is the 1932 *Legend of the Swordsmen of the Mountains of Shu* (*shushan jianxia zhuan* 蜀山劍俠傳) by Huanzhulouzhu (pen name of Li Shoumin). Since the 1990s, romantic *xianxia* has become a staple of Chinese film and television, noted for gorgeous costumes and love between mortals and immortals.

The blurb on the cover of the English translation of Jin Yong's *Legends of the Condor Heroes*, from the *Irish Times*, says it's "A Chinese *Lord of the Rings*." How much of an overlap is there? Certainly there is a general theme of the evil Jin dynasty versus the Song, but little sense of cosmic Good versus Evil. Much of the plot is driven by personal feuds, macho showing-off, and over-sensitivity to insult. Though there is a moralistic rhetoric about personal honor and justice, most of the action centers around the acquisition of martial skills and a compulsion to test those skills in combat. The fights in *LOTR* are rare, and given only a rudimentary description, whereas here we have a fight every few pages, with elaborate technical descriptions of the moves.

So the fit is not perfect. But how about: *Lord of the Rings* is an English *Legends of the Condor Heroes*? One of the key concepts in *wuxia* novels is *jianghu* 江湖, literally "rivers and lakes" but connoting the martial-arts world, which is physically or socially marginal, countercultural, outside of governmental or policing structures, perhaps criminal, and related to *wulin* 武林 the "forest" of marital artists (Teo 2009: 18). Gandalf, "a travelling magician of unknown powers and purpose" (*FR*, I, ix, 157), is in Yilin, "a *jianghu* magician (*moshushi*) of limitless magic power (*fali wubian*) and sinister motives (*juxin poce*)" (Yilin *FR* 197). *LOTR* doesn't exactly have a *jianghu*, except maybe the social world that Aragorn moved in (prior to the start of the story): the Rangers keeping an eye out for villains in the North. Aragorn's wandering away from the centers of power can be seen as the *wuxia*'s years of training and tempering in marginal spaces prior to his ultimate test. Deng translates "Rangers" as *youmin* 游民, wandering people (*FR*, I, ix, 146; Deng *FR*: 188), Yilin as *liulang han* 流浪汉, wandering/ vagrant men (Yilin *FR*: 183), but Zhu gives it as *youxia*, wandering *xia* (Zhu *FR*: 239). Aragorn has multiple names, which is typical of *xia*. His romance with the immortal Arwen fits the *xianxia* mold. When Aragorn decides to pursue the captured Merry and Pippin, that's a *xia* moment. Legolas and Gimli are *xia* blood brother types. The fact that the Oathbreakers cannot pass on until they have fulfilled their oath to the heir of Isildur seems consistent with the *wuxia* code of ethics, which takes oaths very seriously. Gimli's thin-skinned defense of the good name of Galadriel against Éomer's suspicious slander feels like a Jin Yong bit. The gathering of a numbered Fellowship is a common trope. "The Passing of the Grey Company" becomes in the Yilin edition *youxia qishi*, "the wandering *xia* riders."

Aragorn fits the classification well, and to some extent Boromir, Faramir, Thorin, and various others more loosely: Gandalf, Legolas, Gimli. But certainly not the hobbits—at least, not until the Scouring of the Shire. Shippey notes the contrast of the dwarf Balin's grand heroic (*xia*) farewell at the end of *The Hobbit* and Bilbo's mumbling about stopping in at tea-time if you happen to be passing by (Shippey 2003: 86; see also Fimi 2009: 185). It's as if Winnie the Pooh strolled into Tennyson's *Idylls of the King*. In *LOTR*, the hobbits consistently bring down to earth the grand Romantic heroism of the *xia* they're travelling with. Though they become fully realized *xia* towards the end of the story, for most of it they're anti-heroes—or anti-*xia*. If we focus on the hobbit protagonists, it's almost a satire of *xia*—Tolkien uses that contrast for comedic effect, though lightly, so we can still enjoy the heroic characters without irony.

In addition to *xia*, two other traditional genre terms seem particularly relevant here: *chuanqi* and *zhiguai*. *Chuanqi* 傳奇/传奇 is generally close to "legend," in the sense of a traditional narrative with some supernatural elements or other reasons for astonishment. Sometimes the term refers specifically to Tang dynasty short stories. *Chuan* means to pass on, transmit, as of a story in this case; *qi* means strange, surprising. What is surprising may not be strictly speaking impossible, and so some *chuanqi* are not at all supernatural. Notable *chuanqi* stories include "The World Inside a Pillow," in which a man goes to sleep, lives his whole life, and then wakes up—it was all a dream; or "Miss Ren," in which a beautiful fox-spirit negotiates the amorous attention of two human men. There are often convoluted love stories, estranged and reconciled families, the ups and downs of human fortune. *LOTR* might well be *chuanqi*, though far longer than typical. The genre's legendary tone, and the association with the supposed "Golden Age" of the Tang would fit *LOTR*'s Medievalism. *The Chronicles of Narnia* is *naniya chuanqi* 纳尼亚传奇.

Another term is *zhiguai* 志怪, records of the strange (Chung 2013: 53–56). *Zhi* means a record or annals; *guai* has a similar range to *qi* (strange), but more supernatural: it can also mean monster or demon, miraculous, anomalous. The best-known collection of these short stories is by Pu Songling (1640–1715), *Liaozhai zhiyi* (record of the strange from Liaozhai studio), which uses the term *yi* 異/异 (strange, different, unusual), similar to *qi* and *guai*. This collection is a mixture of ghosts, romances, fox-spirits, seduction, uncanny dreams, and mysterious karma. Certainly it is rich with the normally impossible, though it remains a collection of short stories with some thematic overlaps, and in this sense closer to Grimm's fairy-tales than a novel. Reading *LOTR* on the assumption that it is *zhiguai*, the reader would anticipate the demon-like orcs, the giant spider, the ghost-army, the prophecies, and the surprising coincidences.

As for modern translations of "fantasy fiction," in Chinese there seem to be several terms in use. Combined with suffixes *wenxue* 文學 (literature) or *xiaoshuo* 小說 (novel), perhaps most common is *qihuan* 奇幻, strange-imaginary, Western in style or influence. *Mohuan* 魔幻 sometimes implies fiction with Western-style fantasy elements. The phrase combines *mo* (magical/demonic) with *huan* 幻 (unreal, imaginary or illusory). There is also *xuanhuan* 玄幻 (dark/mysterious imaginary), generally referring to hybrid Chinese/translated fantasy, or to online fiction with Chinese-style magical elements (Ni 2020: 1–2; Chung 2013: 43, 59). The distinctions may be further elaborated in terms such as *dongfang xuanhuan* (Eastern fantasy) and *xifang qihuan* (Western fantasy). Certainly the Western-ness of Tolkien's works is obvious in China, and central to fan consciousness of his work. Other new genre terms include *xiuxian* 修仙 (immortality cultivation), *xianxia* 仙侠 (Ni 2020: 2), *yishu chaoneng* 异术超能 (super-normal powers), *mofa xiaoyuan* (magical school campus), *yijie dalu* 异界大陆 (adventures in another world), and *lingyi qitan* 灵异奇谈, supernatural and mythic stories.

While fine distinctions among genre categories may be important in certain contexts, in general we can recognize a family resemblance. We should not impose more precision on the terms than is evident in actual usage, which in any case shifts all the time. In this soup of Chinese native, translated and newly coined categories, where is Tolkien to be found? Predominantly his work is *xifang qihuan* (Western fantasy), but we can recognize elements of *youxia*, *zhiguai*, *chuanqi*, and *xianxia*.

Children's Literature

There is another major classification to consider. Is *LOTR* children's literature? "They belong to the category of adult, or young adult," said Deng. "If you go to a bookstore in Taiwan to look, you might discover Tolkien's books, for example *The Silmarillion*, but when I want to find the English books, they're put in children's books" (2017). Vincent Ferré et al. and Marcantonio Savelli note the general tendency in France and Italy to treat the books as children's fiction (Ferré et al. 2011: 50; Savelli 2020: 10), and undoubtedly this pattern is widespread around the world.

A dragon in a story does not make it automatically for children. But are Tolkien's works children's stories in some other sense? A case could certainly be made for *The Hobbit*. The feeling of "being told a story" is greater in *The Hobbit* than in the other books, in large part because of a certain quality of some of the narration—specifically where the narrator speaks directly to the reader, as if Tolkien was gathering his little audience around his comfy-chair on a winter's eve, even to the extent of interrupting his own thoughts. For example, concerning Bilbo's adventure, "He may have lost the neighbours' respect, but he gained—well, you will see whether he gained anything in the end" (*H*, i, 4; see also Williamson 2015: 130–131). Both Yilin and Zhu reproduce the oral quality here: "Maybe because of this he lost peoples' respect, but he got … oh, you can see what he got in the end" (Yilin *H*: 2). And: "but at least he got—forget it! (*suanla!* 算啦!) In the end you will know what thing he got" (Zhu *H*: 6). Wu's translation is a less oral: "his gains were not a few—reading below you will be clear about whether he did or didn't get what he gained" (Wu *H*: 7).

There are other places where the children's storyteller reaches out through the fourth wall, but not so much in the Chinese translations. Speaking of Bilbo, the narrator remarks parenthetically, "(even the hobbit had never forgotten the magic fireworks at Old Took's midsummer-eve parties, as you remember)" (*H*, vi, 105). *As you remember?* This is the narrator speaking, so "you" is the reader or listener. Yilin has: "Hobbits can never forget" (Yilin *H*: 85). Or, Zhu: "Hence, Hobbits continuously remembered and never forgot" (Zhu *H*: 115). In these lines, the translations remove the second person pronoun which is part of what gives *The Hobbit* its children's-book tone. Yilin and Zhu attribute all of the remembering to the hobbits. Wu, however, keeps the second person: "this you (*nimen*, second person plural) should still remember" (Wu *H*: 135).

The resemblance to traditional fairy stories might also account for their placement in children's literature. *The Hobbit* retains much of a fairy story's tone but is very long compared to traditional fairy stories. Most of the tales collected by the Grimms or by Lang are just a few pages—perhaps assuming that children have a short attention span. Michael Moorcock called Tolkien's work "epic Pooh," in the sense that they have the ingredients and narrative pattern of a much more modest and cozy narrative tradition, but expanded to epic scale (2004: 127). He meant it negatively, but he has a point. Attebery asserts, "The structure of *The Lord of the Rings* is that of the traditional fairy tale" (1992: 15). Structure, and some of the ingredients (elves and talking trees and magic balls and giant spiders), but the *length* not so much: "folk" don't tell "tales" that are 450,000 words long.

What *Mojie* Says about Genre

As it turns out, the stories themselves include some discussion of genre. There is a varied lexicon of narrative types, and also a number of places where the characters directly address the genre of the story they are in.

Boromir refers to stories about Fangorn forest as "old-wives' tales" (*FR*, II, viii, 364). To translate that phrase, we get: "old woman's superstition" (*laotaipo de mixin*) (Deng *FR*: 467); "what old ladies (*laotaitai* 老太太) have heard on the street and spoken on the road" (*daoting tushuo* 道听途说, namely gossip, rumor) (Yilin, *FR*: 456); and "stories told by a nanny" (*baomu* 保母, variant of *baomu* 保姆) (Zhu *FR*: 577). Deng relates the term to religious error, Yilin places them on the unreliable streets, and Zhu locates the tales in the nursery, which makes sense as Boromir immediately explains the term with "such as we tell to our children." But all three retain from the original the implausible notion that old women are somehow less reliable than, presumably, old husbands, or the young. The context in *Fellowship* clearly means to treat any such stories as false, and we are not meant to think of Tolkien as a writer of old wives' tales.

Also talking about Fangorn, Pippin asks if the stories are true. Merry answers, "If you mean the old bogey-stories Fatty's nurses used to tell him, about goblins and wolves and things of that sort, I should say no" (*FR*, I, vi, 108). Once again, we see male skepticism towards the narratives of women—"nurses" here presumably meaning wet-nurses or nannies. All three translations use *baomu* 保姆 (or 保母), nursemaid, literally "protecting nanny or mother." Class is also on display—about stories a servant told the affluent Fredegar "Fatty" Bolger. For "bogey-story" we get a variety of translations. Deng has "out-of-date (*laodiaoya*, old lost-teeth, toothless) monster (*yaoguai*) stories"

(Deng *FR:* 138). Yilin: "those spirit-ghost (*shengui*) stories" (Yilin *FR:* 136). Zhu renders this as, "ghost stories (*guigushi*), legends about things like *yao* who eat people (*shirenyao*) and evil wolves" (Zhu *FR:* 182). In place of eats-people-*yao*, Zhu's earlier translation used *dijing* 地精, goblin, earth-spirit (Zhu *FR:* 2001 169). For the scary creatures in the stories, Yilin uses a set phrase: "tigers, leopards, wild dogs and wolves" *hubaochailang* 虎豹豺狼 (Yilin *FR:* 136).

Faced with the evidence of his senses, Éomer struggles to reconcile such "old wives' tales" with his reality. He names the genres of the story in which he finds himself: "Dreams and legends spring to life out of the grass" (*TT,* III, ii, 423). For "dreams" Yilin and Zhu use *menghuan* 梦幻/夢幻, combining *meng* (dream) with *huan* (illusion) (Yilin *TT:* 29, Zhu *TT:* 47), but Deng opts for "dream lands/domain (*mengjing* 梦境)" (Deng *TT:* 31). In a Chinese context, the use of "dream" to describe a story naturally points us directly to the best-known of all Chinese novels, *Hongloumeng*, The Dream of the Red Chamber. In what sense is that Classic novel about a dream? That novel's title has a strong Buddhist meaning, namely that life is dreamlike—beauty is illusory and all things are vain.

In Éomer's comment and elsewhere, "legends" is rendered uniformly as *chuanshuo*, 传说/傳說, which is also used for "fables," "tales," and even "folklore." "What are the fables of the forest that Boromir had heard?" (*TT,* III, ii, 431); all three use *chuanshuo* (Deng *TT:* 42; Yilin *TT:* 39; Zhu *TT:* 59). This term literally means a saying or story (*shuo*) which has been transmitted or passed along (*chuan*). "Legend," by contrast, derives from what is read (cf. legible) and thereby a story. The Chinese *chuanshuo* of course may be written down, but by nature the term is more oral. You might hear them from your nanny.

The choice of Éomer to voice these skeptical thoughts is astute—in the books (and in Karl Urban's interpretation), Éomer is a blunt pragmatist. Éomer's epistemological crisis continues as he struggles to believe himself inside such a fictional world, or to believe a fiction real; and he ties this dissonance to a question of ethics. "It is hard to be sure of anything among so many marvels. The world is all grown strange. Elf and Dwarf in company walk in our daily fields; and folk speak with the Lady of the Wood and yet live; ... How shall a man judge what to do in such times?" (*TT,* III, ii, 427). (Théoden has a similar reaction after an encounter with ents. *TT,* III, viii, 536–537). The phrase "in our daily fields" recalls Dunsany's ingenious phrase, "in the fields we know," especially as the contrast here is elves actually walking in the fields Éomer knows. It is hard for me to imagine Tolkien did not have some echo of Dunsany in mind here. Rohan was not primarily an agricultural land, after all—why would Éomer think of fields?

Éomer is telling us he can't believe what's happening. How does this challenge to the suspension of disbelief sound in Chinese? Deng:

> Among these many inconceivable matters, what to think is really not easy. The whole world has changed to be strange! Elves and dwarves are companions, who walk in our ordinary make-a-living meadows (*richang guohuo de caoyuan*); yet there are people who have spoken with the forest lady and afterwards are still left with life; ... In this kind of age, how should a person judge for himself what to do? (Deng *TT:* 37)

Deng could have said "field" but chose meadow, which while useful (for livestock) is more leisurely than "field"; yet in place of "daily" she gives us "make-a-living" (*guohuo*, passing [the time] and surviving; managing to get by), returning us to the notion of the utility of a field. Deng's phrase tweaks "daily fields" by accentuating both its pragmatic use and its pleasantness, but also makes it more like Rohan, which is primarily grazing land. Yilin generalizes the phrase as "our world" (*dijie*, Yilin *TT*: 35), and Zhu turns the field into "broad daylight" and a "domain": "Elves and dwarves unexpectedly in broad daylight are companions walking in our domain's land" (Zhu *TT*: 53). Zhu's Éomer is more struck by the open and visible display of elves and dwarves, and by their intrusion into Rohan's territory.

For "marvels," in addition to Deng's "inconceivable matters," Yilin and Zhu use "strange traces" (*qiji*), the latter character *ji* 跡/迹 having the literal sense of a footprint, and by extension any perceivable vestige or evidence (Yilin *TT*: 35; Zhu *TT*: 53). Éomer sees things that are both strange and also evident. He makes this comment soon after Aragorn and friends have gone on an astonishingly long foot journey in pursuit of orcs also on foot, and shortly before Aragorn scrutinizes the ground for some strange footprints/traces left by the mysterious old man (*TT*, III, v, 477) and the escaping hobbits (*TT*, III, v, 478). We might have Éomer say, "among so many strange footprints."

Tolkien could hardly be considered post-modern, but his characters do exhibit a common attribute of post-modern narrative, namely an apparent awareness that they are themselves characters in a story. Treebeard says, "But you speak of master Gandalf, as if he was in a story that had come to an end." He could have just said, "as if he were dead." And Pippin replies: "The story seems to be going on, but I am afraid Gandalf has fallen out of it" (*TT*, III, iv, 455). Pippin seems to be talking about reading *The Fellowship of the Rings*. Deng reproduces the gist of the exchange, though adding a theatrical metaphor: "but I'm afraid Gandalf has already left the stage (*tuichang* 退场)" (Deng *TT*: 74). Zhu similarly uses a theatrical metaphor: "Gandalf already does not have a role (*jiaose* 角色) in it" (Zhu *TT*: 96). Yilin heightens the basic metaphor by calling Gandalf a character: "You just spoke of Gandalf the great master, it sounds like he is a character (*renwu* 人物) in an already finished story" (Yilin *TT*: 69). Similarly, in Lothlórien, Sam says, "I feel as if I was *inside* a song" (*FR*, II, vi, 342). Deng and Zhu present direct translations: "I feel myself as if **placed myself in** a ballad" (Deng *FR*: 438; similar at Zhu *FR*: 543). Whereas Yilin only says, "This is really like what is sung in a song" (Yilin *FR*: 427). Gandalf is himself referred to as a book: Pippin says he's travelled with Gandalf, and "there is much to read in that book, and I cannot claim to have seen more than a page or two" (*RK*, V, i, 744; Yilin *RK*: 20; Zhu *RK*: 39; Deng *RK*: 22).

But the best known passage in which characters speak as if they know they are in a story is when Sam and Frodo reflect on their own journey as it might be narrated later, such as to Sam's children. Here they mouth some of Tolkien's own views about the eucatastrophe essential to the best stories. Sam and Frodo are speaking hypothetically, much as we might speak of our own lives as stories, whereas we read their words with an added layer of knowledge, namely that their "story" (the actions they take) actually *is* a story

Sam recalls certain stories he "used to" call "adventures" (*TT* IV, viii, 696). And he used to imagine that protagonists eagerly went out in search of danger, as indeed they do in many stories. The Arthurian knight-errant typically roams around in search of a noble quest, rather than waiting to be badgered into it. But then Sam says, such stories are not as good as the stories in which the protagonist is forced to take a risk; "their paths were laid that way" by fate, or by the author (*TT* IV, viii, 696). The best stories feature protagonists who dig deep to find courage to go on, and their struggles are what make these stories memorable. But Frodo points out that while we as readers are aware of the story in terms of its genre or its ending, the protagonists within the secondary world of the story don't know; and it would damage a story if they knew, for example, that they would survive their quest and live happily ever after. We understand his point, and indeed some have made that charge against *The Lord of the Rings*: with all its doom and gloom, very few significant characters actually die (Shippey 2003: 154). When we are reading it for the first time, we can imagine Sam and Frodo might die. Even when we read it again and we know the ending, as long as the characters are afraid, we are afraid. Sam and Frodo are speaking of the emotions we feel while we are reading a scene of danger, during which we suspend our meta-knowledge of the text. Sam is making a direct analogy, talking about themselves as protagonists in "old tales and songs" (*TT* IV, viii, 696), but not some Dudley Do-Right or hero of a Henty novel—and not like Aragorn or Boromir, either. Assuming that Tolkien was trying to write a story that "really mattered" (*TT* IV, viii, 696), he cannot have Sam or Frodo as characters who are automatically and absolutely courageous.

Deng adjusts "old tales and songs" to "ancient legends (*chuanshuo* 传说) and ballads (*geyao* 歌谣)"; and for "adventure" uses *maoxian* 冒险, a conventional translation in which both characters mean risk or danger. The characters in those stories "went out and looked for" adventure; whereas Deng's translation has "came out the door and looked for" (Deng *TT*: 393), which is a nice echo of Bilbo's philosophy of adventure: "It's a dangerous business, Frodo, going out your door" (*FR*, I, iii, 72). Ding's translation for the Yilin press ignores the "went out," and Zhu interprets it as "of their own motive (*zhudong*) went looking for" (Zhu *TT*: 464). The passive voice "their paths were laid that way" is retained in Zhu's version: "their road was arranged (*anpai*) like this" (Zhu *TT*: 464). But Deng turns it into "they were only able to go on their road" (Deng *TT*: 394), which also seems to avoid the issue of who laid their way.

Stereotypical knights errant might consider adventure as "a kind of sport" (*TT* IV, viii, 696), which becomes "a kind of amusement (*yule* 娱乐, recreation)" in Deng (Deng *TT*: 393). Yilin makes it a little lighter with "fun (*lezi* 乐子)" (Yilin *TT*: 365). Certainly "sport" is "fun," rather than, say, football. Zhu has a different take: "stimulation (*ciji* 刺激)" (Zhu *TT*: 464). Midway through this passage, however, Yilin goes off track. In the original: "But that's not the way of it with the tales that really mattered, or the ones that stay in the mind. Folk seem to have been just landed in them, usually—their paths were laid that way, as you put it" (*TT*, IV, viii, 696). Yilin is rather creative here: "But in fact, what they did and what people recount (*chuanshuo* as a verb) are really not the same, those legends (*chuanshuo* as a noun) are only thought up out of nothing (*pingkong xiangchulai*); to again put them onto these people's bodies, the only similarity is that the road they go on is the same kind" (Yilin *TT*: 365). Instead of a comment on the difference between a character intentionally going out to find adventure and a character thrown into danger against their will, the Yilin translation here seems to be contrasting the legend and what really happened, thereby emphasizing the pure fabrication of the legends, even though in both cases there might be some similarity of plot or "road." Without defending a mistranslation, the question is: how does this new material change what Sam is saying? The Yilin version casts doubt on the veracity of those stories, as if to say: in real life, nobody is so heroic; all that heroism is just fiction. This introduces a certain (uncharacteristic) cynicism or pessimism in Sam. In Zhu's telling of these lines, the "really true (*zhenzheng zhenshi*) [stories] or the stories engraved on people's hearts (*mingke renxin*) certainly do not develop like this, usually, people all accidentally stumbled (*wuda wuzhuang*, mistakenly hit mistakenly bump) and rushed into a historical whirlpool (or vortex, *lishi xuanwo*), or one could say their road was arranged (*anpai*) like this" (Zhu *TT*: 464). Zhu intensifies the language throughout, from "a bit dull" to "monotonously boring"; characters who "just landed in" the adventures instead accidentally stumble and rush into a whirlpool. In the original, the sense is of people plopped into a situation (by the author, by fate); here the characters themselves blunder into "historical" chaos.

Sam comments on how stories without danger are forgotten, whereas danger makes for better and more memorable stories. "We hear about those as just went on—and not all to a good end, mind you; at least not to what folk inside a story and not outside it call a good end" (*TT* IV, viii, 696). Yilin gives us, "But anyhow, absolutely not all [of the better stories] have good endings. At least speaking of the people in the stories, it was not a good ending; of course people hearing the story all [listen] with keen interest (*jinjin youwei*)" (Yilin *TT*: 365). This last phrase seems to replace the phrase "and [people] not outside it call a good end." Zhu: "We have all heard those stories of people continuing and persisting, but they were certainly not all good endings—at least, for the protagonists (*zhujue* 主角) in the stories and the outside readers not a good ending" (Zhu *TT*: 464). Zhu makes an error of grammar here, apparently thinking that neither category calls it a good ending; he seems to have missed the second "not" in "at least not to what folk inside a story and *not* outside it call a good end." The original "and not outside it" is merely a reiteration of "inside it." Zhu's Sam seems to be saying, both the protagonists and the readers would consider a tragic ending as equally bad. But in the original, Sam is contrasting a good story ending (such as the tragic end of *Macbeth*) and a good final situation for the protagonists (happily ever after). Also, where Sam talks about "folk inside a story," Zhu gives us the more technical term *zhujue*, protagonist, literally the host-role. Similarly, Frodo's "the way of a real tale" becomes the "story's true plot" (Zhu *TT*: 465).

Then Sam describes a happy ending: "You know, coming home, and finding things all right, though not quite the same—like old Mr. Bilbo" (*TT* IV, viii, 696). In Yilin: "Of course there are also [stories that end with] matters all much enjoyed, like old Mr. Bilbo peacefully came back, and also [he] found treasure, the ending was five flowers eight gates (*wuhua bamen* 五花八门)" (Yilin *TT*: 365). The original is describing a good ending: you go home, everything's fine, although you feel a bit different about things now. He cites Bilbo, but it's just as much about how Sam's story ends: "Well, I'm back" (*RK*, VI, ix, 1008). In place of "though not quite the same," we get this *chengyu*, *wuhua bamen*, meaning, "varied, all sorts, much changing"; it originally referred to ancient battle arrays that could change quickly. Now Bilbo returns and finds the Shire in a state of rapid and unpredictable transformation—again, this sounds much more like *Sam's* eventual return to the Shire under Sharkey's rule. Zhu however reads the happy-ending as a "longed-for dream (*mengmei yilai*)" (Zhu *TT*: 465).

As Éomer witnesses actual elves, the collapse of the boundary between "legend" and his own reality gives him a disorienting shock. By contrast, Sam makes the same connection between the epic story of the silmarils and his direct experience of Galadriel's light. "Why, to think of it, we're in the same tale still! It's going on. Don't the great tales never end?" (*TT*, IV, viii, 697). Frodo says they don't end, and his thoughts flow easily from a character in a story he's heard, to himself as a character in a story: "But the people in them come, and go when their part's ended. Our part will end later—or sooner" (*TT*, IV, viii, 697). Here again the theatrical metaphor is stronger in the Chinese: Deng has, "people in the stories come and go (*lailai ququ*): they come out onto the stage (*chuchang* 出场), wait until the portion of their performance (*banyan de bufen* 搬演的部分) is over, then they withdraw from the stage (*tuichang*). A little later, our portion will end—or a bit earlier, we can't say for sure" (Deng *TT*: 394). Similarly, Yilin uses "ascend the stage (*shangchang* 上场)" and "leave (or descend from) the stage" (Yilin *TT*: 365). Zhu is less theatrical, though for "people in [the stories]" he writes of "the cast of characters (*renwu*)" (Zhu *TT*: 465).

Sam says, "I wonder if we shall ever be put into songs or tales. We're in one, of course; but I mean: put into words you know, told by the fireside, or read out of a great big book with red and black letters, years and years afterwards" (*TT*, IV, viii, 697). Deng and Zhu reproduce his very direct "we're in one," whereas Yilin has "in the future, will we be written into a legend or a ballad? Of course we will." This misses the verb tense of "we're in one"—meaning, *already*, namely what they are doing at that very moment. Instead, it's Sam thinking someone will write their story later. And indeed, Sam immediately elaborates on his vision of future narrations, conjuring a picture of a fireside story-time. In black letters, fine, but what's this red ink? Western Medieval hand-written manuscripts often feature headings or key phrases in red ink, a practice known as rubrication. If we assume all books in Middle-earth were hand-written, this may be what Sam is referring to. But in China, writing in red ink was traditionally exclusive to the emperor's comments added to memorials written in black; there is by extension a traditional taboo against writing anyone's name in red ink, because of its associations with the names of criminals receiving death sentences, and also with the names of the hell-bound written by the presiding ruler of hell. Whether in English or Chinese, it is hard to say how much these meanings still attach to red ink.

Conclusions

While there will always be some concerns about the applicability of genre categories across cultures, overall there does seem to be a common ground, a literature which relies on imagining things that don't normally exist, based in a magical or religious idiom distinct from science fiction or realism. The category of fantasy literature and its direct Chinese translations emerged into popular usage quite late (the 1960s in English; and the late 1990s in Taiwan and soon after in China). In both cases, the categories have been retroactive, so that both Peter Pan and *Xiyouji* can be included in a lineage. In English and in Chinese, the category "science fiction" came into being in the early twentieth century, long before "fantasy" (as genre). In both contexts there was a notional relation of science fiction to science, which served science fiction better in China than the West due to the government's intermittent promotion of science fiction as a kind of advertisement for science—though perhaps the state did not really serve science fiction well, with its heavy-handed micro-management of the genre.

The discussions of genre in *LOTR* include a number of categories. Obviously Sam and Frodo couldn't talk about themselves being in a fantasy, but rather in an adventure, and Éomer speaks of being in a dream and a legend, with marvels and strange events. Éomer comes closest to identifying his own genre as a fantasy, precisely because of his skepticism about the reality of elves and magic swords. Éomer sees things that he thought didn't really exist. Though the hobbits having a pint at the Green Dragon think magic belongs elsewhere, they express no disbelief. Though our four hobbit protagonists are astonished by certain things, at no point do they say those things are impossible. Instead, Sam and Frodo speak more neutrally of being in a story or tale, an adventure at most.

The last section of this chapter is some indication of Part Two: the exploration of the new visions opened by the multiple translations, arranged thematically, starting with questions about the various fictional entities of Middle-earth. These extensions of sentience beyond the self include gods, elves, and other "species," magical beings and monsters. Beyond that, we will turn to the afterlife, fate and doom, and language.

Part Two

Reading Tolkien in Chinese

5

Gods and Heathens

Projections of Sentience Beyond the Self

Untethered from reality, we conjure vast populations, whether fictional or (believed to be) real, belonging to fantasy or religion: pantheons, cryptozoologies; what John Francis Davis (speaking of Chinese religion) called "a tremendous et cetera of monsters" (1822: 20). We impute awareness and rationality outwards beyond ourselves, and beyond what can be empirically verified. Setting aside fantastical places, objects, and phenomena, here I focus on *beings*, entities with consciousness and agency.

It is not obvious what classification system would be best for a comprehensive lexicon of imagined life-forms. Or indeed, what the point would be of any such classification. There can only be unstable categories. I find an endless stream of unreal beings, not only from folklore previously unknown to me but also from all the new stories which constantly add to the list: slake-moths, The Ood, Kelpians, the White Walkers, the Pale Man. Each story or franchise features its own unique take and its own particular details. Tolkien's works are obviously not concerned with aliens (*waixingren*, persons of outer stars) or robots (*jiqiren*, machine persons). Among the life-forms of Middle-earth (in addition to humans and ordinary animals), either depicted in the story or referred to, we have a fair spectrum: gods and demons, dragons, giants, various humanoids, ghosts, unusual animals and trees, an "inanimate" object (the Ring), and Lovecraftian "nameless things."

What of the Chinese lexicon? What are the primary categories of weird entities in the translations of Tolkien, and what broad meanings do they have in Chinese? It seems to me that the majority of monster-type entities involve the following terms:

1. *gui* 鬼
2. *yao* 妖 or *yaojing* 妖精
3. *mo* 魔
4. *ling* 靈/灵, *hun* 魂, and other terms for "soul" or "spirit"
5. *guai* 怪

These can be combined in different ways and with a great many other characters. But let us consider them individually.

Gui is a very pervasive word with a wide range of meanings. The noun's core meaning is probably something like ghost, along with demon, spirit, and related meanings. It is used in various negative ways: a *gui*'s words (*guihua*) are lies. The *gui* from over the sea are *yangguizi*, "foreign devils." A lazy *gui* (*langgui*) is a "lazybones." A booze *gui* (*jiugui*) is an alcoholic. The word has a humorous dimension, similar to the jocularly "devilish" qualities of *mo*. One might affectionately call a child a "little *gui*." And indeed when the Lieutenant of Sauron calls the hobbits "imps" in an obviously non-literal sense (*RK*, V, x, 871), Deng uses *xiaogui* (little *gui*) (Deng *RK*: 182). But the term is often modified by monstrous characteristics: *xixuegui*, suck-blood-*gui*; *diaosigui*, died-by-hanging-*gui*; *yuangui*, a *gui* who is bitter due to dying of some injustice. In *Mojie*, the term appears by itself or in various combinations to translate: ghost, bogey(-stories), spooks, goblins, will-o'-the-wisp, dwimmer-crafty, phantom, devilry, (juggler's) trick, miserable slinker, candles (of the Dead ones), haunted, fey, and vampire.

With *yao* 妖 we have a combination of *nü* 女 (female) and *yao* 夭, which can mean tender and young, or to die young. Women who die before marriage—before being tied into the husband's system of ancestral offerings—are homeless spirits prone to hungry wandering. Like *gui*, the term refers to entities known in English as demons and evil spirits, but inevitably carries a gender lacking in *gui*: for example, *yaoli*, which is *yao* plus *li* 麗 / 丽 (beautiful), means seductively charming, dangerously beautiful. A *yaojing* 妖精 is an evil spirit, demon, seductress, siren. The arts of the *yao* (*yaoshu*) are translated as witchcraft. On the other hand, Pokemon (a Japanese portmanteau of "pocket" and "monster") is in China 口袋妖怪 (*koudai yaoguai*, pocket *yao-guai*; *guai* is another general term for monsters). *Yaoguai* is better known in some fan circles by its Japanese pronunciation, *yokai*. And some *yao* in the translations are not female, such as "wight": *shiyao* 屍妖／尸妖 or corpse-*yao*. (Zhu *RK* Appendix: 147; Deng *FR*: 164; Shi and Deng *UT*: 455). The (male) goblins are *xiao yaojing* (little *yaojing*) (Yilin *H*: 76). Trolls are *shirenyao* 食人妖 (eats-people-*yao*) (Zhu *RK* Appendix: 133; Deng *FR*: 238; Wu *H*: 50). Imps are *xiao yaoguai* (little *yao*-monsters) (Zhu *RK*: 231). *Yao* are also described as animals, plants, or so-called inanimate objects that have absorbed magical powers and achieved sentience.

I asked Deng Jiawan to precisely define a *yao*. After a laugh, she said:

> Well. Generally speaking, *yao* or *jing* is a concept opposite to *xian* 仙 or *shenxian* 神仙. In Chinese myth, there is a type of being called *yao* or *jing*; humans usually do not change into *yao* or *jing*. Animals, plants, or objects (jade, mirrors, swords, antiques, etc.) can change into *yao* or *jing*. There are good and bad *yao* or *jing*, it depends on the interests of human beings. What is beneficial to human beings is good, and what is harmful to human beings is evil. *Xian* or *shenxian* are usually good beings. Of course, in tradition, *yao* or *jing* are mainly bad, harm people, and *xian* or *shenxian* help and save people. People can want to become *xian* (*chengxian*). People don't want to become *yao*. (Deng 2017)

Yao is also used in the translations of the Land (of Mordor), bogey (-stories), trolls, sorcery, bewitched, devilry, creature (the fell beasts), and fairy-wife. We see significant overlap with *gui* and other terms considered here.

The character *mo* 魔 was discussed in Chapter 3. Note here that the character includes a semantic element, namely *gui* 鬼. *Mo* is more demonic than *gui*. Perhaps the most common term for demon-like beings is *mogui* 魔鬼, which as you can see has *gui* in it twice. In the translations, *mo* is used in combinations for: magic, Mordor, the Ring, the Dark Lord, evil creature, sorcery, the Great Eye, bewitched, devilry, wizardry, enchantment, spell, wood-demons, hell-hawks, and necromancy.

There are a range of terms involving *ling* 靈/灵, *hun* 魂, and other terms for "soul," "anima," or "spirit," for example *youling* 幽靈 (dark spirit), *shenling* (gods and spirits in general), and of course *jingling* ("elf," discussed in the next chapter). *Hun* 魂 is also soul and spirit; often interchangeable with *ling*. Somewhat arbitrarily *jinghun* is just soul or spirit, whereas *jingling* is elf. Necromancer is *siling fashi* 死靈法師, the magician who deals with dead spirits (Zhu *FR*: 391; Deng *FR*: 313). Wraiths are *siling* 死靈 (dead spirits) (Zhu *RK* Appendix: 187) or *youling* 幽灵 (dark spirits) (Deng *FR*: 231; Zhu *FR*: 291). Dwimmerlaik is *yuanling* 怨靈, resentful or malevolent spirit (Zhu *RK* Appendix: 154). Ring-wraith is *jieling* (ring spirit) (Zhu *RK* Appendix: 177; and Deng *S* 2015: 458) or *mojie youling* (*mo*-ring dark spirit) (Yilin *RK*: 91). Aside from its pervasive use in the term *jingling* (elves), *ling* also appears in terms for: a Power, (Fangorn being) alive, (a funerary) bier, stronger (than Morgul-spells), those who fall in battle, the mind, mortals, growing things, phantom, charm (of Saruman's voice), haunted, ghost, the Dead, shadows, god, and spirit.

And finally, *guai* 怪. *Guaiwu* (*guai*-creatures) is a general category of "strange beings" or "monsters." As noted in the genre classification *zhiguai* (records of the strange), here the sense of strangeness or surprise is prominent; the word *guai* is used in phrases such as *nanguai* . . ., "it would be hard to think it strange that . . ." or more idiomatically "no wonder . . ." *Guairen* (strange people) can be strangers or eccentrics; *guairen* is also the "weird" in Weird Al Yankovic. *Yaoguai* are monsters and also oddballs. The Yilin edition calls giants *juguai*—giant *guai* (Yilin *RK*: 452), and uses the same term for trolls (Yilin *FR*: 233). Zhu uses it for imps: *xiao yaoguai* (Zhu *RK*: 231). In the translations, *guai* also appears in: portents, "he spoke funny," bogey, queer, strange, wargs, wood-demons, wights, and sorcerer.

Regarding the English word "monster" in the source texts, the translations reflect the vagueness of the word. For "monsters" (*S*: 35), in Yilin we get four categories all heaped together: *yaomo guiguai* (Yilin *S*: 32), and elsewhere *guaiwu* (strange creatures) (Deng *S* 2015: 70) and *egui* (evil ghosts) (Yilin *S*: 41), but Deng also gives us the intriguing *yaonie* 妖孽 (Deng *S* 2015: 62; Deng *S* 2002: 44). As noted above, *yao* is a general category of animistic nastiness, sometimes but not always gendered female; *nie* means demon, treacherous, unfilial. It is used in *niezi*, son of a concubine, or an unfilial son. In Buddhist terms, *niebao* is retribution for sins, and *niehai* is the sea of retribution.

One looks in vain for a United Nations Commission on Standardization of Terminology About Monsters. Whereas with a deity there might be at least the attempt by the institutions of orthodoxy to nail down a meaning, there is no stopping the viral permutations of all those non-empirical sentient beings who circulate freely in our nightmares and entertainment. It is hard to get traction at such a high level of generalization. The way to get at some comparison of these different worlds is by examining specific cases, such as those appearing in the works of Tolkien.

On the subject of supernatural beings who might or might not exist, let us consider the oliphaunt in the room: God.

God in *Mojie*

There is one use of the word "god" in *The Lord of the Rings*. It is spoken not by one of the characters but by the narrator, Tolkien, or whatever document Tolkien is pretending to be translating—"the Red Book of Westmarch" or one of its related manuscripts (*FR* Prologue: 14). Théoden, the insecure king with an inferiority complex, has risen to the challenge of facing the army of Sauron. He was goaded into it by Gandalf, and by the presence of Aragorn (the ideal king) who however promptly abandoned him during the muster. There is a beautiful moment in the story where Merry observes Théoden, sees his frailty, and wonders if the old king will quail and sneak back to Edoras. But Théoden's still got it, and he rouses himself and his troops into a charge on the massive forces of Sauron. And he leads the way:

> Théoden could not be overtaken. Fey he seemed, or the battle-fury of his fathers ran like new fire in his veins, and he was borne up on Snowmane like a god of old, even as Oromë the Great in the battle of the Valar when the world was young. (*RK*, V, v, 820)

Who is this "god of old," Oromë? He is one of the high-ranking Valar, one of the gods brought into being by Ilúvatar the primordial mono-deity. These Valar-gods were characterized by their different activities. Oromë was a hunter, known for hunting and killing various monsters in Middle Earth, especially during the sleep of Yavanna (a period of stillness prior to the emergence of the elves). He is known for his beautiful horse Nahar. He was later active in the struggle against Morgoth (McBride 2020: 27–28, 47).

It is often remarked that there is a striking lack of religions among the peoples of Middle-earth (Lobdell 2004: 64–66; McBride 2020: vii–viii). The whole story may be sacramental (Roberts 2013: 12), but as a depiction of a more-or-less Medieval society it suffers from the absence of a priestly hierarchy, cultic rituals, and rival sects. The Valar appear in *The Silmarillion* and related texts, even to the extent of manifesting before mortals, even responding to specific prayers. Tuor has a direct audio-visual encounter with the Vala Ulmo (*UT*: 28–30). The elves have their devotional but somewhat detached meditations on the stars. But here, the narrator refers to Oromë as a god "of old," such as we might say today of Diana or Odin. Catholics don't call Jesus or Yahweh a "god of old." Oromë is not a god considered present or relevant in the world, belonging to myth rather than religion—myth in the popular sense of dead religion, a sacred narrative relocated to a category of general folklore. The lower-case g in "god" also suggests a monotheist's demotion of other peoples' Gods.

By the time we get to Bilbo and Frodo, the Valar have become entirely remote, or simply unknown. None of the hobbits ever seem to call on them, even in the way we might say, "Thank God," when we just mean, "That's nice." It's true, we have a faint residue of prayer when Sam says things like "Bless you"—to which we will return in Chapter 10. Even as Théoden's men prepare to rush into battle against the horde, do they say any prayers? You'd think this would be an urgent moment to call upon whatever supernatural entities they might believe or half-believe in. But no. Théoden makes a speech about how it's a good day to die—sounding like the more "pagan" side of *Beowulf* (*RK,* V, v, 818; White 2010: 116). Tom Shippey describes them as "virtuous pagans" (2003: 199; also Abbott 1989: 25–26). But it's not clear they are *actively* pagan. Their whole culture seems to be lapsed heathen. Théoden reminds them of the oaths they swore, "to lord and land and league of friendship" (*RK,* V, v, 818), but not to any god. Doesn't anyone want to hedge their bets just in case Oromë is looking down? Haven't they heard of Pascal's wager?

But what did the three translations make of this, the only direct reference to a "god?" The Yilin edition, here translated by Tang Dingjiu: "But from start to finish they could not catch up with Théoden. He seemed to be very excited (*xingfen*), perhaps his ancestors' kind of battle fury also rose up like a flame in his blood, he sat erect on Flying on Snow (*xueshangfei* 雪上飞), like an [countword *zun* 尊] ancient god (*gulao de shenqi* 古老的神祇), even like the great Oromë in the war of the Valar in the early period of the world" (Yilin *RK*: 115). The use of the count word *zun* adds a minor touch to the translation—when saying "a" god, you have to specify a count noun (like "one *piece* of paper"). While *zun* also means senior, elder, esteemed, and to venerate, it is used as a count noun for objects such as icons and gods. Deng and Zhu basically ignore the word "a," but because of context, I will retain the word "a" (or "an") in my back-translations.

Deng gives us this: "But there was no person able to keep pace with [or catch up with] Théoden. He looked crazy (*diankuang*, demented, furious), or a new life (*xinsheng*) fire just like his ancestors' (*xianzu*) battle fury, rushed through his whole body's veins. He rode on the back of Snow-mane (*xuezong*), like (an) ancient god (*gudai de shenming* 古老的神明), just like when the world was still young, the great Oromë in the Valar's great war" (Deng *RK*: 117).

The original has "battle-fury of his fathers." The most common word for father, *fu* 父, can be used metaphorically for men of one's father's age, but not normally for ancestors in general, who tend to be known by the term *zu* 祖, or *zong* 宗, or combinations such as *zuxian* 祖先. In a Patrilineal system, the important ancestors are male, so "fathers" becoming "ancestors" is not a stretch, in Chinese or in Middle-earth. Zhu gives us a variation. Like the other translators, he reads "fathers" as ancestors but extends it into a four-character duplicative phrase "many ancestors and many lineages" (*liexian liezong*).

Zhu writes: "But none could catch up with Théoden. To look at, he was like an unstoppable crazy person (*kuangren*), the many ancestors and many lineages' blood was all inside his body boiling (*feiteng*), he rode on Snow-mane's back just like an ancient god (*gudai de shenling* 古代的神靈), even like when the world began to be made, the great Oromë in the great war of the lord gods (*zhushen*)" (Zhu *RK*: 156). The phrase *zhushen* 主神 "lord gods" or "[one who] hosts spirits" is possibly a typographic error for the common phrase *zhushen* 諸神, "the many gods." The phrase Zhu used for "fey" and which I have translated as "unstoppable" is *wanfu modi* 萬夫莫敵: "among ten thousand warriors none could resist." This certainly describes Théoden's charge (though he dies soon after).

For "god" (of old) we get *shenqi, shenming,* and *shenling.* They all mean something like "gods," but are there nuances between them? Chinese-English and Chinese dictionaries give virtually the same for each phrase: "gods, deities, divinities." They all use *shen* 神 (gods, spirits, souls). *Qi* 祇 is a less used term with a specific meaning of God of the earth, much like *she* 社, a god of the earth. Ming 明 has the sense of radiance; spiritual lights. *Ling* 靈 has the general sense of a soul, a consciousness which survives death. The translations generally do not use *shangdi* or *tianzhu*, being much too explicitly Christian and monotheistic, though there is an exception (see Chapter 10). The use of the lower-case g and the added descriptor "of old" also help to exclude Christian theology, but to get at what "a god of old" or the Valar in general feel like in Chinese, and to reconsider the many powerful entities in Middle-earth, requires some generalization about gods in Chinese.

Divinity in Chinese

First, a common attribute of the God of Christianity and other monotheisms is that He created everything. In contrast, the creation myths of Chinese religion, related for example to Pan Gu, have very little to do with the deities people actually worship. When people pray to Guandi or Mazu, it is not because these gods created the world. And Buddhism can scarcely be said to have a creation myth at all—at most, a cyclical regeneration. Similarly, the Deistic Ilúvatar created the world but remains a remote figure. The creator of their world appears to be almost entirely irrelevant to the people in Middle-earth.

Second, in China there is a marked continuity between humans and gods. In Christianity one may aspire to be *with* God, but certainly not to *be* God. God has always been God and nothing else; whereas in many cases Chinese gods used to be human, and have origin stories rooted in history (Hansen 1990: 48–78). In Chinese religion, divine incarnation in human form and vice versa are relatively common affairs. Though there is no possibility of a Middle-earth human *becoming* a Vala, yet the complex spectrum of powerful beings reduces the sense of an absolute chasm between humans and gods.

Third, as in most polytheistic cultures, Chinese deities have division of labor and individual personality. Gods are not all helpful for all purposes: people pray to one God for success in an exam, to another for safe childbirth. Chinese gods are not omnipotent. Each has its own quirks, and not all of them are automatically interested in your wellbeing or your soul. There are other differences, but in short we might say the Chinese pantheon is more like the Classical Greco-Roman, or the Indian pantheon, or many others, including the Valar. Thinking globally and historically, polytheism is the norm; monotheism is the anomaly.

Moving to the lexicon, what are the words for things like "gods" in Chinese?

Shen 神 is a term used in many combinations such as *caishen* (wealth god) and *menshen* (door gods). *Shen* is the preferred translation of God in evangelical Protestantism. *Shen* can be a powerful spiritual entity to whom one might pray, or the "spirit" within each of us—more like a "soul," "mind," or "consciousness." A human being, possessing a *shen*/soul, dies and the *shen* continues, either as an ancestral spirit (a family god) or as a more "public" spirit worshipped by anyone. A soul-*shen* is not qualitatively different from a god-*shen*. The term *ling* 靈/灵 is similar. This ambiguity—or rather, what appears as an ambiguity when considered in English—is not coincidental, but arises from some fundamental ideas about divinity in Chinese culture. Uses of *shen* in *Mojie* range from the religious to the psychological with some anomalies along the way: the Valar (Zhu *RK* Appendix: 5), the One (Deng *S* 2002: 3), spirits (Yilin *S*: 23), Power (Deng *FR*: 59), magic (ring) (Zhu *FR*: 62), temple (Deng *RK*: 64), sacred (Deng *TT*: 123), mind (Deng *FR*: 51) and thought (Deng *TT*: 121).

Laotian 老天 and variations of *tian* 天, means sky, heaven, the beings in heaven; also day, season, weather, and inborn or natural. Strictly speaking, heaven itself doesn't have any consciousness or intention, unless by heaven we mean the beings that reside in it, and indeed we do speak of heaven having a mind: "heaven knows" or "heaven help us." This synecdoche is close to a common Chinese use of *tian* as the collective consensus of the many divine beings in the heavens, and also by extension the natural order. *Tian* is very frequently used in the translations, as an ejaculation translating words such as "Ah!" (*FR*, II, x, 388; Yilin *FR*: 484), "blimey!" (*H*, ii, 39;. Yilin *H*: 31), "Behold!" (*RK*, V, vi, 822; Zhu *RK*: 158), "Alas" (*TT*, III, i, 403; Yilin *TT*: 3), and in phrases such as "thank goodness" (*FR*, II, i, 216; Deng *FR*: 275; Yilin *FR*: 269; Zhu *FR*: 344) and "good gracious me!" (*H*, i, 7; Wu *H*: 12; Yilin *H*: 4).

To translate "God" (or "Deus"), Catholic missionaries coined the neologism *Tianzhu*, "lord of heaven." *Zhu* 主 means lord, host, owner, presiding person, and in the relevant religious contexts, Yahweh or Allah. In Catholic usage, *zhu* is short for *tianzhu*. Here, the qualities of ownership, political authority and hosting are divinized, as they are with divine titles such as *gong* 公 ("duke"), *jun* 君 (lord), or *di* 帝 (emperor). *Shangdi* 上帝 (emperor on high) also refers specifically to the God of Christianity—particularly of Protestants—though this word is also used rather generically. Here, height (as a metaphor of great age or supremacy), rulership, and ancestry are foremost. I have found no *Tianzhu* and only one *Shangdi* (Yilin *FR* 131; see Chapter 10) in the translations, being perhaps too culturally specific—too close to capital-g God.

Some Daoist deities are named after stars, such as *shouxing*, long-life-star, or *kuixing*, one of the stars in the Big Dipper. This resonates with the star contemplation of the elves. Upon awakening, the elves first saw starlight. "Therefore they have ever loved the starlight, and have revered Varda Elentári above all the Valar" (*S*: 45). Both versions by Deng have *re-ai* (warmly loved) and revered (*zunchong* 尊崇) as the verbs here. Yilin's version is less intense than Deng's, saying the elves "extremely liked (*xihuan*) starlight" (Deng *S* 2002: 57–58; Deng *S* 2015: 72; Yilin *S*: 43). Still, a star can also be a negative supernatural influence, as in translations of "bane"—*zaixing*, star of disaster.

If there is no single, living God intimately involved in the daily lives of the characters of Middle-earth, there are nonetheless gods "of old," deities belonging to dead religions. None of the humans seem to believe in them, not having read *The Silmarillion*. In the ancient days, people could call upon the Valar and receive direct responses, but that seems to belong to a day gone by. Even the elves' contemplation of the Even-star is primarily contemplative. Mentioning Oromë to Éomer would be like mentioning Thor to me. Are we supposed to imagine Oromë like Thor, god-like but so downgraded that these days one can treat him as a mere superhero? Are the Valar the gods of dead religions? If the worship of the Valar has disappeared, was it shunned? And if, so who shunned it?

What is a Heathen?

We have two explicit references to this category of wrong religion, spoken by Denethor and Gandalf. Shippey calls the use of this word a "significant anachronism" (2003: 173; also Reynolds 1993: 50).

His mind poisoned by Sauron's influence, Denethor becomes suicidal. He counsels everyone to give up the fight, and goes to immolate himself with the (not-quite) corpse of Faramir. "We will burn like heathen kings before ever a ship sailed hither from the West" (*RK,* V, iv, 807). Who are these "heathen kings" of so long ago? Denethor is probably referring to the rulers of the humans deemed unworthy of going to Númenor, and who stayed in Middle-earth. These second-rate people fell under the domination of Sauron, until the Númenoreans sailed back from the West to reassert their enlightened rule and stamp out the "heathen" worship of Morgoth. In fact, eventually the Númenoreans were also corrupted by Morgoth and the "worship of the Dark" (*S*: 325). The non-heathens in this case were those humans who were faithful to the Valar (Amendt-Raduege 2018: 36). And yet, since there seems to be no surviving worship of the Valar by humans in the time of Frodo, we might conjecture that the concept ought to be meaningless.

"Heathen" is derived from words in Old English, Old Frisian and other languages, meaning "dweller of the heath," which is to say, of rural or wild lands where pre-Christian religion persisted long after urban Europe was Christianized. Inevitably, "the word *heathen* tells the tale of a pagan exodus" (Holmes 2011: 122). As early as the tenth century it was a general category for all of those who are not Christian, Jewish, or Muslim. And hence "uncivilized" and "savage." In Middle-earth, the term cannot mean "not Christian." Perhaps, as Dickerson observes, "Tolkien may have had in mind its more literal, nonreligious, and certainly derogatory meaning: ... associating Denethor ... with the uneducated traditions of the heath" (Dickerson 2007: 267). But Denethor was not saying, "like the rural kings," or "like how the hicks think of kings." While we can safely ascribe a certain urban snobbery to Denethor, "heathen" remains a religious term.

How do the translations deal with this word "heathen"? Deng and Zhu share the same term. Deng: "We will be cremated like those kings of wild and savage people (*yemanren* 野蠻人) when the first ship had not yet sailed west to this land" (Deng *RK*: 101; similar at Zhu *RK*: 135). Yilin takes a different approach: "We will be cremated like the strange-teachings-followers' nation's kings before western ships sailed here" (Yilin *RK*: 99). Strange-teachings-followers is *yijiaotu* 异教徒, *yi* = foreign, different, strange; *yijiao* is often given in dictionaries as heathenism or paganism, but literally meaning *different* teachings—different in a pejorative sense, like "weird" or "alien." It is also used to translate heterodoxy and heresy.

A little later, Gandalf says to Denethor, "only the heathen kings" committed suicide along with their kin (*RK*, V, vii, 835). The translations each take different stabs at this: Deng says, "those nation's kings without (religious) faith (*meiyou xinyang* 没有信仰)" (Deng *RK*: 136). Yilin has, "those uncivilized rulers (*yeman diwang*, wild and savage emperors and kings)" (Yilin, *RK*: 133). And Zhu goes for, "those fallen (*duoluo* 堕落, degenerate, decadent) rulers (*junwang*)" (Zhu *RK*: 178).

So for "heathen," we have: wild and savage people without faith (Deng); wild and savage strange-teaching-followers (Yilin); and wild and savage people who are fallen (Zhu). All of the translators interpret the two uses of the word differently in the two different contexts. All three include the use of the term *yeman*, a term derived from *ye* 野, meaning open country, wild land, uncultivated, unruly, rude, uncivilized, and rough—a range with an obvious overlap with "heath" or "wild"; and *Man* 蛮/蠻, having the senses of: savage, fierce, brute, reckless, but also a term for non-Han ethnic groups in what is now Southern China (more about *Man* in Chapter 7). When Deng interjects "without faith," the term for faith, *xinyang*, is primarily religious, rather than in the sense of trustworthiness. Similarly, Yilin identifies the kings as following a weird/foreign/heretical religious teaching. Zhu's term *duoluo*, fallen, has possible association with the Biblical Fall. As a set of interpretations of "heathen," these are reasonable choices. But does the Chinese then preserve the "significant anachronism"?

Contrasting the English with the three Chinese texts taken together, the difference in the tones of the two speakers is clarified in the Chinese: Gandalf's use of the word seems plainly judgmental—the heathen kings were faithless degenerate savages (*meiyou xinyang, duoluo, yeman*), you should not imitate them. Denethor seems to have embraced the ancient ways proudly, even if they were savage, weirdly heterodox, and of another ethnic group (*yeman, yijiaotu, man*). There is religion in the translations, but the problematic implication of pre- or non-Christian never arises.

Wizards

To assist in his own funeral, Denethor calls upon no experts. More or less *ad hoc*, Gandalf crowns Aragorn. In all the weddings, funerals, healings and other rituals, there are no priests or monks (let alone priestesses or nuns). There are however a few "wizards." Of the five in Middle-earth in physical form, we meet Gandalf, Saruman, and Radagast (McBride 2020: 52–57). But what is a wizard?

The *OED* on "wizard" starts from fifteenth-century Middle English, giving several meanings over time: philosopher, sage (often contemptuous); a man skilled in occult arts; male counterpart of a witch; a man who 'does wonders' in his profession; a witch-doctor or medicine man; a professional conjurer. The word follows a common pattern: it was used to mean someone who does real magic, and gradually became used for anything impressive, including trickery. Gandalf self-identifies, "I am a wizard" (*H* vii, 130; Yilin *H*: 103; Zhu *H*: 139; Wu *H*: 164). In this context, the primary sense of a wizard such as Gandalf would seem to be: a man skilled in occult arts. Though Gandalf is sagely and even tricky, his wonders are real.

What do our texts tell us about this category? First, like "elves," the word "wizard" is presented as a translation: "the *Istari* or Wizards appeared in Middle-earth" (*RK* Appendix B: 1059). Deng and Zhu agree on "Istari or *wushi*" (巫师) (Deng *RK* 445; Zhu *RK* Appendix 72; on *wu*, see Shao 2018: 90–95), whereas Yilin skips "Istari" and uses "*shushi* (术士)" (Yilin *RK*: 426). The Istari are among the Maiar, lesser among the Valar. In the *Unfinished Tales*, we read that they were "persons of the 'angelic' order, though not necessarily of the same rank. The Maiar were 'spirits', but capable of self-incarnation, and could take 'humane' (especially Elvish) forms" (*UT*: 394; Shippey 2003: 151; Ruud 2010: 143–144). Deng and Shi give "angelic" as "angelic type (*tianshi bande*)," adding, "of the same clan forming a group (*zulai chengyuan*), but not necessarily belonging to the same rank (*dengji*). Maiar are '*shenling* (spirits),' but can chose to use a flesh-body form (*roushen xingti*), and can take "person/human form" (*renxing*) (especially the elven outer form)" (Shi and Deng *UT*: 511). Similarly, "angelic people" becomes "angelic clan (*tianshi yizu*)" (*UT*: 395; Shi and Deng *UT*: 513). For Gandalf as a Messenger, they use *shizhe* 使者 (envoy) (*UT*: 389; Shi and Deng *UT*: 505). The common element of angel and messenger is *shi* 使 which means to send or tell (someone to do something), to use or cause; and hence as a noun: envoy, messenger, ambassador. An angel is thus a messenger or envoy of heaven (*tian*). Whereas in English we do not read "messenger" and think of angels, in the Chinese the association is stronger. There is perhaps a clearer hint of Gandalf's angelic nature in the Chinese.

They are not quacks or charlatans, though one of the old hobbits in the pub says: "that old wandering conjuror, Gandalf" (*FR*, I, i, 24). Deng gets the trivialization implied by the phrase, with *lao liulang bianxifa de* 老流浪变戏法的, old wandering conjurer/juggler—one who puts on a show (*xi*) of magical transformations (*bian*) (Deng *FR*: 29). Yilin is similar: *yousifang de dashushi* 游四方的大术士, the great master of techniques (*shushi*) who travels in all four directions. (Yilin *FR*: 27). *Shushi*, literally a master of (unspecified) techniques or arts, can refer to a Confucian scholar, but more often to magician, necromancer, or alchemist. But Zhu uses *lao wushi* 老巫师, old shaman (Zhu *FR*: 52). Later we read he was generally regarded as "a travelling magician of unknown powers and purpose" (*FR*, I, ix, 157). Deng somewhat overspecifies: "a wandering magician (*moshushi*, master of *mo*-techniques) with unknown magic powers (*fali weizhi*), with sinister/ulterior motives (*juxin poce*)" (Deng *FR*: 201). Yilin is similar, except for naming Gandalf's milieu as the dangerous Jianghu world (Yilin *FR*: 197). Zhu sticks closer to the original here: "magician (*fashi*) whose power and goals are all unclear" (Zhu *FR*: 256).

Wormtongue says to Théoden, of Gandalf: "This wizard has bewitched you" (*TT*, III, vi, 508). Here, all use *wushi* 巫师/巫師 (Deng *TT*: 144; Yilin *TT*: 133; Zhu *TT*: 179). *Shi* 師 means master, teacher; a close variant is *shi* 士. But *wu* is the key word, used in *wupo* (*wu* + old woman, hence witch, shamaness), *wuyi* ("witch-doctor"), *wudu* ("voodoo," literally shaman-poison). (On early uses of *wu*, see Strassberg 2002: 6–7, 51–53; Michael 2015.) In ancient uses *wu* had a female connotation, but this seems to have been lost. The bad people call Morwen "Witchwife," which is rendered as *wupo* (*UT*: 105; Shi and Deng *UT*: 138). The translation of *wu* as shaman is common, but problematic, as both words blur distinctions among different traditions; hence, some Sinologists use the portmanteau *wu*-shaman.

Clearly it would be an error to expect too much precision when mapping a fuzzy set in English onto a fuzzy set in Chinese. In the Harry Potter books, "wizard" is *wushi* (巫師) (Rowling 1999: 3; trans. Peng 2000: 19)—that might be a better way to judge what the term means in *Mojie* than whatever the *Shiji* said. Etymology does not determine meaning. Both Dumbledor and Gandalf are *wushi*, despite their differences. Tolkien wrote "wizard"; the translators turned that into *shushi* and *wushi*; we try to determine how to say *shushi* and *wushi* in English, and we come back with not only wizard but also Confucian scholar, necromancer, alchemist, shaman, witch, conjurer, magician, medicine man, clairvoyant, astrologer, physiognomist. If we go back into Chinese with these terms, we will inevitably come up with *shushi* and *wushi* but also others.

Among this jumble of words is necromancer, which also appears in Tolkien (*H*, vii, 152). Zhu and Wu give *siling fashi* 死靈法師/死灵法师, dead souls master (Zhu *H*: 161; Wu *H*: 188). Yilin is inconsistent, using a meaningless transliteration: *nikeluomansi* (Yilin *H*: 120), but elsewhere *mofashi*, master of *mo*-method, *mo*-magician (*H*, i, 29; Yilin *H*: 23). "Sorcery" receives a rich variety of treatments. The Necromancer is also a "black sorcerer," (*H*, vii, 152), for which we get both our main terms for wizard: Zhu gives *xie-e yao shushi*, evil *yao* master of techniques (Zhu *H*: 161). And Yilin: *xingyao zuogaui de nanwu*, male *wu*-shaman who raises *yao* and makes *guai* (Yilin *H*: 120). This latter would be more fitting as a paraphrase of necromancer, one who raises monsters (from the nether-world). One line below "Necromancer" as *siling fashi*, Wu turns "black sorcerer" into *siling fashi* as well (Wu *H*: 188). And when Gandalf calls the witch-king a "sorcerer" (*FR*, II, ii, 250), Deng and Zhu use *fashi* (magician, dharma master) (Deng *FR*: 322; Zhu *FR*: 401). Wormtongue refers to Galadriel as "the Sorceress of the Golden Wood" (*TT* III, vi, 502), and all translations use female *wu*-shaman (*nüwu*) (Deng *TT*: 137; Yilin *TT*: 126; Zhu *TT*: 170). In the *Unfinished Tales*, "witch" is the same—*nüwu* (*UT*: 68; Shi and Deng *UT*: 91).

Even "shaman" or *wu* is an understatement. Gandalf's divine nature is revealed from time to time. As he speaks the words on the Ring, his voice changes: "Suddenly it became menacing, powerful, harsh as stone. A shadow seemed to pass over the high sun, and the porch for a moment grew dark. All trembled, and the Elves stopped their ears" (*FR*, II, ii, 248). The descriptors of Gandalf's voice here, "menacing, powerful, harsh as stone," show quite a wide variation: "fierce (*xionghen*), strong, harsh like stone" (Deng *FR* 318), "full of power, overbearing (*duoduo biren*, arrogant), voice was crude (*shengying*, unnatural, blunt, rigid) like rock" (Yilin *FR*: 309), and "evil (*xie-e*), strong, like rock cold-hearted and ear-piercing (*lengku ci-er*)" (Zhu *FR*: 397). But where Deng uses *wushi* and Yilin uses *shushi*, Zhu again uses *fashi* 法師. The *shi* is the same "master," and *fa* has a range of meaning (method, law, model, Dharma, and magic arts). *Fashi* often means a Buddhist Dharma master, but *fashi* has some flexibility in usage. In fact, Buddhist monks through history have been known to do magic. It is tempting to call Gandalf a *chanshi* (Zen Master), as many of his pronouncements are like koans. But the transformations of Gandalf's voice and appearance, combined with his angelic aspects, suggest a Buddhist bodhisattva rather than a Chan master.

And also suggest Jesus. In *Matthew* chapter 17, Jesus is transfigured before three of the apostles. Jesus' face shone and his clothes turned white; and "a bright cloud overshadowed them." When this display is concluded, it's just Jesus again. Gandalf is not meant as an allegory of Jesus, but he likewise periodically manifests some of his divine nature. When the Fellowship is surrounded by wargs, Gandalf grows to become "a great menacing shape like the monument of some ancient king of stone set upon a hill" (*FR*, II, iv, 291). The translations give us three interpretations of that royal monument: Deng has *shidiao fengbei* 石雕丰碑, stone-carved monument-stele (Deng *FR*: 374); Zhu has memorial stele (*jinianbei* 紀念碑) (Zhu *FR*: 464); Yilin has stone carved image (*shidiaoxiang* 石雕像) (Yilin *FR*: 365). However, the Valar wanted wizards to stay undercover: "their emissaries were forbidden to reveal themselves in forms of majesty" (*UT*: 389). For this we read: "their emissaries (*shizhe* 使者) were forbidden to manifest (*xianlu*) their true body (*zhenshen* 真身) full of power (*weishi*, power and influence)" (Shi and Deng *UT*: 504). The trope of someone suddenly radiating light and glory, and then deflating back to an ordinary person, seems to be one of Tolkien's favorites. Galadriel does it, Gandalf does it (see also Hooker 2003: 140–141; Petty 2011: 5–59). It is also a common attribute of deities in Chinese religion, who "dim their radiance" in order to communicate with us effectively. Indeed, *zhenshen* (true body) is part of the terminology of the Buddha's three bodies—the term *zhenshen* is a synonym for either the formless body (*fashen*, dharma body), or god-like body (*baoshen*, body of reward), in contrast with the relatively human form which he assumes so as not to overwhelm us (*huashen*, body of transformation).

There are two anomalous but godlike figures, not named as wizards but who have the status of Maiar, namely Tom Bombadil and Goldberry. Goldberry is given a variety of names. When the hobbits consider her "a fair young elf-queen clad in living flowers" (*FR*, I, vii, 121), Deng calls her an "elven empress (*wanghou*)" (Deng *FR*: 155) and Zhu, for a change, resists promotion: "elven queen (*nüwang*)" (Zhu *FR*: 201). Yilin calls her "a heavenly sylph descended into the world" (*xiafan tianxian*) (Yilin *FR*: 152). When she is called "fair lady" (*FR*, I, vii, 121), we get the close match *furen* from Deng (Deng *FR*: 156, 157), but "sylph-woman" (*xiannü*) from Yilin (Yilin *FR*: 153), and, oddly, from Zhu: "miss" (*xiaojie*) (Zhu *FR*: 202, 203). (More on sylph/*xian* in the next chapter.) Still, this is the hobbits' perception—she is not in fact an elven queen, or even an elf at all. What is she? "I am Goldberry, daughter of the River" (*FR*, I, vii, 121). Deng and Zhu preserve the ambiguity: "I am the river's daughter (*he zhi nü*)" (Deng *FR*: 156; cf. Zhu *FR*: 201–202). But Yilin makes her status clearer: "I am the daughter of the river-god (*heshen de nü-er* 河神的女儿)" (Yilin *FR*: 152). In Tolkien's legendarium, the Vala Ulmo is associated with waters, though primarily the seas. Unless there is some other river-god, this suggests that Goldberry might be Ulmo's daughter which is unlikely, as alone among the Valar, Ulmo took no spouse. In Chinese traditional terms, however, the river-god need not be Ulmo, since all bodies of water have powers in them, namely *long* (dragons). The Yilin translation hints that Goldberry is a dragon-king's daughter. The most famous of such daughters is mentioned in Chapter 12 of the *Lotus Sutra*. Another such daughter is the Jade Maiden (*Yunü*), associated with the Jade Emperor. If Goldberry is the dragon-king's daughter, she too must also be at least half-dragon. Though shape-changing is normal for Chinese dragons and one of the many secondary or occasional attributes of dragons in the West, we see no such thing in Middle-earth. Smaug is immutable. But in one Chinese version, Goldberry might at any point go outside and soar serpentine in the stormy sky.

Conclusions

Religion and fantasy overlap in positing superhuman beings known as gods, demons, angels, and magical-ritual specialists such as shamans and saints and wizards with powers beyond our own. Such beings have always extended the shape of the human imagination. The populations of genre fantasy easily blend into the long-established categories of religion, whether theological or demonological—more so than in science fiction, certainly. Yet to make these deities function as characters in stories requires a significant limitation of their power. The image of the demi-god, divine but not nearly omnipotent, and not automatically morally good, has been marginalized in Christian theology. They are angels or demons, clearly serving one side or the other—or they simply don't exist. On the other hand, traditional Chinese polytheism is crowded with such beings of moral complexity and indeterminate power. In traditional Chinese lore, we often find beings much like those of Middle-earth—capable of marvels but far short of any monotheistic idea of a God. Even the three most common terms for the Christian God hint at this more ambiguous divine society, since God is the lord ruling heaven (which is full of lesser beings), or a supreme ancestor (among many ancestors, even if supreme), or a Spirit (among countless spirits who might not merit the capital-S).

The empirical non-existence of such beings makes denotation impossible, and therefore in both lexicons we find haziness of definition. There is considerable latitude in naming these beings in Chinese, with much overlap between apparently distinct species—such as when *yao* is used in terms for goblins but also vampires and ghosts. There is a feeling of the various categories being more intimately related than in the English. We might hesitate to define the difference between a troll and a giant, a wood-demon and a hell-hawk, but the frequency of lexical overlap in Chinese gives them all either a certain flatness (since they no longer seem so distinct), or a certain internal coherence (as belonging to a system).

When we name a goblin, troll or imp using *gui*, we see them as scary but also closer to us—since a *gui* is essentially a *shen* (spirit) in a malevolent mode. A good ancestor *shen* can become a bad wandering *gui* if not properly tended. As we will see in the next chapter, the term for "elf" also spiritualizes the category and brings it closer to the human.

The example of Oromë indicates a being certainly understood as real, but no longer worshipped—as the "old gods" are not worshipped. They are not disbelieved, but irrelevant. There are no surprises in the translations of "of old" but then, in Chinese traditional religion, why would there be? All the gods are "of old." There are certainly deities in China whose worship dwindled long ago, but such gods do not form a distinct pantheon. In the original text but not in the translations, "of old" implies a worship long abandoned, belonging to a "heathen" past referenced by Denethor and Gandalf. Yet, heathenism is a problematic and anachronistic term in a world where Christianity has not yet appeared. The translations have to be creative here, drawing from the literal meaning "of the heath," and also from suggestions of ancient savages, degenerates, and heretics. The translators certainly pick up on the pejorative values of "heathen," relying on some sense of contrast with the orthodox or true, but drawing from a different history of othering—a somewhat less dichotomizing history, perhaps, being less about a contrast with Christianity.

The nearest we come to any kind of priest or shaman, anyone claiming to channel the voice of the gods, is the category of wizard, a term whose meaning shifts in translation, bringing it much closer to an explicitly religious quality. The translations occasionally seem slightly Buddhist, a little Daoist, or vaguely Confucian—lessening the contrast in English between "wizards" (and witches) who are of course *in the wrong* compared to priests and monks and nuns of Christianity.

In the next chapter, we turn to a category of beings certainly beyond human power: elves, including beings such as Galadriel whose power puts her in the ranks of the angels.

6

Elves and "Men"

What Exactly is an Elf?

The word teeters between Santa's little helpers and immortal superheroes, though we would hardly mistake Galadriel for a Smurf. But of course there is an older history. The "reality" of elves gradually declined during the nineteenth century due to what Tolkien called "rationalisation" (*OFS* 29), though the story is more complicated than viral empiricism. Shakespeare's Puck was in many ways the turning point, in which figures who were basically thieving monsters began to become representatives of nature (and therefore pre-rational), and eventually perceivable only by children (whose rationality was undeveloped). Puck even *apologizes* for possibly causing offence! In the nineteenth century, they shrank, ever more ephemeral, eventually to the point that (according to Peter Pan) merely saying you don't believe in them causes them to die. The Cottingley photographs of fairies, faked in 1917, fooled a few people briefly but otherwise proved fairies were a fraud (Purkiss 2000: 284–293; Magliocco 2018: 343). Lacking the institutional power of gods, by contrast fairies have not fared well. They were pinched between the anti-pagan Reformation and the anti-magical materialism of science. Their only escape route was "fiction," a category which self-consciously advertises in advance its own made-up-ness, like the legal disclaimer on fortune-telling sites saying "for entertainment purposes only." And even then, with literary modernism emphasizing "realism" in fiction, the escape was mostly into children's fiction. "She never found a place in modernism; indeed, she represented pretty strenuously everything modernism was against" (Purkiss 2000: 304).

Fairies shared the fate of many "small gods": "they are found within the encompassing, totalizing framework of a world religion that tends to find problematic the relationships characteristic of animism, and therefore seeks to condemn, contest, or marginalize continued belief in 'small gods'" (Ostling 2018a: 10). The elves of Middle-earth are fading away (as they did in Europe) but without any demonization or exorcism by Christianity or Science. The closest to their demonization is when people like Éomer voice their suspicion of the sorcery of the elves—or in the orcs' doomed war on elves. But the elves are not being *driven out*. In our history, the erasure of the small gods of Europe is unthinkable without Christian pressure, and globally unthinkable without colonialism. In Middle-earth, their disappearance is their own choice, to make way for the Dominion of "Men," a general ascendancy of humans which is the main characteristic of the Fourth Age.

The Chinese term for "elf," *jingling* 精靈/精灵, is a traditional term that had nothing to do with anything like elves. The use of it to translate "elf" is modern. There is nothing closely corresponding to "elf" in the traditional Chinese lexicon (Chen and Lei 2020: 88). I don't know when *jingling* began to be used to translate "elf," but I suspect the late nineteenth or early twentieth centuries, perhaps via Japanese, as part of the general project of translation of Western knowledge in which many new terms were coined.

Jingling is composed of *jing* (refined, spirit, essence, smart, excellent, skilled) and *ling* (mind, soul, spirit, deity, numinous, spiritually effective, nimble). Hence: agile spirit, excellent mind, refined soul—although one cannot take *these* words—spirit, mind, soul—too precisely, for they are also subject to the same ambiguities of translation. When we go back and forth, in the absence of a real referent, we never find a fixed point. *Jingling* is also used for leprechauns. Smurfs are *lanjingling*, "blue elves." To make matters worse, in common parlance (and in the Yilin translations), *jingling* is often prefixed by *xiao* 小 "little." As Gao Sifei points out, the use of *xiao* moves the elves away from Tolkien's intentions (2011: 134). Elves had the ill fortune to enter Chinese at the very nadir of their cultural power.

The oldest meaning of *jingling* is glossed as *guishen* 鬼神 (spirit, god, ghost)—and that particular usage has great antiquity. The term is also glossed as *jingshen* 精神 (animal spirit, vitality, vital energy of the body, anima). In fact, *jingshen chongbai* 精神崇拜 (the worship of *jingshen*) is a translation of "animism." You might wonder if it had something to do with the worship of elves. There is also a Buddhist use of *jingling*, referring to that part of each of us which is conscious and vital, and which survives after death and is reborn—an idea also known by several other variations.

But in Middle Earth, the elves are *not* the spirits of the dead or of "inanimate" objects, nor do humans have an animating *elf* inside them. Elves are a species or quasi-species distinct from humans, whereas in older Chinese terms, each of us has a *jingling*, and after death this *jingling* (at that point renamed *linghun* 靈魂/灵魂 or a similar term) either transmigrates or becomes a powerful spirit. The use of the term makes the elves less physical. In Tolkien, they have a kind of perfected physicality, but they are not beings of pure spirit or energy. The Chinese term is also therefore less "racial," in that there is less sense that elves are a distinct species or race. So, overall, *jingling* as "elf" is rather odd, though it is now entirely natural. Is there any better option? Not really—though I consider *xian* 仙 below. Deng remarked that the choice of *jingling* for elf was already customary, not a matter of her own ingenuity: "I just followed the word that people already recognize" (2017).

For "High Elves" (*RK*, Appendix B, 1057), Deng and Zhu both use: *gaodeng jingling* 高等精灵/靈, "high-level or high-grade elves" (Deng *RK*: 442; Zhu *RK* Appendix: 69), whereas Yilin gives the term a more "genetic" sound: *chunzong xiaojingling* 纯种小精灵, the pure-bred little elves (Yilin *RK*: 423). For "Silvan Elves" (*RK* Appendix B, 1057), Deng and Yilin transliterate: *si-er-fan* elves (Deng *RK*: 442; Yilin *RK*: 423), whereas Zhu adds a stealth gloss, "forest elves (*senglin jingling*), wood-elves (*mu jingling*) of the *xi-er-fan* elves" (Zhu *RK* Appendix: 70). For "The feasting folk were Wood-elves" (*H*, viii, 182), again Zhu uses *mu jingling* (Zhu *H*: 192). *Mu* 木 can mean tree, but also timber, wooden, as well as plain, even slow-witted or unthinking, so *mu jingling* does carry a hint of "wooden elves." Whereas Yilin prefers "forest little elves" (*senglin xiaojingling*), improving on *mu* but sadly still burdened with "little" (Yilin *H*: 144). In this line, Wu moves "wood" from an attribute of the elves to describe the location of their feast, with "in the forest feasting were these elves" though the same paragraph refers to them as forest elves (*senglin jingling*) (Wu *H*: 226).

Bilbo goes on to assess the moral or cultural qualities of the Silvan elves: they are not "wicked" but are xenophobic and suspicious of "strangers"—either *wairen* (outsiders) (Zhu *H*: 192) or *moshengren* (strangers, literally people born on the road) (Yilin *H* 144; Wu *H* 226). Mostly they "were descended from the ancient tribes that never went to Faerie in the West" (*H*, viii, 182). For "Faerie in the West," Zhu and Wu give *xianjing*, "Western sylph-domain" (more about *xian* and "sylph" below), but Yilin awkwardly transliterates the term as "Western regions' *fei-rui-ai*" (literally, radish-auspicious-dust, but easily recognizable as a transliteration of "Faerie"). In that place lived "the Light-elves and the Deep-elves and the Sea-elves" (*H*, viii, 182). Zhu gives us bright elves (*guangming jingling*), extensively learned (*boxue*) elves, and ocean (*haiyang*) elves (Zhu *H*: 192). Wu follows this except that "Deep" becomes "deep and broad" (or "erudite") (*yuanbo*) (Wu *H*: 226). Yilin differs significantly only in interpreting "deep" as "dark" (*hei-an*) (Yilin *H*: 144).

Let us delve into Tolkien's elves in translation. A great deal of what it means to be an elf has to do with death, but I leave that discussion for Chapters 8 and 9.

The Nature of Tolkien's Elves

Tolkien explained a lot of his world-building in the Appendixes, including a crucial passage on the word "elves." (The Yilin edition omitted many of the latter appendixes.) He begins with a slightly apologetic concession that "elves" is not the ideal "translation" of certain truer words. He tries to neutralize the possibility of logical contradictions by claiming the whole thing is a translation from other (fictional) languages. This insulates or liberates his use of the word "elves" from other understandings:

> *Elves* has been used to translate both *Quendi*, 'the speakers', the High-elven name of all their kind, and *Eldar*, the name of the Three Kindreds that sought for the Undying Realm and came there at the beginning of days (save the *Sindar* only). This old word was indeed the only one available, and was once fitted to apply to such memories of this people as Men preserved, or to the making of Men's minds not wholly dissimilar. (*RK* Appendix F, II, 1111)

So, if I follow this correctly: the words "Quendi" and "Eldar" are Romanizations of words originally written in an elven script; the one meaning "the speakers," and the other a proper noun (meaning "of the stars"). Are we to understand that whenever the text says "elves" we are to wonder which word was "actually" spoken, Quendi or Eldar? Are we to understand that there is no single word for elves in any of the languages of Middle-earth? Yet the "old [English] word" *elves* is adequate as long as we think of an older understanding of such beings (retained faintly in our cultural memory of the Quendi), or use our imagination in a certain way. The exact way in which our imaginations should be used to understand the word "elves" in *LOTR* is presumably best indicated by *LOTR* itself. Deng's collaborator, Shi Zhongge, interprets this passage with clarity, perhaps more clarity than the original text:

> The author selected and uses the term "*jingling*" to translate two terms: one is "Quendi," the meaning is "ones who can speak," this is the name for that entire race (*zhongzu*) of high elves; and one is "Eldar," this is the name for the three big lineages (*zongzu*) who went seeking the not-dying realm and at the beginning of the making of the world (*chuangshi zhichu*) reached that place (only except the Sindar). In fact, this ancient word was the only choice; once (chosen,) it was as if custom-fitted (*liangshen dingzuo*), used to describe memory impressions (*jiyi yinxiang*) preserved by humans about this race (*zhongzu*), so as far as human minds go it was not completely unfamiliar (*mosheng*, foreign-born, strange)." (Deng *RK*: 527–528)

Shi strengthens the word "fitted" into a set phrase, *liangshen dingzuo* 量身定做, "made by measuring the body," emphasizing the closeness of the fit between the word and certain human memories, and giving the relatively abstract sense of closeness of two understandings a certain physicality, as if the English word "elves" *clothed the body* of the words Quendi and Eldar. It is an interesting image of translation. As for "to the making of Men's minds not wholly dissimilar," Shi reads this as meaning, "still familiar to human minds," setting aside the hint in the word "making," which I read as "imagining" or even "sub-creating."

Of course it is odd to imply that Tolkien used the word *jingling*; she means Tolkien used an English word which is customarily translated as 精靈/精灵 (Romanized as *jingling*). Zhu on the other hand chooses to preserve the Romanized word, and adding the Chinese in parentheses: "[In Roman letters:] Elves (*jingling*) this word is used to translate [also Romanized:] Quendi, '*yongzhe* (those who chant, recite, narrate in poetic form),' the name in high-level elves' language for all of this race (*zhongzu*)" (Zhu *RK* Appendix: 141). He also gives Eldar in its Romanized form. Zhu sets the word "Quendi" apart from the rest of his Chinese text by retaining it in Romanized form, foreignizing the word in a way comparable to Tolkien's assertion that when he says "elves" he really means either "Quendi" or Eldar," originally in an elven script. Interpreting the difficult second sentence, Zhu writes, "Really, there was only this word suited to the present-day situation, people will use it to describe in memory a small number of histories about elves, or a past not at all similar to humans" (Zhu *RK* Appendix: 141). He has misread the understated double-negative "not wholly dissimilar" (which means, "somewhat similar") as "not similar at all." Here, Zhu's Tolkien is saying, the word is suited to our usages, because it is used in a few old stories, or used about an unfamiliar past—the word is good because it is obscure. These translations do not resolve the problem of two words in elvish being "translated" as one word in English or Chinese.

Tolkien goes on: "But it has been diminished, and to many it may now suggest fancies either pretty or silly, as unlike to the Quendi of old as are butterflies to the falcon—not that any of the Quendi ever possessed wings of the body, as unnatural to them as to Men" (*RK* Appendix F, II, 1111). Hence, we must therefore reject more recent understandings of elves, which Tolkien in "On Fairy-stories" called "flower-and-butterfly" (*OFS*: 29; also de Rosario Martínez 2010). Here, Tolkien refers to some unspecified history of human amnesia in the Fourth Age and beyond, but simultaneously to the rationalization of elves and fairies in Industrial Europe. There are two kinds of gap here: between our modern trivialization of elves and the pre-modern seriousness; and between even our best understandings and the lost language of the elves themselves. The Chinese translations have another layer of complication.

Shi continues: "But the meaning (*hanyi*, implications) of the term '*jingling*' has already faded (*tuise*), today many people consider that word suggests lovable or silly (*yuchun*) fantasy (*huanxiang* 幻想, illusion), and the difference between this and the ancient Quendi, really is like the difference between a butterfly and a swift hawk/falcon (*xunjie yingsun* 迅捷鹰隼)" (Deng *RK*: 528). She correctly reads the dominant meaning of "fancies" as fantasies rather than decorative trivialities. The Chinese *huanxiang* covers a range very similar to fantasy: illusion, fantastic imagination, fancy. She expands "the falcon" to *xunjie yingsun*, fast or agile falcon, for euphony and emphasis.

Having urged us to set aside our modern understandings, Tolkien describes the elves as he wants them to be: "the older Children of the world, ... the People of the Great Journey" (*RK* Appendix F, II, 1111). Both translators stay close to the original, though "Children" is of course not capitalized (nor not capitalized). Zhu introduces a potentially awkward anachronism, in translating Great Journey as *changzheng* 長征, the same term used for the Long March—the retreat of the Red Army from the Nationalists in 1934–1935. The Long March was later mythologized by the Communist Party, as a crucible in which the spirit of the Revolution was forged. Shi uses a less loaded term, *daqianxi*, great migration. The descriptions of the elves' physical appearances are straightforwardly translated, with only the change that "their voices had more melodies" becomes in Shi's voice an idiom, *wanzhuan dongting* 婉转动听: "their voice was sweet and pleasing to the ear" (Deng *RK*: 528). This doesn't quite get to the idea that their very voices had melodies, but it's not bad. In contrast, Zhu's "their voices were more beautiful-marvelous (*meimiao*)" (Zhu *RK* Appendix: 141) is bland.

The elves we meet in Middle-earth perceive themselves as exiles. Gildor explains, "We are Exiles, and most of our kindred have long ago departed and we too are now only tarrying here a while, ere we return over the Great Sea" (*FR* I, iii, 79). For "Exiles," Deng and Zhu use *liuwang* 流亡, composed of *liu* (= flow, hence drift, spread, and to be banished into exile); and *wang* (flee, lose, die), a fairly close match to "Exile." We know from other passages where they will return, but Zhu specifies: "We are exiles, the most part of our fellows (*tongbao* 同胞, those born of same parents, or fellow countrymen) long ago left, we are only staying (*douliu* 逗留) here for a short while before we go to the sylph domain (*xianjing*) beyond the sea" (Zhu *FR*: 138. Cf. Deng *FR*: 100). Yilin softens the implication of exile: "We are wanderers (*liulangzhe* 流浪者, same *liu* [flow] but with *lang* [stroll, ramble]), many people of my tribe (*jiazu*) long ago have left, we are only staying (*liu* 留) in this place, and then will cross the sea to return to the old place (*guli* 故里 native place)" (Yilin *FR*: 99). The term *liulangzhe* used by Yilin carries a sense of wanderers, even vagrants. "Those who wander" in the famous line, "Not all those who wander are lost" (*FR* I, x, 167), is *liumang* 流氓 (vagrant, hoodlum, even gangster) in the Yilin translation (Yilin *FR*: 209). Zhu and Deng use the somewhat kinder *langzi* 浪子 (loafers, wastrels) (Zhu *FR*: 271; Deng *FR*: 214).

As a description of the two perfect specimens, Celeborn and Galadriel, we read:

> Very tall they were, and the Lady no less tall than the Lord; and they were grave and beautiful. They were clad wholly in white; and the hair of the Lady was of deep gold, and the hair of Lord Celeborn was of silver long and bright; but no sign of age was upon them, unless it were in the depths of their eyes; for these were keen as lances in the starlight, and yet profound, the wells of deep memory. (*FR* II, vii, 345)

Zhu continues his pattern of promotion, here opting for *nühuang* (empress) over Yilin's and Deng's *furen* (lady). When Éomer calls her the Lady of the Wood (*TT* III, ii, 427), Deng keeps the Lady a lady (*furen*) (Deng *TT*: 37), where Zhu promotes her to forest empress (*nühuang*) (Zhu, *TT*: 54), and Yilin reflects Éomer's awe by divinizing her with "forest goddess (*nüshen*)" (Yilin *TT*: 35). The original pictures no "sign of age" on them; all three of these use *henji* 痕迹/痕跡; *hen* has a sickness radical and implies scars, bruises—a distinctly more damaged sense than "sign of age" (Zhu *FR*: 548; Deng *FR*: 443; Yilin *FR*: 432). The sense of vision is also different. In the original we have: the depths of their eyes, keen as lances, profound. In Yilin we have, *muguang* 目光 (eye-light) revealed (flow-show-out). Zhu has, eyes glistening (shining keenly). Rather than a sense of something going into the depths of their eyes, there is more of a sense of their vision as a substance emitted from their eyes. Boromir would certainly agree, perceiving her gaze as intrusive telepathy (*FR* II, vii, 349).

As mentioned in Chapter 2, to evoke the signs of age in the depths of their eyes, Yilin uses the phrase *cangsang*, short for *canghai sangtian*, 沧海桑田, the deep blue sea becomes a mulberry field. Zhu says the mark of time was deeply stored in their eyes. As for their eyes being like wells of memory, Yilin took "well" literally and added "never drying up": "like an eternally not-drying-up memory well" (Yilin *FR*: 432). Zhu added that the well was "old" (*gu*), which is not only idiomatic of wells in Chinese but also very appropriate to the story. He also adds that their eyes were "hoarding/storing up" (*yuncang* 蘊藏) the memories, just as Deng adds that the memories have been "accumulated" (*jilei*) (Deng *FR*: 443). All three of them have to specify that the deep well is a simile, using "like ...," whereas the original is directly metaphorical. Their eyes *were* wells of memory. Common Chinese metaphors for eyes include 目光似箭 *muguang sijian*, eye-light/gaze like an arrow (but not a lance). But for clear, sparkling eyes: like stars in clear sky of a summer night (夏夜晴空中的星星) and like flowing water of a little stream on an autumn day (秋天小溪流水). Wells (*jing* 井) are used as metaphors of orderliness, perhaps because of the appearance of the character itself, but not usually for eyes. Overall, though Tolkien's metaphors for their eyes are not quite idiomatic in Chinese, there are overlapping elements: sharpness, depth, and stars.

Elves and Altered States

There is some question of how the elves are related to magic. Usually the term used for "Elf-magic" (*FR* II, vii, 352) is *jingling mofa* (Yilin *FR*: 440; Zhu *FR*: 558; Deng *FR*: 451).

Let us recall the consideration of *mo* 魔 from Chapter 3: the basic distinction between conjuring-entertaining-magic and serious-powerful-magic closely corresponds to the Chinese *moshu* 魔术/魔術 (*mo*-arts) and *mofa* 魔法 (*mo*-methods), both of which rely on the complex character *mo*, with its own unique range of meanings related to the "devilish" as in the truly demonic as well as in "a devilishly clever crossword."

But we are fortunate, for the word itself is questioned in the story. Galadriel remarks to Sam that she is unclear about the word. "For this is what your folk would call magic, I believe; though I do not understand clearly what they mean; and they seem to use the same word of the deceits of the Enemy" (*FR* II, vii, 353). All three translations use *mofa* (i.e., serious magic), with only minor differences in interpretation of these lines (Deng *FR*: 452; Zhu *FR*: 560; Yilin *FR*: 441). That the same word is used for elven magic as for "the deceits of the Enemy" is stronger in Chinese, because the *mo-* of *jingling mofa* (elves' magic) retains some sense of the demonic. The magic of the elves is neither evil nor mere conjuring, which might explain Galadriel's puzzlement. Elves ("Good People") using a method (*fa*) which relies on *mo* is a greater contradiction than the use of "magic" by both the elves and "the Enemy."

But Sam reflects on the magic of elves, and reaches an important insight. Sam begins to discern diversity within his previously homogeneous category:

> Now these folk aren't wanderers or homeless, and seem a bit nearer to the likes of us: they seem to belong here, more even than Hobbits do in the Shire. Whether they've made the land, or the land's made them, it's hard to say, if you take my meaning. It's wonderfully quiet here. Nothing seems to be going on, and nobody seems to want it to. If there's any magic about, it's right down deep, where I can't lay my hands on it, in a manner of speaking. (*FR* II, vii, 351)

Sam perceives that the elves have a relationship to the land, in contrast to his previous perception of them as exiles or wanderers. For "wanderers" here, Deng and Yilin use the term *liulang* (roam, whether positive or negative), and Zhu uses the more positive and idiomatic "taking the four seas as their home"—"four seas" in the sense of everywhere; all the land between the seas. In the original, elves belong in Lothlórien even more than Hobbits belong in the Shire. Yilin turns "belong" into *yilian* 依恋, rely on and love, long for, but the comparison is accurately retained. Deng and Zhu have "belong" (*shu* 属/屬, be under, belong to), but Zhu equalizes the two: elves belong in Lothlórien the same as Hobbits belong in the Shire (Yilin *FR*: 439–440; Deng *FR*: 451; Zhu *FR*: 558).

As for Sam's speculation "Whether they've made the land, or the land's made them," Deng's version is very close to literal, whereas Yilin expands on "the land" a little, with: "the water and earth," emphasizing its physical substance. Zhu writes, "It's difficult to say in the end if the environment molded (*huanjing suzao* 環境塑造) them, or that they molded the environment" (Zhu *FR*: 558). "Environment" gives it a more modern sound. Environmental determinism (or pathetic fallacy) is pervasive in Tolkien. Did the orcs make Mordor such a horrible place, or did such a horrible place naturally produce such horrible people?

As for the elves of Lothlórien, the strong sense of belonging, together with its idyllic beauty and peace, evokes some aspects of Daoist utopian lore, such as the short story

"Peach Blossom Spring" by Tao Qian (365–427), or in *Daodejing* chapter 80: a place separated from the stressful common world, in which time seems to pass differently, where people "Will find relish in their food / And beauty in their clothes, / Will be content in their abode / And happy in the way they live" (trans. Lau 1994). If there is something Edenic or heavenly about Lothlórien, Chinese readers might have these and other images in the background: the abode of various deities such as the garden of Xiwangmu (Queen Mother of the West) wherein grow the peaches of immortality, or Penglai, the "isle of the immortals" in the Eastern sea.

In the original, "If there's any magic about, it's right down deep, where I can't lay my hands on it," becomes, in Yilin: "If I were to say there was some kind of magic (*moli*), then, it comes from underground, comes from a place I can't grasp" (Yilin *FR*: 440). Certainly "deep" implies underground, but may be more subtle than that. Zhu makes the phrase more ontological: "If this place has magic (*mofa*), then as far as I can see, it really is in a deep place of things (*zai shiwu de shenchu* 在事物的深處), not a place where I could judge (*pingduan* 評斷)" (Zhu *FR*: 558). Zhu keeps the subtlety, as "in a deep place of things" suggests "deep" in the sense of "inherent" or "fundamental." Deng similarly leaves "deep" open to interpretation. But Zhu changes the physical "lay my hands on" to "not a place where I could judge." Certainly, grasping is a natural metaphor for understanding or controlling, and it would be natural for Sam to think and speak in physical ways. Also, since he's talking about the physical place, "lay my hands on" or "grasp" would seem more appropriate than "judge." He's talking about what is intangible in this tangible place. Still, Sam trying to "judge" suggests his mental effort to make his mind up about Lothlórien, rather than the possession implied by "lay my hands on it."

Sam notes that his perception of time was affected by Lothlórien, and Legolas clarifies: time never stops, but in different places the pace of change differs. For elves, things change both quickly and slowly. "Swift, because they themselves change very little, and all else fleets by: it is a grief to them. Slow, because they do not count the running years, not for themselves. The passing seasons are but ripples ever repeated in the long long stream" (*FR* II, ix, 379).

Yilin: "To speak of fast, it is because their own bodies (*zishen*, own persons) almost don't change, and all surrounding is fleeting (*shaozong jishi* 稍纵即逝), because of this they feel sad; to speak of slow, it is because they have never counted the passing (*shiqu*) years and months, or at least they themselves do not count. The changing of the seasons is only a repeatedly stirred up (*fanfu jiqi*) little bit of ripples (*lianyi* 涟漪) in the long river in time" (Yilin *FR*: 474). The ripples of the passing seasons are now "stirred up." Yilin develops "all else fleets by" into a more physical metaphor with *shaozong jishi*, "slightly relax the grip and it's gone," a more vivid image, or at least less passive—though perhaps the elves have grown passive. Zhu also adapts the phrase a little: "all other things are as if flying away (*rufei erqu*)" (Zhu *FR*: 598). Thinking of fleet horses, Deng uses a common *chengyu*: "all other things are like [glimpsing] a white horse passing a gap in a fence (*baiju guoxi* 白驹过隙)" (Deng *FR*: 487). Each of these three variations on how elves perceive the changing world has its own appeal: a moment can be grasped but that moment is gone when they relax their attention; the world flies away in the air; they see things only as tantalizing glimpses.

The passing seasons are ripples in a long stream; Yilin makes the stream a river, but otherwise is close, except for diminishing the ripples to "a little bit"; and specifying the river is "of time." Zhu makes the passing of time into an "unceasing repeated frothing/bubbling (*paomo* 泡沫) in a slow and long flow of time"—also implying a wider river than a stream. Ripples and frothy bubbles are not the same. Ripples imply effects, repercussions, karma—a sequence of events. Froth and bubbles are old Buddhist metaphors for the world as transitory, valueless, a fuss about nothing, which here might emphasize the elves' detachment.

We can get a sense of the elves also by looking at their effects on others. Spending time with a traveling band of elves early in *Fellowship*, the hobbits experience various drug-like effects: amnesia, bliss, a sense of unreality, hallucinations, and distorted perceptions of time (*FR* I, iii, 81; Deng *FR*: 102; Zhu *FR*: 140; Yilin *FR*: 101). The elves' song-like language, and especially their singing, is like a magical spell (*FR* II, i, 227). In Chapter 12, we will return to this passage. For now though, let's see what happens to the "spell." Deng: "immediately entered a lost state (*rulemi*, entered a trance)" (Deng *FR*: 288). Yilin: "immediately lured (*yin*) him" (Yilin *FR*: 282). Zhu: "was lost in it" (Zhu *FR*: 361). Rather than a spell holding him, Frodo moves into the spell.

Indeed, the singing gradually creates a vision of a whole world. The experience escalates until Frodo is completely overwhelmed and his mind shuts down. This world-sized vision "drenched and drowned him. Swiftly he sank under its shining weight into a deep realm of sleep" (*FR* II, i, 227). The vision of the world magically created by the elves' spell forces him out of consciousness. For "drenched and drowned," Deng and Zhu are close to literal, but Yilin aerates the imagery: "made him [feel] as if he fell into a five-colored mist (*wucaiwu* 五彩雾), in this bright shining cloud-light, he very quickly sank into the sleep country (*mengxiang* 梦乡, sleep village)" (Yilin *FR*: 282). Zhu also lightens the weight, making them rays of light: "In those shining rays of light, he very quickly sank into an unlimited dream land (*mengtu*)" (Zhu *FR*: 361). Yilin and Zhu compromise the steady downwardness of the original, which Deng retains: "By its shining weight pressed down (*ya*), he quickly sank into the kingdom (*wangguo*) of sleep" (Deng *FR*: 288). Sleep is a realm, a rural area, or a land, or a kingdom, not the mere loss of consciousness.

The blurring of waking and dreaming is one of a number of tropes which make the elves ambiguous and beyond linear rationality. Frodo's pearl of wisdom specifies their ambiguity: "Go not to the Elves for counsel, for they will say both yes and no" (*FR* I, iii, 83). Isolated from context, the strange English word "yes" is a very abstract concept. "No" seems easier, or at least, "not." Deng translates this as: "Do not look for elves' counsel (*zixun*), they might say it is, also might say not (*huishuo shi, you huishuo bu* 会说是，又会说不)" (Deng *FR* 105). Zhu: "they may not posit whether [something] can [be] or not (*buzhi kefou* 不置可否)" (Zhu *FR*: 143). The abstract "yes" has to turn into "it is" or "it can be." Yilin gives a rhyming 7-character couplet which resists any elegant or even grammatical back-translation: "Don't look for elves' advice, the ambiguous two possibilities are both the way (*moleng liangke dou shi dao* 模棱两可都是道)" (Yilin *FR*: 104). Perhaps I should capitalize that last word, the Way—the Dao. Hence, both mutually exclusive possibilities are harmonized in the elven Way. This idiom harks back to an idea from Daoism (but also other schools) that before the division of yin and yang, reality embraced every possibility without contradiction, in a primordial "chaos" before even the first binary. In Daoism, the reversion to the non-binary is associated with immortality. This idiom positions the elves in primordial time, immortal because they include both life and death. Do not ask the elves for advice because asking "yes or no" divides the world in a way they have transcended. Here at least, the elves are more Daoist than Confucian.

What Exactly is a *Xian*?

Having remarked on the oddity of using *jingling* for "elf," one obvious alternative is the character *xian* 仙. This character is frequently used for fairy, such as Yilin's *xiannü* (Yilin *H*: 2) for "a fairy wife" (*H*, i, 5). In that instance, Zhu however has the more menacing "*yaojing* acting as a wife," *yaojing dang laopo* 妖精當老婆, using *laopo* (old woman) for "wife" (Zhu *H*: 7). Elsewhere, Zhu uses *xianjing* (*xian* domain) for Faerie (e.g. *H*, viii, 182; Zhu *H*: 192), perhaps because *xianjing* is an established idiom, but *yaojing-jing*, the domain of *yaojing*, is not.

But what is a *xian*? Setting aside irrelevant or derivative meanings, in Chinese a *xian* is generally but not absolutely associated with Daoism; through Daoist cultivation a *xian* has achieved a transcendent state characterized by not dying, and by freedom from limitations. They typically fly, exist on refined nutrition such as air, dew or *qi*. A set group, the eight *xian* (*baxian*), is well-known from art, games, comics, and films.

Let's use translations of Wu Cheng-en's sixteenth-century novel *Xiyouji* (*Journey to the West*) by Arthur Waley, Anthony Yu, and Timothy Richard. In these three translations, the word *xian* is rendered as: immortal, magic, fairy, enchanted, Eternal, and divine. *Xianshi* 仙石, Yu gives as "immortal stone," Waley as "magic rock," and Richards "stone egg" (Yu *JW*: 67; Waley *JW*: 11,; Richards *JW*: 3). *Xianshan* 仙山, Yu gives as "immortal mountain"; Waley as "fairy mountains" or "enchanted hills." Richard says, "the Eternal Mountain" (Yu *JW*: 73; Waley *JW*: 14; Richards *JW*: 7). Monkey addresses a man as *laoshenxian*, 老神仙 and Yu and Waley agree with "Reverend Immortal" (Yu *JW*: 78; Waley *JW*: 16). *Xiantong*, 仙童 Waley gives as "fairy boy," Yu as "immortal youth" (Yu *JW*: 80; Waley *JW*: 18). *Xianshu*, 仙術 Yu has "divine magic"; Waley and Richard have "magic arts" (Yu *JW*: 103; Waley *JW*: 34; Richards *JW*: 30).

We find *xian* used in many translations from English to Chinese, such as Liang Shiqiu's 1936 translation of J. M. Barrie's *Peter Pan*, where fairies are *shenxian* 神仙 (trans. Liang 1936: 19). Tinkerbell is a little *xian*-girl (*xiao xiannü*). "Fairy dust" is *xianchen* 仙塵 (Barrie [1911] 2011: 36; trans. Liang 1987: 42). Queen Mab is glossed as a *xian*-queen or -empress (*xianhou* 仙后)" (115). I find a very comparable set of terms in Zhu Shenghao's 2012 translation of *A Mid-Summer Night's Dream*. The Fairy Queen = *xianhou* (Shakespeare, trans. Zhu 2012: 31). The Fairies are *shenxian* (39). Or, a fairy is *xiaoxian*, little *xian* (47). However, when Puck says, "Spirit!" in Chinese he says *jingling*, the term otherwise used for "elf" (31). In Peng Qianwen's translation of *Harry Potter and the Chamber of Secrets*, green *xian* (*lüxian*) appears to translate "pixies" (2000: 128; cf. Rowling 1999: 101). Fu Hao's translations of the poetry of W. B. Yeats uses *xian* for Fairy, but also specifying the female gender; a poem urges a "human child" to go "With a faery," which is "With a *xiannü* (female *xian*)" (2000: 36–38).

Translations of *xian* into English seem to gravitate around these three core ideas: immortal, magic, and fairy. Yet each of these meanings is very different. There seems to be a loose consensus or habit of translating elf as *jingling* or *xiaojingling* and fairy as *xian* or *xiannü*. The routine feminizing of *xian* into *xiannü* does not seem to be the case with *jingling*—I have not found any *jinglingnü*. And there remains a fundamental mismatch of *xian* and fairy: traditionally, elves and fairies don't have souls, whereas in Daoism, "becoming a *xian*" (*chengxian* 成仙) is the very definition of spiritual success for your soul. "Immortal" is not quite right either: in Daoist usage, although a *xian* has survived beyond the death of their body, yet a *xian* may still die. A *xian* may have extreme longevity but not automatically by strict definition immortality.

There is in some circles of Sinology a use of the word "sylph" to translate *xian*. A word from the seventeenth century, sylphs are a race of beings inhabiting the air, belonging to the element of air. This sense correlates to *xian* in some ways, because *xian* are frequently believed to be very light and able to fly, subsisting on the ether itself. Yet again, since some of the *xian* used to be human, *xian* are not a "race" distinct from the human race. Sylph is not our solution. And yet one thing makes "sylph" appealing—its very obscurity. We are less likely to impute misguided meanings, simply because most of us aren't very sure what sylph means. I will use sylph specifically for *xian*.

There are many examples of using *xian* in translations of *The Lord of the Rings*. The elves sing a hymn to Varda, queen of the Valar: "We sing to thee / In a far land beyond the Sea" (*FR* I, iii, 78). Zhu renders the line as: "Let us present a ballad-entertainment (*quxiang* 曲響) for the spirit-empress (*shenhou*) of the sylph domain (*xianjing*) beyond the sea" (Zhu *FR*: 135). Here, *xian* is used not as a direct translation but as an interpolation to elaborate on the nature of the Undying Lands. Elsewhere, when the hobbits refer to Goldberry as "a fair young elf-queen" (*FR* I, vii, 121), Deng and Zhu use *jingling* for elf, but the Yilin edition has: "a heavenly sylph descended into the world (*xiafan de tianxian*)" (Yilin *FR*: 152). The Yilin edition seems to show a greater propensity to conflate *jingling* and *xian*. Aragorn says that after the deaths of Beren and Lúthien, they spent some time together and eventually "together they passed, long ago, beyond the confines of this world" (*FR* I, xi, 189). The Yilin edition has this as: "together left the fetters (*jiban*, shackles, yoke) of the dusty world (*chenshi*), and passed away (*xianshi* 仙逝, sylph-died; died and became *xian*)" (Yilin *FR*: 238). Though in the vast majority of cases, elves are *jingling*, we find *xian* at the edges of the semantic field, suggesting an alternative Legolas.

What Exactly is a (M/m)an?

Along with elves and trolls and gods, *The Lord of the Rings* references another strange creature: human beings, or, as Tolkien calls them, "Men." Obviously this usage, "man" or "men" when referring to human beings in general, now feels very dated—although outside of the academy it isn't quite dated enough. "Man" was used either to mean *males (not females)* or *all human beings*, to suit the male establishment: for example all "men" have to pay taxes, obviously including women, but allowing "men" to vote naturally excluded women (Srinivasan 2020: 35). The 1970s and 1980s saw an uptick in resistance to this androcentrism. It would be hard to imagine Jacob Bronowski's *The Ascent of Man* (1973) being broadcast by the BBC today, and Huston Smith's 1958 *The Religions of Man* became *The World's Religions* in its revised edition of 1991.

Elrond says, "Farewell, and may the blessing of Elves and Men and all Free Folk go with you" (*FR* II, ix, 274). For "Men," all three Chinese translations of this line give *renlei* 人類 (humankind, a gender-neutral term; Deng *FR*: 353; Zhu *FR*: 438; Yilin *FR*: 344). Clearly, Elrond cannot mean, the blessing of (all) Elves (of any gender) and (only) male (not female) people. The Chinese language is certainly capable of encoding patriarchy into its characters and usages, but in this particular case it does not. Yet, not all uses of "Man" in *The Lord of the Rings* are quite so easily gender-neutralized. Indeed, one of the key plot points of the whole story hinges on the androcentric ambiguity of "Man."

And here, we should recall that one of the fundamental differences between Chinese and English is that English has capital letters, and Chinese does not. This is not a trivial difference. The text itself problematizes the term and its upper or lower cases. Introducing Pippin to the soldiers of Gondor, Gandalf says: "His name is Peregrin, a very valiant man." The Gondorian soldier Ingold asks, "Man?" And Pippin replies: "Man! ... Man! Indeed not! I am a hobbit" (*RK* V, i, 733). Gandalf seems to be using "man" (lower case) to mean, male person. He might have said, "a very valiant fellow." Ingold takes it to mean "human," and doubts it; and Pippin confirms that sense: he's not speaking of gender but race (or species). (Fimi notes Tolkien's inconsistency in naming what elves/men *are*: races, peoples, kindreds; 2009: 132.) Sometimes "man" is ambiguous because of gender, and sometimes because of species. The ambiguity of *ren* (人) is clearly not about gender, but it can mean "human" or it can mean "person." Even without the suffix -*lei* (-kind), *ren* has a sense of "human," because after all, in the real world, most "people" are human. In Deng's translation: "His name is Peregrin, [he] is an extremely valiant *ren*." "*Ren*?" ... "*Ren*! Am not! I am a hobbit person (*huobite ren*) ..." (Deng *RK*: 7; Yilin *RK*: 5 is basically the same). Zhu specifies more: "[he] is an extremely brave *ren*." "*Ren*?" "Human! (*renlei*) ... Human! Am not! I am a hobbit person (*habi ren*)" (Zhu *RK*: 22). Here, Gandalf uses *ren* to mean "person," Ingold takes *ren* to mean "human," and Pippin adds -*lei* (-kind) to confirm Ingold's understanding, though also rejecting the categorization. In any case, here the issue is not his gender—he's not objecting to the attribution of masculinity.

When a contrast with elves or dwarves is made, such as in: "for Men multiply and the Firstborn decrease" (*FR* II, ii, 238), the full term is used. Deng: "because the human population (*renlei renkou*) increases, the first children (*shouxian ernü*) daily gradually wither" (Deng *FR*: 305; also *renlei* in Yilin *FR*: 296; Zhu *FR*: 381). In the *Silmarillion*, the line, "But the sons of Men die indeed" (*S*: 36), is given in Yilin as *ren* (Yilin *S*: 35), but both of Deng's versions say: "humans (*renlei*) and their sons and grandsons" (Deng *S*: 2015: 64; Deng *S*: 2002: 46).

Poor blinkered Éomer is having trouble adjusting to the presence of elves and dwarves. In such a strange world, "How shall a man judge what to do in such times?" (*TT* III, ii, 427). He probably just means, "How can I know what to do?" He isn't assuming that women might have figured it out already, or lack curiosity. Yet, so soon after he has mused on elves and dwarves, surely it also means, "How can human beings know?" Deng uses the gender-neutral *ren*: "In this kind of age, how should a person (*ren*) judge for [him]self what to do?" (Deng *TT*: 37). Yilin avoids the grammatical subject: "These years, it is hard to say what to do?" (Yilin *TT*: 35). But Zhu accents and genders Éomer's self-identification: "How can a common man (*fanfu suzi* 凡夫俗子, common-male common-son) under these circumstances, make a true judgement?" (Zhu *TT*: 54). An additional category used by hobbits such as Pippin for all sorts of non-hobbits is "the Big People" (*FR* I, iii, 74). Deng's choice is gender-neutral: *dazhongren*, big-type people (Deng *FR*: 93). Zhu uses the not-quite gender neutral *dajiahuo* 大傢伙, big fellows (Zhu *FR*: 129). When Pippin says "Big People," Yilin uses a term gendered male: *dahan* 大汉, big male fellows (Yilin *FR*: 93; cf. *haohan*, below), but three lines below Frodo uses both "Men" and "Big People" and Yilin gives both as *darenzu*, the big people race. They all avoid simply *daren* (big people) because *daren* means adults (not children). But at the start of *The Hobbit*, the narrator mentions "the Big People, as they call us" (*H*, i, 4)—"us"?!—and Yilin gives *daren* (Yilin *H*: 2). Zhu uses *dajiahuo* (Zhu *H*: 6) and Wu uses *dazhongren* (Wu, *H*: 7).

The muddle of Pippin's classification as it moves into Chinese might be no more than a slight distraction, another example of a source text using a single word which must be translated into different words in the target language, depending on context. But there is one place where this problem is crucial to the story itself, in the scene surrounding the death of Théoden, he of the permanent inferiority complex: "A lesser son of great sires am I" (*TT* III, x, 566). All three translations can identify the notion of failing one's ancestors with precision, invoking the powerful virtue of filial piety. Deng: "an unworthy descendant (*buxiao zisun* 不肖子孙) of great fathers' generations" (Deng *TT*: 223; identical at Zhu *TT*: 268; similar at Yilin *TT*: 205).

His niece Éowyn falls in love with Aragorn but is gently rebuffed, and she begins to actively seek her own death in battle. She dresses up as a man—shades of Mulan—and joins the army as Dernhelm, along the way taking pity on Merry who has likewise been excluded from military service. Finally they plunge into the Battle of Pelennor Fields. Théoden is mortally wounded and lies unprotected. When the monstrous Witch-King approaches to finish him off, Éowyn confronts the enemy:

[Éowyn:] Do what thou will; but I will hinder it, if I may.
Hinder me? Thou fool. No living man may hinder me!
... But no living man am I! You look upon a woman. Éowyn I am ... (*RK* V, vi, 823)

Why is the Witch-king so very confident he can't be killed? Long before, the powerful elf Glorfindel made a prophecy. The Witch-king was fleeing a defeat, and Glorfindel told others not to pursue him. "Far off yet is his doom, and not by the hand of man will he fall" (*RK* Appendix A, I, iv, 1027). Here, we have the ungrammatical "man," neither "a man" (male person) nor "Man" (human beings). We might blame the transcription of Glorfindel's utterance—after all, we can't actually *hear* upper and lower cases. Tolkien wanted to leave it ambiguous, and so he seems careless here. Glorfindel's words are buried away in an appendix, but Gandalf repeats it in the story itself: "not by the hand of man shall he fall" (*RK* V, iv, 801).

The problem is that when Tolkien/the Witch-king says, "no living man can hinder me," he thinks (and we think) it means "no one" or possibly "no human being," but when Éowyn says, "no living man am I," she is saying, "I'm alive and I'm human, but I'm not male, I'm female." As if no one had ever imagined a woman might stab him. So the original contains a kind of verbal trick or riddle. Tolkien plays bait and switch, so as to obscure the possibility that Éowyn might kill the Witch King, and to heighten the sense of danger to Éowyn—she's up against someone *no one* can kill!

When the Witch-king seems about to kill her, Merry gets a stab in—then Éowyn stabs the Witch-king, and the body vanishes. When Merry stabs him, it's again as the bad guy said (while being loose about the capital M), no "man" can stop me—Merry is not a "Man" but a hobbit, as Pippin vigorously insisted earlier—a difference of species, not gender. Between them they kill him: a Man who's not a man, and a man who's not a Man. Perhaps also, since the hobbits are frequently referred to as "halflings," "only children to your eyes" as Aragorn remarks, Merry is not fully a "man" in another sense: not yet an adult (*TT* III, ii, 424). He's a half-man. In the Appendixes as a footnote to Éowyn's title "The Lady of the Shield-arm," we read that Glorfindel was right: "the Witch-king would not fall by the hand of man. For it is said in the songs of the Mark that in this deed Éowyn had the aid of Théoden's esquire, and that he also was not a Man but a Halfling" (*RK*, Appendix A,II, 1045). So, in the Mark they took "man" to mean "Man" in order to include Merry even if it excluded Éowyn? Or vice-versa? Within a single footnote, we see how the rules of the game change according to the players.

Éowyn's femininity functions as a kind of magic here, a kind of partial immunity (see Gitter 1984). She cuts off the dragon-like fell beast at its "long, naked neck" (*RK* V, vi, 822)—a kind of castration? (And if so, whose penis is severed?—The Witch-king's? Or "Dernhelm's"?) Then she removes her "helm," and "her bright hair, released from its bonds, gleamed with pale gold upon her shoulders" (*RK* V, vi, 823; on the power of her unbound hair, see Colvin 2020: 135–136). When Éowyn says she's a woman, "the Ringwraith made no answer, and was silent, as if in sudden doubt" (*RK* V, vi, 823). Éowyn's announcement that she is a woman functions as her awakening wisdom that she should not after all have tried to be a male; and once she has recovered from her wounds she goes straight into the arms of her future husband Faramir, as a War Bride (Smith 2007; Johnson 2009: 117). And they lived happily ever after.

How do the translations handle this?

In the Yilin translation, here by Tang Dingjiu, the key moment of dialogue (quoted above) is:

In the world there is not that person (*meiyou neige ren* 没有那个人) able to stop me!
… Then just wait for me to deal with (*shoushi* 收拾, put in order, settle up) you! [Yilin skips "You look upon a woman"] I am Éowyn … (Yilin *RK*: 118)

So, the Yilin edition has: no person (*ren*) can stop me—this is not gender-specific, but also only loosely species-specific, since he does not quite say no *human* (*renlei*) can kill me. And Éowyn's reply ignores the issue. She just says, wait til I deal with you! No one can stop me / I'll give it a try. Yilin's version of Glorfindel's prophecy has: "the hand of ordinary/mortal people (*fanren de shou* 凡人的手) cannot seize him" (Yilin *RK*: 381). It's not much of a prophecy: under the circumstances, it could just mean, "let him go, no ordinary person's going to be able to get hold of him." It sounds like a bit of a put-down: it'll take more than you ordinary people to catch him—and recall, he's talking to Eärnur the last king of Gondor. For Gandalf's repetition of the line (*RK*, V, iv, 801), Yilin is not much better: "other people (*bieren*) cannot strike him dead (*da busi ta*)" (Yilin *RK*: 91). The trick is gone, and we are left with merely a prophecy that turned out to be false—unless arbitrarily the king of Gondor is an "ordinary person," but Éowyn is not—which I could certainly accept.

Yilin having otherwise read "man" as gender-neutral *ren*, the footnote to Éowyn's title rather inconsistently reads "by the hand of man" as "by a male person (*nanren*)'s hand" but goes on to say of Merry ("not a Man" in the original) that he "was not a human (*renlei*), but was a ... Halfling person (*hafulin ren*)" (Yilin *RK*: 407). This footnote places both Éowyn and Merry as candidates for the prophecy, and the translator is forced to name both contradictory meanings in quick succession.

Zhu comes at the problem in a different way:

'All the world's masculine heroes (*yingxiong haohan* 英雄 好漢) have no way to stop me!'
... 'I am not some kind of masculine hero! Before your eyes is a woman—I am Éowyn ...' (Zhu *RK*: 160)

The phrase *yingxiong haohan* is strongly masculine. *Han* has the sense of maleness, as in *laohan* 老漢 (old man) and *dahan* 大漢 (big man). *Ying* means hero; *xiong* means male, virile, as used in combinations for male animals, in medical terms such as testosterone, and in words starting with andro-. "Maleness" itself is *xiongxing* 雄性, *xiong*-nature. So Zhu gets the gender issue: no masculine hero can stop me / I'm not one of those masculine heroes, I'm a woman. But Zhu cannot capture the shift from man-as-person to man-as-male. It's not as if the Witch-king fears some cowardly back-stabber might do him in. Zhu's translation of Glorfindel's prophecy also uses *yingxiong haohan*, and Glorfindel's words remain a somewhat accurate prophecy because Éowyn is not male (Zhu *RK* Appendix: 28), though as it turns out, she is one of the greatest heroes of the whole story. Zhu's version of the note about Éowyn's title also uses *yingxiong haohan*, but here saying that not just Éowyn but also Merry was not "some kind of masculine hero" either (Zhu *RK* Appendix: 54), which at least has the merit of consistency. Though Merry is male, he's not yet the heroic warrior we see later during the Scouring of the Shire.

Even Deng cannot fully solve this puzzle. Deng's version of Glorfindel's remark is: "he cannot die by a person's hand (*renshou* 人手)" (Deng *RK*: 395. also Deng *RK*: 93). Here, Glorfindel is simply incorrect. Then:

There is no living person (*huoren* 活人) that can stop me!
... But I am not a living male person (*huozhe de nanren* 活着 的 男人)! What you face is a women (*nüren* 女人). I am Éowyn ... (Deng *RK*: 121–122)

The witch-king says no one alive can kill me, and Éowyn says I'm not alive-and-male. Deng is fully aware of the problem and resolves the issue in two ways, by slipping in "male," and by inserting a footnote on the phrase *huoren* ("living person"): "*Huoren* ([in English:] living man [but actually, living *person*]) can also be translated as 'living male person'. Here it has two connotations" (Deng *RK*: 121). However, her assertion here is somewhat ad hoc—there is nothing inherently gendered about *huoren*. More precisely, she interjects her own note into the footnote on Éowyn's title: "what Glorfindel said to King Eärnur a long time ago came true: the witch-king could not die by a person's hand (*renshou*). (In English 'man' can be translated as 'humankind (*renlei*)', and also can be translated as 'male person (*nanren*)'—translator)" (Deng *RK*: 423). Even though I don't agree with Eco that a footnote is "always a sign of weakness on the part of a translator" (Eco 2001: 50), it registers as an interruption. And in the end, this glaringly contradictory footnote can only be presented as: this trick only works in English.

So, pretend now that the first time you are reading this is in the Chinese—or even, imagine that Tolkien wrote it in Chinese. The Yilin edition ignores the gender aspect and emphasizes Éowyn's suicidal fury, because she shows no sign of any hope: I am invincible! / I don't care. Éowyn had been seeking her own glorious death at least since Aragorn rejected her. This is surely the Northern Theory of Courage—not Éowyn cottoning on to the trick with a glimmer of hope, but persisting in the face of apparently inevitable death. Zhu catches the gendered aspect, but also features Éowyn's denial that she is a hero—this, after her previous protestations about not being allowed to fight in the war, and her angry assertions of her own martial skills (*RK* V, ii, 767). Zhu's translation hints that she might be wising up a little—and indeed, after she has recovered, she moves into a traditional romantic relationship with Faramir. It also implies she has no hope: if all these great macho heroes can't kill you, what chance do I have? Yet I will try. Deng's version blurs the question with a non sequitur insertion into Éowyn's reply of the adjective "male"; but Éowyn also seems to deny that she is *alive*—perhaps showing her full embrace of the inevitability of her death. By the very inability to reproduce the trick of Man/man, the Chinese versions are forced to depict Éowyn as even more despairing and therefore even braver than in the original. At the cost of Glorfindel's credibility, perhaps.

Conclusions

The Éowyn case is a good example of reading the translations in their own right. Although I started with a sense of a trick in English that cannot be easily replicated, I ended the case with a sense of enlarged possibilities. "Man" can mean male or human, and the translators are forced to decide. But more often we find ambiguities in one language mapping imperfectly onto ambiguities in another. "Magic" is another example, questioned in the text itself. Sam sees it less as a matter of manipulation of the material world (that old and hostile attitude towards magic, used to differentiate it from religion), but rather as a place-based rootedness, more environmental, more natural. "Belonging" is made explicit for example by Zhu with "the environment molded (*huanjing suzao*) them." The Chinese translations of elf, fairy, and wizard put these beings more into religious, animistic, or "small god" categories, rather than those of race or species.

But there are different histories of marginalizing the small gods; one a mixture of Christianity and the Enlightenment, science, and the industrial revolution; the other including skeptical influences of Confucianism, rapid adoption of science (as an ideology as much as a practice), the anti-religious movements of the twentieth century, and Communist materialism. Perhaps in the West now, fairies can be understood in neo-Pagan terms as nature spirits, loosely aligned with feminism and environmentalism, and it would certainly be interesting to inquire into contemporary neo-Paganism in China and Taiwan today—and the neo-Pagan influence of Tolkien, if any.

Legolas' waking/dreaming state is a perfect synthesis of empirical perception and imaginative wandering. He dreams with his eyes open: a double vision. We might compare the elves' altered states to reading as an altered state. When the hobbits fall into the elven trance, is it like "believing" in a world of fiction? The effects are similar: amnesia, bliss, a sense of unreality, visions, and distorted experiences of time. In Chinese, "entering into" a trance is often expressed as *mi*—a lost state, a meandering mind. Like "suspending disbelief" (or "believing") in a story as we read it, the elves' minds are non-rational, beyond logical binaries. I will return to words as spells in Chapter 12.

7

Race

The famously blunt director Hayao Miyazaki wrote, "if you read the original novels you can also tell that the people being killed are really Asians and Africans" (Miyazaki 2008: 288). The literary theorist Sue Kim describes *LOTR*'s racial coding as "cringe-inducing" (Kim 2004: 875). In 2015, a discussion thread on the *Baidu tieba* forum for fans of *Mojie* starting with the post: "First let me say, I really liked watching *Mojie* ... but reading *Mojie* I discovered, it has some classist perspectives (*dengji guannian*) and racism, why did Tolkien write this?" Among the responses: "You see the bad guys who do evil are Eastern people, Southern people, black-skinned people, yellow-skinned people, and the good guys are Western people with golden hair and blue eyes (*jinfa biyan*), doesn't this clarify the question?" (I have translated from various posts on this forum, 2015–2022, but do not cite each post.)

Much has been written on questions of Tolkien, race, and racism. Here, I focus on the narrower context of Tolkien in Chinese. How do the translations deal with black, dark, or "sallow" skin, "slant" eyes, and the general hostility to both the East and South? How do the translations mediate the implications of these racial categories? To what extent do Chinese readers see that coding, and perceive it as anti-Chinese or anti-Asian? How do Tolkien's terms interact with Chinese racial and postcolonial attitudes?

This chapter differs from the others in introducing voices from the *Baidu* Post Bar fan forum. Within the limited parameters of an online fan forum, the discussions of race do go into some detail: different concepts of perspective, the role of historical context, the politics of the ideas, mixed in with inarticulate reactions, tangents, and jokes. One finds a spectrum of views, broadly similar to online forums in English. Discussions of racial discrimination sometimes go along with questions of class, which might not always be the case on English-language forums, but is of course more normal in China.

As we all know, one person's post does not represent a whole culture or even the specific fan forum. Yet, I would risk a general impression: I see more of what I would consider obvious anti-black racist discourse by Chinese posters than on mainstream English-language sites. Certainly there are comments that would be deleted by the moderators of, say, the OneRing.net. This *general impression* (and it can be no more than that) is at least confirmed by other scholars: Yinghong Cheng writes, "For historical and ideological reasons, the Chinese people are aware of their history of being victims of Western and Japanese racism but are often blind to their own racism, and society does not provide anti-racist education or promote public awareness of sensitivity to racism" (2011: 562). Shanshan Lan writes, "Existing work on racial neoliberalism has noted the prevalence of a race-mute culture in the public sphere and the relegation of discussions of race and racism to the private domain.... China echoes this race-mute culture due to its official denial of racial problems in the country and its externalization of issues of race and racism to the Western world" (2021: 4; also Henry 2021: 147). Robeson Taj Frazier writes, "Racism, the CCP alleged, was a Western disease that had not taken hold among Chinese people" (2017: 95; also Shih 2013: 156; Sautman 1997: 79–80). When it attracts too much attention, there is official censorship of Chinese racism, and foreign reports on Chinese racism are described as simply "anti-China." In all cultures there is racism and denial of racism; what is distinctive here is the official line, that racism *cannot* exist in China, a dogma which may lead to less self-censorship of racial discourse. I am not attempting to say anything about "the Chinese people," or to position "the West" as fundamentally different.

Regarding the problem in the source texts, a basic observation is widely stated online: "the easterners in *LOTR* are Asians, westerners are Europeans." And: "all the [main] roles are white people; the orcs, strongmen, wild barbarians and stupid fools, are Black people." In response to the accusation of racism, there are simple denials with no elaboration, and hostility to the very question. It's "something I've had my fill of." "It really is a stretch." "It's too easy to go into the perspective of a conspiracy theory (*yinmoulun*)." But other posters quoted various of Tolkien's statements against fascism and racism (cf. Fimi 2009: 135–138), or certain passages from the works to nuance the discussion. Some seemed to say that it is anachronistic to use modern thinking to understand an old work; the author was born during the Qing dynasty.

Another type of answer is: *LOTR* being a fantasy novel should not be subjected to anything as serious as primary-world questions of race. One poster said, "this is something from the time of the Cultural Revolution," referring to a period when works of fiction were judged using rigid political criteria. Such ideological vetting was pervasive in the Maoist period, especially under the influence of his wife Jiang Qing. All forms of artistic expression served political goals, and the desire to read a book for mere enjoyment was dangerously bourgeois. Another distinctive term which comes up in the discussions is *xuetonglun* (literally, "blood-lineage theory"). Though here it is generally about inherited genetic characteristics (and hence, a more "scientific" proxy for "race"), the term recalls a vicious debate in the Cultural Revolution about whether or not one's fundamental politics was inherited and hence predestined by ones lineage. It was a loaded term which deliberately attempted to naturalize or geneticize a political identity.

Moral Geography

At Boromir's funeral, Aragorn and Legolas sing of the West wind, the South wind, and the North wind, but not the East wind, because the East is associated with Mordor (*TT* III, i, 408; see Lobdell 2004: 71–81). But there is another East beyond Mordor, from which come the Easterlings. And "the East" is not just part of a fictional geography, since it inevitably evokes a long history of "East–West" antagonism and binary symbolism. In modern area studies and other academic fields, "East–West" is so profoundly reductive that it lacks any analytical utility, though it continues to be used as a sketchy shorthand.

In translating Tolkien's ethnonym "Easterlings," its diminutive suffix is eliminated, with *dongfang de renlei*, "humans of the East," and *dongfangren*, "Eastern people" (*RK* Appendix A, I, iv, 1021; Deng *RK*: 387; Yilin *RK*: 374; Zhu *RK* Appendix: 21). Similarly, the suffix is removed from "Southrons" (*TT* IV, iv, 645) which becomes merely Southern people (*nanfangren*) (Zhu *TT*: 387) and Southern fellows (*nanfanglao*) (Yilin *TT*: 302). This reduces the sense that "Easterlings" and "Southrons" are specific groups, and makes the mercenaries merely people from the East and South. Deng however chooses a Chinese ethnic category, *nanmanzi* 南蛮子, the Southern *Man* (Deng *TT*: 327), a term with nuances of Northerners' contempt for Southerners, often translated as "Southern barbarians," since *Man* and "barbarian" have a similar range of connotations and a similar vagueness. But *Man* is more specific than just Southerners. *Man* names a purported non-Han ethnicity in the South or to the South of China, not Europeans. ("Barbarian" derives from Barbary, that is, the North African coast, directly and immediately South of Europe.) Both terms have been broadened to indicate a savage people lacking in culture, which is a flattening generalization very much in line with perceptions of orcs, according to Mills' analysis (Mills 2022: 13). Note that the radical for the character *man* 蛮/蠻 is *chong* 虫, insect, a little piece of xenophobia embedded in etymology.

One *Baidu tieba* poster wrote: "There certainly is discrimination, but racial discrimination is not like regional discrimination ... Tolkien's worldview is like this: the closer to the Valar, the more the goodness and wisdom, the closer to ... Sauron, the more evil and dark, therefore in *Mojie* the eastern-born elves are not so good, the western ones are lots better." There was some effort to naturalize the anti-Eastern implications by making the prejudice merely geographic rather than racial: "This isn't racial discrimination, it's the geography of the Eurasian continent. Easterners think foreign things are all from the West, Western people think foreign things are from the East. This isn't strange." Indeed, this isn't strange—it is entirely "natural." The East–West opposition fits a strong official nationalism which consistently presents China against "the West." "It's based on European history, they always had enemies in the East." The implication here is that readers should not consider Tolkien as specifically demonizing the Chinese. One poster proposed the choice as almost arbitrary: "As for why Easterners are the enemy, writing a novel you always need an enemy, if they're not from either the East, West, North or South, then you can't write it." In other words, enemies have to come from *somewhere*. Somewhere *else*. According to one poster, if you say that *LOTR* is prejudiced against Easterners, "then I would consider *Sanguo yanyi* to be prejudiced against Northerners"—that is, *Romance of the Three Kingdoms* (a 14th-century novel of Southern vs. Northern states within China). At times, the fictional East–West is treated as overlaid on geo-political distinctions in the real world; at other times the East of *Mojie* has no relation to the East of the Eurasian continent. Indeed, we get very little information about the East or South, not just for basic plot reasons (no one ever talks to those people) but also because there is nothing to talk about. The maps show almost nothing to the South and East, only white space: "the white spaces signify the unpeopled character of these countries, a signal to the reader that we need pay no attention to their claims" (Mills 2022: 25). We'll never know their version of history.

"Can we say Tolkien discriminated against Easterners? Buddhism talks about the Western paradise, can we say Buddhism discriminates against the East?" The poster of this sarcastic gem concludes: "This is all just the habits of Western white liberals (*xifang baizuo*)." This term, *baizuo*, is literally white-left, "white left-wingers," but by broader connotation: naïve, self-righteous Western liberals, of the same kind that criticize Chinese human rights violations but buy cheap Chinese products. The term shows up repeatedly: "Saying *Mojie* is racial discrimination is completely letting white lefties put poison in your tea. I've had my fill." "Really pointless. You read a story and there's racial discrimination? Isn't that letting white lefties brain-wash you?" And: "last year or the year before, there was a white lefty author scolding Tolkien's racial discrimination." (I suspect this might be a reference to China Miéville.) And it's not just white lefties who can't shut up about race; "One reason Black people don't have a good reputation now is that they like to always talk about racial discrimination."

Concepts of Race

The Lord of the Rings uses the word "race" twenty-two times, nine of them specifically for Númenoreans (Fimi 2009: 147). Their "blood" "decayed" when mixed with "lesser men" (Fimi 2009: 148). Clearly, there is an assumption that some "blood" is inherently superior or inferior. In place of "blood," today we might say "genes," though that substitution risks normalizing racial discourse as "scientific." Within Middle-earth, Tolkien validated the genetic superiority of the Númenoreans by giving them great longevity. Their exact life span changed during Tolkien's life, but it was at least 200 years or more at the start, and the Kings lived for up to 420 years. Even among the Númenoreans, the royalty were also of better "blood." Aragorn, already far removed from Númenor, nonetheless died aged 210.

Fimi makes the case that Tolkien had in mind the "Great Chain of Being," a medieval theory ranking beings according to their spirit and their matter (2009: 141). The first-born have the greatest longevity, and certainly, she notes, "The Elves' supremacy over the other anthropomorphic Middle-earth beings is taken for granted" (ibid., 142). The closer to God and the origin of the world, the longer is life. Adam lived to be 930, Noah 950, but Moses only 120, David only 70, and by this time in the narrative we are within realistic numbers, "threescore years and ten" (Psalms 90:10), if you're lucky. It is hard to say what an orc's natural lifespan is, since we never see one die of natural causes, but presumably it's short.

Race as a scientific, descriptive term was accepted or at least not significantly challenged until after the Second World War (Fimi 2009: 132–133). And race was widely seen as hierarchical. It has never been a neutral descriptive term. In the early twentieth century, it was associated with the eugenic movement, now widely reviled though never completely dead. Broadly speaking, the modern concept of race began as a "scientific" concept, before being recognized as a "cultural" concept, though said reconceptualization is far from universally accepted, and many still perceive race as a natural and scientific term. Dikötter writes, "a language grounded in science is shared by global racism" (2011: 34). The connection to science is important in China due to the overwhelming cultural authority of "science"—a term which of course has many meanings. "Science" is often a cultural marker, an appeal to authority which may have nothing to do with formal scientific methods or even the current consensus of working research scientists.

Western race science did not arrive in China in a single, coherent package. Neither did Chinese intellectuals passively accept Western ideas. Instead, a pre-existing discourse on lineage fused with certain imported ideas, constituting a local use of the "pseudo-scientificity of a global discourse" (Müller 2011: 236). The translation of the term "race" was coined in Japan. Various terms were tried: *renzhong* 人種 (human-kind), *zhonglei* 種類 (kind-category), *minzu* 民族 (people-lineage) (ibid., 237). The term *zhongzu* 種族 (kind-lineage) became the most common. *Zhong* often means "kind," "type," but also has the sense of seed, and *zu* has a sense of lineage, as found in terms for clan, ethnicity, tribe, and genealogy.

The rulers of the last dynasty (the Qing) were descended from an ethnicity known as Manchu (Manju), and they maintained a distinction from their Han subjects through strategies such as not binding the feet of Manchu women, and imposing the queue onto Chinese men, as well as maintaining distinct administrative units and housing segregation. They rigidly imposed rules of lineage (*zu*) as a way to distinguish Han, Manchu, Mongol, and Tibetan (Dikötter 2011: 27; Hayton 2020: 80–81). The Qing classified subjecthood on the basis of ancestry, not place of birth, nor any purported "natural" physical differences of appearance. After all, the government had to impose a *hair style* in order to visually differentiate people. Only later, in interaction with Western ideas of race, did the idea of *zu* became "racialized," in service of the political agendas of reformers such as Liang Qichao (1873–1929) and Kang Youwei (1858–1927) who wanted to create a new form of Han identity in opposition to the Manchu. Imported evolutionary theories and late-Qing politics encouraged a sense of "the world as a battlefield in which different races struggled for survival. They also appealed to patrilineal culture in order to represent all inhabitants of China as the equal descendants of the Yellow Emperor" (Dikötter 2011: 32). There was easy acceptance of the classification of humans into five "colors" (white, yellow, red, brown, and black), but the scheme was adjusted to: yellow vs white competing for control over black, brown, and red.

One debate was over who exactly belonged to this newly concocted "yellow race." The inclusion or exclusion depended entirely on the politics of the person making the claims. Strategically sometimes it made sense to say Han and Manchu and Japanese are all one "race;" at other times, no, they are different "races." Indeed, "The very notion of a Han race emerged in a relational context of opposition both to foreign powers and to the ruling Manchus" (Dikötter 2011: 33; also Müller 2011: 238, 241, 243–245).

Ideas first circulated over a century ago are still common. Modern Chinese racial attitudes are "informed by a racial discourse that was constructed in the early stage of modern Chinese history to define China's place in the world order" (Cheng 2011: 561–562). Race is alive and well today as a "scientific" reality because it is ideologically useful to China's rulers, for example in asserting rule over Taiwan, and in making claims of "racial loyalty" from overseas Chinese, all based on "blood" (Sautman 1997: 80). The Party claims all *huaqiao* ("overseas Chinese") as somehow still belonging to China because of race. "In speech after speech they [Chinese officials] display an understanding of Chineseness that is overtly racial. It is not about which passport someone holds but about their 'blood'" (Hayton 2020: 76).

Just as whiteness, in America for example, functions as a default or unmarked category, so too does "Han" in China (Leibold 2010: 542). Within China, Han is not an ethnicity—only minorities have ethnicity; but Han becomes an ethnicity vis-à-vis foreigners (Henry 2021: 148). In recent years, there has been a Hanfu (Han clothing) movement, rejecting Manchu and Mongol influences (for example, in historical dramas on television). It is a movement aligned with Han-Centrism; China is multiethnic but Han is the "core race" (*zhuti minzu*) (Leibold 2010: 549). Han nationalism reproduces a rhetoric of pure blood and anti-hybridity, including the kind of replacement theory paranoia so familiar to observers of American racism (ibid., 555–556).

Skin Color: Black

Keisha Brown identifies two main themes in twentieth-century Chinese views of black people: inferiority (blacks are inferior, proved by the fact of their colonization and slavery), and sympathy, "largely based on an imagined shared experience of oppression" (2016: 22; also Shih 2013: 157). Under Mao, there was expression of solidarity not so much against anti-black racism per se as against Western imperialism, particularly after the Bandung Asian-African Conference in 1955. The Chinese press maintained a steady stream of reportage about the situation of blacks in America. Some black Americans visited Communist China, most notably W. E. B. DuBois. Mao voiced support for the US civil rights movement (Frazier 2017: 92). In 1968, there was a mass rally to condemn the assassination of Martin Luther King. But the CCP viewed African-American civil rights activism as a fight against American imperialism (Brown 2016: 24; Frazier 2017: 95). Chinese awareness of Africans was undoubtedly influenced by propaganda posters featuring black/African men and women opposing racism and imperialism, or cheerfully collaborating with Chinese aid workers. Within China, these signaled the CCP's international leadership; outside of China, they helped assert the solidarity of the CCP with victims of colonialism and racism (Frazier 2017: 94).

After the death of Mao, there were multiple riots against African students in China, in the late 1970s onwards. There was resentment that the African students were getting better scholarships from the government, a fear of black male sexuality, and various rumors of violence. Shih writes, "the main agenda was racial" (2013: 159). The best documented was the "Nanjing Incident" in 1988 (Cheng 2011: 562). Triggered by African students bringing Chinese women into a dorm, there was a melee with several thousand students, and authorities had to evacuate African students. "The blacks were stigmatized as sexual predators and a relationship between a black man and a Chinese woman was socially unacceptable" (ibid., 565).

As in America and elsewhere, Chinese anti-black racism dwells on assumed drug-dealing, crime, illegal immigration, competition for scarce resources, undeserved aid from the government, sexual pollution, and venereal disease, all of which bring "shame" to "our country" and "our ancestors" (Cheng 2011: 567; also Frazier 2017: 111). On the internet there is open discourse of racial hierarchy, in which white and Chinese are superior, and others below—rhetoric directly out of a hundred years ago. Online content by Chinese working in Africa includes accusations of discrimination against Chinese in Africa: we give them aid but they racially profile us. Cheng notes that while there was some Chinese online pushback *in* China against these views, more came from Chinese *outside* China (2011: 571).

There was a 2020 thread debating concerns over the new Amazon series *The Rings of Power*, including the casting of black actors. While most of the posters were basically OK with there being black people in the series (as orcs, villains, or minor background characters), there was a near-unanimous objection specifically to casting black actors as elves. It is "a wicked trick" (*yaoezi*); "the most important thing is they're filming Black elves"—followed by three angry emojis. And a classic "I'm not a racist, but" statement: "I really have no racial discrimination . . . but I beg Amazon not to let Black people play elves." Even in the midst of all this, there is an awareness that the label "racist" is toxic (cf. Cheng 2011: 572).

Chinese, like English, uses "black" in various negative ways, in contrast to white, closely related to darkness in contrast with light. In *LOTR*, the color-coding is thorough: the feathers of the orc arrows are black (*TT* III, i, 404). Orc blood is "dark" (*TT* III, ii, 411). An orc cloak is black (*TT* III, ii, 413). Gollum refers to Sauron's hand as the Black Hand, for which Deng and Yilin have *heishou*, black hand (*TT* IV, iii, 627; Deng *TT*: 304; Yilin *TT*: 280), whereas Zhu uses *heizhang*, black palm or "clutches" (Zhu *TT*: 360). Gollum simply refers to Sauron as "the Black One" (*TT* IV, iii, 629). Yilin uses *heishou* (black hand) again (Yilin *TT*: 283). But Deng finds "One" a little vague perhaps, and opts for *heian mowang*, dark *mo*-king (Deng *TT*: 306). Zhu similarly has *heianwang*, dark king (Zhu *TT*: 363). And they come from the Black Land (*FR* II, ii, 246), the "dark place" (Deng *FR*: 317; Zhu *FR*: 395) or "black domain (*heise guodu*)" (Yilin *FR*: 307).

Yet, there are places where some of the translations read "black" for its metaphorical senses and thereby actually remove the blackness. When Gandalf says "already, Frodo, our time is beginning to look black" (*FR* I, ii, 50), Deng's translation is almost word-for-word: "our age is changing to dark (*heian*)" (Deng *FR*: 63). But the Yilin edition paraphrases without reference to color: "The current situation is critical (*shiju jinpo*)" (Yilin *FR*: 62). And Zhu also shifts the meaning: "the shadows already begin to envelop the long river of our history" (Zhu *FR*: 94). For the term "black sorcerer" (*H*, vii, 152), Wu retains the word black (Wu *H*: 188), while Zhu and the Yilin translator treat the word "black" as a metaphor of evil: *xie-e yao shushi*, evil *yao* wizard (Zhu *H*: 161), and *xingyao zuoguai de nanwu*, male *wu*-shaman who raises *yao* and makes *guai* (Yilin *H*: 120). Similarly, Treebeard says of Saruman. "And now it is clear that he is a black traitor" (*TT* III, iv, 462). Zhu basically retains the color: "he has sunken into the way of darkness" (Zhu *TT*: 107). But Deng does not: "he is an evil traitor" (Deng *TT*: 84). And likewise Yilin: "an evil poisonous traitor" (Yilin *TT*: 78). Given that blackness has extended metaphorical meanings, and translators may choose to state the connotation, the translations may slightly reduce the frequency of the color symbolism.

Turning to blackness and darkness as physical attributes, sometimes it is applied to orcs and sometimes to Southrons. It is sometimes attributed to their skin, or to their whole person. When Pippin sees "a large black Orc" (*TT* III, iii, 437), Zhu and Deng stay close to the original, but Yilin is more specific: "dark-skinned (*pifu youhei*)" (Yilin *TT*: 46; cf. Zhu *TT*: 68; Deng *TT*: 49). The gaffer says Frodo has been "chasing Black Men [i.e. Nazgûl] up mountains" (*RK* VI, viii, 990). Deng and Zhu directly ascribe darkness to them, but Yilin shifts it to the place they come from: *heian wangguo de ren*, people from the dark kingdom (Yilin *RK*: 332; cf. Deng *RK*: 340; Zhu *RK*: 410).

"Swarthy Men" (*RK* V, iii, 782) results in a range of options: Yilin switches to the proper noun *Halade*—the pseudo-ethnonym Haradrim (Yilin *RK*: 68), Zhu calls them *yeren*, wild people (Zhu *RK*: 97), and Deng sticks closest to the original: *heifurenlei*, black-skinned humans (Deng *RK*: 70). Likewise in *The Children of Húrin* she translates Swarthy Easterlings (*Húrin*: 61) directly: "those dark skin-color east-comers (*fuse youhei de donglaizhe*)" (Deng *Húrin*: 54; see also Fimi 2009: 146–147). Frodo and company see some Southrons marching to Mordor. Gollum says, "Dark faces. We have not seen Men like this before ... They are fierce. They have black eyes, and long black hair, and gold rings in their ears" (*TT* IV, iii, 631). The translations are all very close to literal, using "black" (*hei*) for "dark" (faces) (Zhu *TT*: 366–367; Deng *TT*: 309; Yilin *TT*: 286). We see a dead Southron, with "black plaits of hair" and "brown hands" clutching a sword (*TT* IV, iv, 646).

Sam and Frodo see two orcs in Mordor, noting one in particular: "it was of a small breed, black-skinned, with wide and snuffling nostrils: evidently a tracker of some kind" (*RK* Vi, ii, 903). Note the pronoun "it"—the other orc is given the pronoun "he," but this one only "it," not just in this line but consistently. Also note the dog-like implication—having wide nostrils means it's a tracker animal, and a "breed." Deng preserved the "it" as *ta* 它 in that same paragraph, though this line in particular elides the pronoun: "One was a short orc, black skin, nostrils very big, sniffed without stopping, obviously was some kind of tracker (*zhuizongzhe*)" (Deng *RK*: 225). However, Yilin and Zhu switch the "it" to "he." Yilin's translation has nothing of note here, translating "black-skinned" directly (*heipifu*) (Yilin *RK*: 219). But Zhu has a little burst of verbosity: "his physique (*tixing*) was relatively small, skin dark-black (*youhei* 黝黑, swarthy), nose alae (*biyi*, nose-wings, refers to width of nose) with big nostrils opening and closing without stopping, very obviously was a species (*wuzhong*) specializing in being responsible for tracking" (Zhu *RK*: 279). Returning to the question of "it," this is not the only use of a dehumanizing pronoun, with similar translations: Sam refers to Gollum as an it. "Tie it up" (*TT* IV, i, 600). Deng uses 'it' (*ta* 它) (Deng *TT*: 268), Zhu uses "he" *ta* 他 (Zhu *TT*: 319), and Yilin's phrasing avoids the pronoun, with "tie up" *kunqilai* (Yilin *TT*: 247). Contrary to the pallid CGI body of the films, Shagrat refers to Gollum as a "little thin black fellow" (*TT* IV, x, 721), translated straightforwardly (Zhu *TT*: 505; Deng *TT*: 429; Yilin *TT*: 397).

King Aragorn II grants clemency to surrendered human servants of Sauron, but not orcs. There is some debate in *LOTR* about Gollum's redemption; none about the orcs. Whatever evil acts Gollum might have committed, Gandalf holds out the hope of redemption, and councils mercy. Whereas the Southrons and Easterlings are treated as humans, orcs are subhuman. Tolkien could not have given them much real humanity for fear of making Legolas and Gimli monstrous and macabre. "Tolkien's heroes, without the least pang of conscience, dispatch Orcs by the thousands" (Tally 2010: 17). For the sake of the heroic battle, the killing of orcs had to be irrelevant to morality, like the zombies or robots of action films, or indeed "the enemy" in most war films. It is worth looking at orcs in more detail.

Deng and Yilin transliterate "orc" as *ao-ke* 奥克 (Deng *FR*: 276); and *ao-ke-si* 奥科斯 (Yilin *FR*: 269). Zhu uses half-beast-people (*banshouren*) which he also used for "goblin," blurring the two categories and increasing the explicit animality of the category (Zhu *H*: 103). Similarly, Deng and Yilin transliterate Uruk-hai as *wuluke* (Deng *TT*: 48, Yilin *TT*: 46), whereas Zhu riffs on his term for goblin with *qiongshouren*, "strong beast person" (Zhu *TT*: 67).

There is considerable uncertainty about the origin of the orcs (Shippey 2003: 233–234). One version has orcs derived from elves, corrupted by Melkor. Treebeard tells us that orcs were made by "the Enemy" "in mockery of" elves, analogous to trolls. Similarly, "Trolls are only counterfeits, made by the Enemy in the Great Darkness, in mockery of Ents, as Orcs were of Elves" (*TT* III, iv, 474). For "counterfeit," Deng and Zhu use a close translation, with Deng's choice *fangzhipin* 仿制品 emphasizing the sense of imitation and copying, and Zhu's *fangmaopin* 仿冒品 accentuating the forgery and fakeness, whereas Yilin simply calls them "things" (*dongxi*) made by imitating (*mofang*) (Deng *TT*: 100; Zhu *TT*: 128; Yilin *TT*: 93). The orcs are racial in their conception, but to some extent the translations defuse the issue: when the original says, "the hideous race of the Orcs" (*S*: 47), the translations skip over the word "race" (Yilin *S*: 45; Deng *S* 2002: 60; Deng *S* 2015: 74).

What was the nature of this process of "corruption"? Melkor "perverted" elves to make them (*S*: 43). Yilin: "lured onto the evil road (*yinshang xielu*)" (Yilin *S*: 41; similar at Deng *S* 2015: 70), though earlier Deng used "distorted (*niuqu* 扭曲, twisted, warped)" (Deng *S* 2002: 54). Later, Tolkien decided that the horrible orcs could not have derived from the elves (Fimi 2009: 155; Bergen 2017: 113–114). He tried other ideas: orcs were corrupted humans, low-level Maia, or automata. Christopher Tolkien said the final view was corrupted humans (Tally 2010: 18). In a letter Tolkien called them "Mongoltypes," and Fimi connects this to "mongol" as an early name for Down Syndrome. J. Langdon Down (1828–1896) himself used it; he thought it was a regression to an earlier human stage (Fimi 2009: 156). "Mongolism" was dropped from use by the World Health Organization (WHO) in 1965, though its use persisted well into the 1980s. Even so, there is no redeeming this idea.

It would bring the whole story crashing down to view the orcs in realist terms, as real people from brutalized childhoods, living in a land on the brink of starvation, socialized into violence, and powerless to resist a military dictatorship (Roberts 2013: 156; Bissell and Alexander 2003). The detailed backstory so lovingly crafted in the novel is absent for the orcs, "in keeping with their ontological shallowness" (Mills 2022: 24). Yet, Tally points to the rare occasion when we actually hear what orcs are saying to each other, when Merry and Pippin are captive, and when orcs come to fetch Frodo's paralyzed body. These conversations do not show them to be noble souls, but they voice resentments fairly typical of oppressed workers everywhere: the higher powers keep their secrets and make mistakes, and the low-ranking orcs will suffer the consequences. They show skepticism. They fantasize about living a better life without being bossed around. They "have deeply human feelings, conventions, and cultures. In fact, perhaps even more than the Elves, whose near-perfection marks them with a profound otherness, Orcs are shown to be human" (Tally 2010: 20). Nonetheless, these episodes are rare and fleeting.

The lore of Middle-earth includes many assertions of life after death for humans, but no mention at all of an afterlife of orcs, who are "intrinsically evil, without any hope of salvation" (Fimi 2009: 157). Tolkien wavered on the question of the orcs' redeemability (Bergen 2017: 114). But he also wrote that Ilúvatar could not have given orcs souls. One of the standard features of racism is the denial of the "humanity" of others. The orcs are "rendered as ontological zeros" (Mills 2022: 24). The soullessness of the orcs seems to be central to the utter lack of remorse in killing them. But also, if orcs have no souls, can they be saved?

Or, to put it another way, does an orc have buddha-nature? East Asian Buddhism asserts the potential for enlightenment in all sentient beings, even as it articulated a rich and colorful demonology. Technically, even demons shouldn't be demonized. In this context, *of course* orcs have buddha-nature. They are sentient enough to talk, strategize, be devious, obey or disobey orders, hope for something better, and so on. They are certainly capable of suffering. Orcs seem close to the *pretas*, the "hungry ghosts" of the Six Paths—creatures who, if scary to the ignorant, deserve pity rather than violence. Nonetheless, this theoretical possibility in Buddhism does not preclude the historical dehumanization of enemies by actual Buddhist rulers and nationalists and soldiers. The doctrine of karma can be invoked to assert that if you find yourself in a miserable body, you are simply getting what you deserved. The opportunities for orcs or pretas to create good karma or even have the mere thought of enlightenment seem very limited, so they should not expect a better rebirth anytime soon.

Skin Color: "Yellow"

The returning hobbits see "half a dozen large ill-favoured Men lounging against the inn-wall; they were squint-eyed and sallow-faced" (*RK* VI, viii, 981), clearly belonging to a certain physical type. Primarily used for skin color, "sallow" means more than yellow or pale brown, but also unhealthy; the OED considers it "now *offensive*" due to its racist implication. The translations are matter-of-fact: *diaoxie yan, lahuang lian* 吊斜眼，蜡黄脸, hanging slanted (or squinting) eyes, waxy-yellow faces (Deng *RK*: 329), *yanjing henxiao, lianse fanhuang* 眼睛很小，脸色泛黄, eyes very small, face-color shallow and yellow (Zhu *RK*: 396), and *lianse huihuang, hai xiezhe yanjing* 脸色灰黄，还斜着眼睛, face-color grey-yellow, with slanting eyes (Yilin *RK*: 319). Similarly, dealing with "slant-eyed" (goblin-soldiers) (*TT* III, i, 405), the Chinese translators chose not to edit out the racist slur which has been applied to East Asians. Two translations go straightforwardly with "eyes slanting" (*xiediao*) (Deng *TT*: 8, Yilin *TT*: 6), while a third has "eyes very small" (or thin and small, *xixiao* 細小) (Zhu *TT*: 19). For "squint-eyed rascal" (*RK* VI, viii, 982), the same terms are used, but in Zhu's translation becomes *xiasanlan* 下三滥 lowlife, rascal—no reference to eyes (Zhu *RK*: 397; cf. Deng *RK*: 330; Yilin *RK*: 321).

In fact, early Western travelers did not say the Chinese were "yellow" (Dikötter 2011: 26). Sixteenth-century European visitors to China called them white, except in the South where they were "brown" because of the sun, "like the Spanish" (Demel 2016: 20). Skin color was described as varying, much like in Europe. However, "In the eighteenth century the Chinese were denied the predicate 'white,' because they were no longer considered to be cultural equals" (ibid., 36). There is some unclarity about how the term "yellow" got applied to the Chinese, but the key players include Carl Linnaeus (1707–1778), Johann Friedrich Blumenbach (1752–1840), and also Jesuits reporting on the positive cultural associations of the color yellow in China. One of those positive associations was the Yellow Emperor, who was reconceived in the twentieth century as a racial ancestor, worshipped in newly invented rituals as a lineage god of the "Han race" (Sautman 1997: 83–84). While Chinese readers surely notice that the "sallow" and "slant-eyed" characters are all villains, and may perceive this as part of a Western hostility, the term "yellow" is not nearly as controversial in China as it is today in America's atmosphere of violent anti-Asian racism. Nonetheless, of course I use the word with trepidation, always understood as *so-called*, a cultural category rather than a scientific fact.

Skin Color: White

One of the most common forms of in-person encounter between Chinese and foreigners in China is the language classroom. China's TEFL market gives advantage to whites and discriminates against non-white Westerners (Lan 2021: 2; Henry 2021: 151–152). Several sources note the phenomenon of white-face or white monkey jobs, where companies and schools hire white people just to project a certain image (Lan 2021: 9–10). Non-white Westerners are marginalized due to a "conflation of whiteness with Westernness in China" (Schmidt 2013: 654). In official and popular media, foreigners are implicitly white, but non-white foreigners are identified by country of origin, or "black" (Lan 2021: 5). The figure of the blonde woman has been particularly loaded with complex meaning (Schein 1994: 144). Another widespread manifestation of color-coding is the skin lightening industry (Cheng 2011: 565; also Glenn 2008: 298; Picton 2013: 91).

Reading Tolkien, sometimes one may say, "white" is not particularly associated with any moral value, such as the "white horses" (i.e. teeth) of Bilbo's riddle (*H*, v, 82), or white mists (*TT* III, ii, 412). There is the exceptional case of Saruman's insignia, "the White Hand" (*TT* III, iii, 439). But there are far more examples of white as a color of objects associated with goodness and purity. Galadriel and Celeborn are clad in white (*FR* II, vii, 345), a white light comes from Glorfindel (*FR* I, xii, 204), snow-white is an attribute of the Vala Elbereth (*FR* I, iii, 78). The star Sam sees in Mordor (*RK* VI, ii, 901), the shores of the Undying Lands (*RK* VI, ix, 1007), the Tower of Minas Tirith, the White Tree, are all translated directly as *bai* (white). Horses participate in the coding: Snowmane and Shadowfax are white. Éomer's helmet had a plume of white horse hair (*TT* III, ii, 421). Meanwhile, the plundering orcs naturally prefer black horses (*TT* III, ii, 426). While it may be possible to distinguish between color in a "purely" or "merely" symbolic sense and color as a direct reference to racial categories, "the opposition of a symbolic and a racial blackness is, in a sense misleading, because, for Tolkien's characters, it can be said, *ontology recapitulates physiology*" (Mills 2022: 18).

White may be applied to people, such as when Gandalf announces himself Gandalf the White (*TT* III, x, 569). But the translations generally attribute the whiteness to his clothes: "white-robed (*baipao*) Gandalf" (Deng *TT*: 227; Zhu *TT*: 272), and "white-clothed (*baiyi*) Gandalf" (Yilin *TT*: 209). Gimli says Gandalf is "all in white," and Gandalf says, "Yes, I am white now" (*TT* III, v, 484)—which comes out as, "white robed" (Deng *TT*: 112) or "only wear white clothes" (Zhu *TT*: 142), though Yilin has, "Yes, I am whole-body pure white (*yishen subai*)" (Yilin *TT*: 104). If Gandalf is "the White," we note also that Radagast is "the Brown," and other wizards are "Blue" which surely cannot mean skin color. While Gandalf is presumably white of skin, his whiteness is meant more metaphorically, or (in the translations) primarily about his clothes. Similarly, Faramir calls Galadriel the White Lady (*TT* IV, v, 664), which Zhu turns into white empress, *bai nühuang* (Zhu *TT*: 416). Yilin uses "*baifuren*" (white lady)—in quotes in the text: you have spoken to the "white lady" (Yilin *TT*: 326). And Deng shifts to clothing as she did with Gandalf: *baiyi furen*, white-clothed lady (Deng *TT*: 352).

But whiteness is more specifically applied to her skin. Gandalf praises Galadriel: "White is the star in your white hand" (*TT* III, vi, 503). Deng's collaborator Du renders this as "On your white (*su* 素, plain, pure) hand the bright star is white and clean (*baijing*, used for fair skin)" (Deng *TT*: 138). Yilin also uses *baijing* (Yilin *TT*: 127). But Zhu refers to her "pure white jade hand" (Zhu *TT*: 171). In translating "She lifted up her white arms" (*FR* II, vii, 355), Zhu continues his jade reference: "She lifted up pure white (*jiebai* 潔白, clean white) jade arms (*yubi*)" (Zhu *FR*: 564), whereas Deng uses a slightly literary *baixi de shuangbi*, 白晳的双臂, her pair of white-complexioned arms (Deng *FR*: 456). *Bai* = white, *xi* = fair-skinned, light-complexioned. Yilin's "white arms" implies a cosmetic look, with *fenbi* 粉臂" (Yilin *FR*: 444) *Fen* as a noun = powder, cosmetics, flour; as an adjective = white or pink. Hence, perhaps: her powder-white arms.

Schein notes in modern China "the motif of golden hair (*jin toufa*), an emblem of racialized difference... which has, in the evocation of gold, an unequivocal connotation of value" (Schein 1994: 144; see also Colvin 2020). Galadriel's golden or rather blonde hair is part of her whiteness too. Her blondeness is part of the ambiguity around the adjective "fair," used extensively. In English, "fair" has a clear double meaning, both beautiful and blond. Fair-as-beautiful is very old in English, applied to men and women, as is the meaning from the twelfth century on: "Of hair or complexion: light as opposed to dark in colour" (*OED*). To the extent that women's light complexion is valued as beautiful in China, there may be the same polysemy, but the English double meaning of "fair" makes the association direct, whereas it is indirect in the Chinese—the translators must choose one of the two meanings.

Faramir calls Galadriel "perilously fair" (*TT* IV, v, 664), and the translations all read that as beautiful: *meide weixian*, dangerously beautiful (Deng *TT*: 352); "this dangerous beautiful person (*meirenr*)" (Yilin *TT*: 326); and "so beautiful (*mei*) that it makes people feel danger" (Zhu *TT*: 417). Yet, the explicit descriptor of the Quendi, "fair of skin" (*RK* Appendix F, II, 1111), becomes white skin (Zhu *RK* Appendix: 141; Deng *RK*: 528). Not surprisingly the translations gender the word "fair," so that for "Boromir the Fair"

(*TT* III, i, 408), Zhu has *junzhuang* 俊壯, handsome and strong (Zhu *TT*: 23) and Deng has *yingjun* brilliant/handsome/talented (Deng *TT*: 11), though Yilin reads the word entirely differently, using *gongzheng* 公正, fair in the sense of fair-minded and just (Yilin *TT*: 9). In the funeral verse about Boromir, "his face so fair," all three translations elide the word in the context of a looser translation (*TT* III, i, 408; Yilin *TT*: 10; Deng *TT*: 12; Zhu *TT*: 23). Yet, as applied to Éowyn, "Very fair was her face" (*TT* III, vi, 504), all three read the word as beautiful (*meili* or *mei*) (Deng *TT*: 139; Zhu *TT*: 173; Yilin *TT*: 128).

Dwarves and Jews

There is a debate in Tolkien scholarship about the relationship of Dwarves to Jews. Dwarves were the product of a misguided enthusiasm by the Vala Aulë; Ilúvatar put them to sleep as he judged them to be not according to plan—the elves are supposed to be the "First Born." The dwarves were thus an earlier and lesser attempt at what later appeared in radiant glory as elves. They were initially without souls, but later granted souls by Ilúvatar (Coutras 2016: 68). "The narrative of the creation of the Dwarves steeps itself in the sort of supersessionist dynamic that early Christian writers used to separate Christianity from its origin within Judaism" (Brackmann 2010: 87). An oppressed people, scattered and shunned, seeking to return to and re-establish their ancestral home—this suggests Zionism. In the *Hobbit* films there are strong desires for revenge on the evil Smaug and the reclaiming of a homeland, but the book foregrounds their desire for gold and gems. The Dwarves speech, Khuzdul, has a distinctly Semitic sound.

Rebecca Brackmann made the argument that *The Hobbit* relied on antisemitic stereotypes, and *LOTR* was in part a corrective (2010: 85). Certainly in the image of Gimli we sense a revision in process: Legolas and Gimli discuss the beautiful caverns of Helm's Deep, and Legolas assumes that if the dwarves knew about them, they would ruin them in their greed, but Gimli refutes this view, emphasizing the sense of beauty which would move Dwarves (TT III, viii, 534–535). While not disputing the basic association of dwarves and Jews, Renée Vink disputed Brackmann's argument. Still, she remarks, "whether there is racism to be found in his works is debatable, although they are certainly rife with racialism, or racial categorization" (2013: 129).

In China, popular consciousness about Jews is a complex story involving Protestant missionaries, Jews as a model for Chinese immigrants (Eber 2020: 226; Zhou 2016: 9), Japanese anti-Jewish articles circulated in China in the 1930s, the presence of European Jewish refugees in Shanghai, and the politics around Israel as a proxy of US imperialism. As we saw with the concept of race, Jews emerged in Chinese culture as a fusion of Western and native Chinese agendas, without internal coherence. Zhou Xun notes how "Jewish" can mean all sorts of things in China (2016: 6). And as we saw with Africans and black Americans, Chinese solidarity with Jews could be based on an appeal to a shared experience of Western imperialist oppression. Popular Chinese discourse on Jews today tends to be a mixture of simplifications, generalizations, exaggerations, and stereotypes—often more positive than negative. There are books on Jews and getting rich (Ross 2016: 26–27; Song 2016: 206–207). Jews are praised for valuing education, like the Chinese, but even this can be put in competitive terms, as in articles and blog posts about how Jews win so many more Nobel prizes than Chinese (Chung 2014: 793–794).

There is much less to say here about the issue of Dwarves and Jews in the translations. Although the association of Dwarves and Jews in Tolkien's works is indisputable, it is not particularly evident in the translations as such. The evidence of the association of Dwarves and Jews is located in a history of stereotypical images, but not at the level of word choice in the stories. It is quite possible to read the books and watch the films and never have the thought that the Dwarves represent a Jewish stereotype (positive or negative, with or without nuances). The argument, once made, cannot be refuted, but for most people, the argument *needs* to be made, by those who are already receptive to the clues, or at least by those already inclined to read the scholarship or popular media which make the case. In the absence of a critical mass of public scholarship and popular awareness, the association passes by. Awareness of the association is hardly widespread in America, even among consumers of the franchise; how much less does it enter into Chinese culture?

Conclusions

The Chinese reception of racial aspects of Tolkien's work can be approached through examination of the decisions of translators and through a sampling of fan posts. In some ways, the translations have reduced the color-coding, though in an incidental rather than systematic way. Positive and negative representations of skin colors remain mostly consistent, for the most part simply representing what is already there in the original. There is in China a widespread consciousness of geopolitical antagonism making use of the reductive binary East–West, yet the translations make almost no effort to obscure the negative coding of East, and Tolkien fans appear to shrug this example off. Instead of any concern over the possible racial politics of the works, there is more often a defensive reaction against the "political correctness" or "wokeness" of raising the question.

8

Hell and Other Theories

Hell

In Middle-earth, there is no universal notion of death or the afterlife. The most frequently articulated ideas about the afterlife relate either to a Valhalla-like place, in which men such as Théoden "go to my fathers" (*RK* V, vii, 836); or to the Undying Lands to the west, where souls go to the Halls of Mandos and then (for mortals) beyond to an unknown fate. But we also find other images. We are not looking at a carefully articulated doctrine of death belonging to one denomination or theologian; rather, the ideas about death belong to a range of somewhat familiar Western European ideas. The question is, what kinds of new stories emerge when we move into Chinese and into what is broadly intelligible in Chinese?

Chinese ideas about the afterlife cannot be reduced to a single image or logically consistent narrative. We are looking at stories rather than what people necessarily believe. One common view is that when a person dies, their spirit often remains in proximity to the corpse, at least until a funeral can be arranged. What happens next? If we follow Pure Land Buddhism, and if the dying person called the name of Amitabha, the deceased may be reborn into the Pure Land, a very fortuitous rebirth close to a buddha. Some mourning families will include some Pure Land ritual, but also other rituals designed to guide the dead through a more complicated journey. In this more pessimistic story, we die and somehow find our way to the first level of hell, a court where we are judged. We may walk there, or wake up there, or just appear there mysteriously. In this court, our past sins are revealed, usually in a mirror, and we are given an opportunity to plead our case. On rare occasions there are bureaucratic errors such as mix-ups with other people of the same name, in which case the dead person is sent back to live for a while longer, or judged virtuous and allowed to skip hell and pass on to their next life. But how many of us are that good? Most of us should expect some suffering before the debt is paid and we get to move to our next life. Justice tends to be treated as quantifiable: a particular sinful act equals x number of years of a particular pain before the next rebirth. It may last a long time but is not strictly speaking eternal.

The hells vary widely: cold hells, hot hells, molten metal, axes and saws, fierce animals, and fire-breathing demons. Popular storytelling and iconography dwell on these horrors, providing endless permutations. These hells are underground. The term for hell is *diyu*, "earth-prison." The images of horned fiery demons and legions of nasty underlings skulking around in their underground domains are surely as familiar to

Western readers as Chinese readers, with much the same general vocabulary, but with much less of a sense that you are in hell as an eternal punishment for not believing in Jesus. And of course it must be said that all of these views coexist in China with many varieties of religious ideas, and with entirely materialist understandings of death.

Let's start with something explicitly hellish. When the forces of Sauron are trying to break into Minas Tirith, they bring forth a great battering ram. "Grond they named it, in memory of the Hammer of the Underworld of old" (*RK* V, iv, 810). Yilin renders this as: "They named it *ge-lang-de*, to commemorate the ancient underground world's great hammer (*gudai dixia shijie de dachui*)" (Yilin *RK*: 103). Zhu: "In order to commemorate the far-ancient times' hell's hammer (*yuangushi de diyu zhichui*), they gave this city-wall-destroying hammer (*pocheng chui*) the name *ge-long-de*" (Zhu *RK*: 140). And Deng: "They gave it the name *ge-long-de*, to use it to commemorate that (*bing*) ancient 'hell's hammer' (*diyu zhichui*)" (Deng *RK*: 105). All three transliterate "Grond" but Zhu and Deng slip *long* (dragon) into the name, which is more awesome than Yilin's *lang* 朗 (bright, clear), though also somewhat misleading in that Grond (the battering ram) is designed to evoke a wolf. (If they wanted the sound *lang*, one wonders why Yilin did not use *lang* 狼 wolf.) Deng's use of the count noun *bing* 柄 (used for things with handles or stems) gives the hammer a grammatical particularity missing in the others. Without the count noun, in Yilin and Zhu, it might possibly refer to hammers.

At this point, however, we are focused on what the "Underworld" might be. As we might expect from Tolkien, there is an answer to that: Grond was also the name of a mace used by Morgoth, also referred to as "the Hammer of the Underworld" (*S*: 180). Showing a copyediting inconsistency, the Yilin edition of *Silmarillion* gives the name as: *Ge-lang-en-de* and calls it "hell's hammer" (*diyu zhichui*) (Yilin *S*: 166). Deng's simplified character version of *Silmarillion* is the same as in *Return of the King*: "'hell's hammer' *ge-long-de*" (Deng *S* 2015: 200). But her earlier *Silmarillion* has: *Ge-long-de*, "the hammer of the dark world (*heian shijie zhichui*)" (Deng *S* 2002: 223), and the same book includes a glossary which explains "Grond" as: "Morgoth's great metal hammer, ... also called 'the metal hammer of the *yin* place (*yinjian de tiechui* 陰間 的 鐵鎚)" (Deng *S* 2002 Index: 35–36).

So, we have four distinct Chinese translations of "Underworld": *dixia* ("underground," in an ordinary sense used for basements, groundwater, "underground" political groups); *diyu* (literally "earth-prison," but most commonly understood as hells or "a hell," or "hell"); *heianshijie* (the dark world); and *yinjian* (the *yin* place, here implying the world of the dead, contrasted with the *yang* world of the living; dictionaries freely render it as Hades or the nether world). We can safely say "the Underworld" (with its capital U) means a lot more than just "underground"! But within Tolkien's legendarium, matters are further complicated by the fact that "Underworld" refers to Utumno, the fortress of Morgoth which (in Quenya,) means "low-lying, deep"; the Sindarin cognate Udun has the sense of a deep pit. It's where the balrogs emerged; Gandalf calls the balrog he meets in Moria "flame of Udun" (*FR* II, v, 322). In transliterating "Udun," Deng and Zhu use the word *wu* 乌/烏 (black, crow) to represent both the sound U- and the meaning of darkness (Deng *FR*: 412, Zhu *FR*: 511). The -dun is represented by *dun* 顿/頓 (sudden, pause, to stamp [the ground]); hence, black-sudden or black-stamp. Where "Udun" might mean "deep" in Sindarin, the word doesn't mean anything to us—actually

I think of udon noodles; here, the translations add value. Yilin also uses the same *wu*, but choses a less meaningful *dun* 敦 (sincere, honest) (Yilin *FR*: 402).

So, Grond (the battering ram) is named after Grond (the mace, hammer) of Morgoth, whose mostly underground fortress is called Utumno, which has root meanings of deep pit. The original uses hellish words but stops short of hell. The words "the Underworld" do not absolutely require us to think of our going there after death, whereas *diyu* (earth-prison or hell) and *yinjian* (among the *yin*/dead) certainly suggest it. What we see in some of the Chinese versions is a more explicit hellishness and association with the afterlife. Similarly, "abyss" is translated as hell by Yilin. Gandalf tells the witch-king, "Go back to the abyss prepared for you!" (*RK* V, iv, 811). Zhu and Deng use *shenyuan* 深淵/渊 (deep pool) (Zhu *RK*: 141; Deng *RK*: 106). But Yilin has "Return to the hell (*diyu*) prepared for you!" (Yilin *RK*: 104). Gandalf's curse puts "abyss" in parallel with "nothingness," so it may mean simply death without afterlife, or an afterlife beyond all light—but in one of the translations it is again more explicitly hell.

During his youthful battles against orcs, Túrin is wrongly assumed to have been killed. "Then many wondered, saying, 'Can the spirit of any man return from death; or has Húrin of Hithlum escaped indeed from the pits of Hell?'" (*Húrin*: 85–86). Deng renders this as: "how is it there are people who can come back from being a ghost and be born again (*huanhun fusheng*)? Or, how is it real that Hithlum's Húrin escaped from the deep pit of hell (*diyu de chenkeng*)?" (Deng *Húrin*: 78). This question puts "death" and "the pits of hell" in direct parallel, and thus excludes the possibility that "hell" here merely refers to Utumno.

Other Theories

What other ideas circulated in Middle-earth? Gollum might be the least reliable witness for Middle-earth folklore about the afterlife, but even he has an odd remark to add. As they are crossing the Dead Marshes, Gollum advises: "Very carefully! Or hobbits go down to join the Dead ones and light little candles" (*TT* IV, ii, 614). Deng, "Otherwise hobbit people will fall down to be companions with those dead people, light little candles" (Deng *TT*: 286). Yilin is similar (Yilin *TT*: 264). Zhu gives us something a little different: "fall down to add to their [number] (*jiaru tamen* 加入它们), themselves will light little ghost flames (*guihuo* 鬼火)" (Zhu *TT*: 340–341). *Guihuo*—*gui* as in "ghost" + *huo*, fire—is translated into English as phosphorescent light, ignis fatuus, will-o'-the-wisp, jack-o'-lantern, but Gollum speaks of lights not above the water but below (Sinex 2005: 93; Amendt-Raduege 2018: 86, 88). In the original, Gollum seems more or less idiosyncratic in attributing the lights to the dead. In British folklore, they are more often attributed to fairies or pixies—by extension, elves perhaps, although not *dead* fairies or elves. Given that the Marshes are filled with the dead (a mixture of elves and humans and others), the Chinese term *guihuo* fits the situation well—more accurate than "little candles," though lacking the poignant image of lighting candles in a church in memory of the dead. The fate of these particular dead people might not be that of all dead people; and neither are they underground, but overall it is a grim prospect. One would not want to be a member of that fellowship.

Yet, there are somewhat better images of the collective dead. Speaking to the Fellowship, Celeborn speculates on a coming last battle to defend Lothlórien, after which: "Then they may return to their own lands, or else go to the long home of those that fall in battle" (*FR* II, viii, 358). Presumably he means, those who fight will either survive and go home, or die. Zhu's translation elaborates with an odd redundancy: they can "go ahead to (*qianwang*) the hall of the victorious souls (*yingling dian*) of the victorious souls who died in battle (*zhansi yinghun*)" (Zhu *FR*: 567). Zhu skips "long" and makes the home a hall (which evokes the Halls of Mandos). He also makes the dead victorious rather than merely fallen. Zhu uses "victorious" (*ying*) twice. There is an additional awkward duplication in my back-translation, with "souls" twice, yet the Chinese terms are different: the hall of souls (*ling*) of the victorious souls (*hun*). They are indeed very close synonyms. The word *yingling* refers to the spirits of the brave departed, or martyrs' spirits. Zhu is clearly thinking of Valhalla. Those who fell in battle while fleeing the enemy, or died in a battle their side lost, do not seem to be admitted. Valhalla-like glory in afterlife for warriors is supported in various ways, such as when Théoden exhorts the Riders: "the glory that you reap there shall be your own for ever" (*RK* V, v, 818; Yilin *RK*: 113; Zhu *RK*: 152; Deng *RK*: 115).

The Yilin edition renders "go to the long home of those that fall in battle" as: "together with the people who fell on the battlefield have the long sleep (*changmian* 长眠) together" (Yilin *FR*: 448). To "the long home," Yilin adds long sleep. *Mian* can also mean hibernate. Sleep is an easily understood metaphor for death, whether in tombstone euphemisms or Chandler's *The Big Sleep* (1939). Elsewhere, Voronwë refers to freezing to death as "the snow-sleep" (*UT*: 39), or *changmian xuedi*, the long-sleep snow-place (Shi and Deng *UT*: 56). Deng's Celeborn says they can go home, "or fall in battle, and return to a forever-peaceful place (*yongyuan anxi zhisuo*)" (Deng *FR*: 459), which sounds more like heaven than Valhalla's feasting halls. Valhalla is for "those that fall in battle"—far from automatic for every mortal (however virtuous), yet in Deng's version admission is not reliant on the question of victory which Zhu adds. Now, in the Chinese, we see the old warriors in that banquet hall are fast asleep, or victorious, or forever peaceful. They don't seem to be quaffing or telling war stories. There is no reference to women going to be with their mothers. If Éowyn had died in battle, would she have broken that particular glass ceiling?

Théoden's dying words include: "My body is broken. I go to my fathers. And even in their mighty company I shall not now be ashamed" (*RK* V, vi, 824). Zhu is a bit casual in describing his "broken" body as "not OK," "not working" (*buxingle*)—is Théoden being humorously understated here? (Zhu *RK*: 162). Though "my fathers" clearly means his ancestors, which Deng and Zhu give as *xianzu* or *zuxian* (ancestors, a term not explicitly gendered as male, though in a patrilineal system the maleness can be assumed). Yilin makes the term more generational with "my father's generation (*fubei*)" (Yilin *RK*: 120). Rendering what is (in my opinion) one of the most moving lines of the whole story, we have: "Now, even if I ascend my self to their great ranks (*hanglie*), I will have no shame (*kui*)" (Deng *RK*: 123). Zhu: "Even though I will be beside the great rank of ancestors (*liezu liezong*), I will not feel the least shame (*xiukui*)" (Zhu *RK*: 162). And Yilin interprets their "mighty" quality in terms of eternal glory: "Their heroic names live forever (*yingming changcun*), but now I have no shame (*kui*) to be one among them" (Yilin *RK*: 120).

A certain number of references to the afterlife involve ancestors, imagined as a group of spirits who gather, as if in their own private Valhalla. Regarding Balin, we read, "Here he must lie in the halls of his fathers" (*FR* II, v, 314). The Yilin translation sticks with simply reclining: "He must lie (*tang*) here, lie in his father's generation's (*fubei*) great hall (*dating*)" (Yilin *FR*: 393). But both Deng and Zhu add a somnolence: "He must long-sleep (*changmian*) in his ancestors' (*xianzu*) hall (*tingtang*)" (Deng *FR*: 403); "Here he must together with his ancestors (*xianzumen*) peacefully sleep (*anmian*)" (Zhu *FR*: 500). In this case, to lie in the halls of one's fathers simply means being interred in a common tomb in Moria, hence more to do with tombs than the afterlife, but sleeping strikes me as somewhat more than merely lying there dead. And where the original uses sleep as a metaphor of death, the translations often make the sleep "long." Gandalf approaches the tomb-mounds near Edoras: "We are come to the great barrows where the sires of Théoden sleep" (*TT* III, vi, 496). Just "sleep." Deng and Yilin let them sleep "long" (Deng *TT*: 129, Yilin *TT*: 119). Zhu modifies its depth rather than length: "We have already reached the place of Théoden's previous kings' (*xianwangmen*) deep sleep (*chenmian*)" (Zhu *TT*: 161).

The notion of joining an assemblage of one's ancestors is very familiar in Chinese religion. Funeral rituals may include an installation of the recently deceased among a larger crowd of ancestors. The classical model of the ancestral temple is structured in a horse-shoe shape. At the head of the hall sits the founding "primal ancestor" (*yuanzu*) of the lineage. On either side are arrayed the six most recent ancestors. When a newly deceased person is added to this line, the least recent of that six is bumped into a general collectivity of ancestors. We do not see this pattern as such in Tolkien's stories, but there is certainly a strong concern with ancestry and lineage. Everyone is "son of so-and-so" or more rarely, "daughter of so-and-so." Elrond recites his elven lineage, which seems to take priority for him over his human one, even if it overrides the patrilineal norms of such declarations. He says, "my mother was Elwing, daughter of Dior, son of Lúthien of Doriath" (*FR* II, ii, 237). Just as in the case mentioned in Chapter 2, both Zhu and Deng have to restate the subject (Dior), "My mother was Dior's daughter Elwing, and Dior was Doriath's Lúthien's son" (Deng *FR*: 304; similar at Zhu *FR*: 379–380). But the Chinese of the Yilin edition has, "My mother was Elwing, she was Doriath's Lúthien's son Dior's daughter" (Yilin *FR*: 295). In describing Elwing's ancestry, the English has: her father, then her grandmother; In the Yilin edition, it has her grandmother and her father. The sequence of names of Elwing's lineage is changed so that eldest is listed first. This is a consistent pattern: on the next page is a less complex example, the proper noun followed by a subordinate clause "Meneldil son of Anárion" becomes the noun-phrase "Arárion's son Meneldil" (*FR* II, ii, 237; Yilin *FR*: 297; Deng *FR*: 306; Zhu *FR*: 382). While this reordering accords with the traditional discursive strategy, it must also be said that subordinate clauses of this kind are generally more awkward in Chinese. Conversely, A's son B's son C is odd in English. The elves are extremely conscious of their ancestry, and in that sense rather "Chinese," though apparently the reverence for their ancestors did not manifest in the sequence of their names.

We get some details about funeral customs from the description of Boromir's improvised funeral (Amendt-Raduege 2018: 22–28, 74–76). Aragorn puts him in a boat with "the weapons of his vanquished foes" (*TT* III, i, 405), which in the Chinese is described as *peizang* 陪葬, a term referring to objects (or in ancient times, people) to be buried with the dead (Deng *TT*: 8, Zhu *TT*: 18), though Yilin just names them as "weapons" (Yilin, *TT*: 6). The translations rely on the Chinese tradition (and vocabulary) of placing objects into a tomb to accompany the dead into the next life—a tradition we also associate with Vikings—to give a little more definition to what is implicit in Aragorn's words. These weapons are also called "trophies of his last battle" (*TT* III, i, 406), and all three name "trophies" less euphemistically as *zhanlipin* 战利品 war-profit-objects—making "trophy" more like booty than a display of victory (Yilin *TT*: 7; Deng *TT*: 9; Zhu *TT*: 20).

Amongst the tales that Bombadil tells the hobbits, we read, "Gold was piled on the biers of dead kings and queens" (*FR* I, vii, 128). Here is an image of gold piled up as *peizang* on royal biers—namely, the portable frames on which coffins or corpses are placed for burial or cremation or transportation to the grave; it might refer to the frame itself or the frame with a corpse on it. Deng: "yellow gold was piled up on dead-and-gone lords-kings and queen's coffin stands (*guancai jia* 棺材架)" (Deng *FR*: 164). Yilin refers to "coffins (*lingjiu* 灵柩, coffin containing a corpse) buried in yellow earth" (Yilin *FR*: 161). Yilin introduces a parallel between the yellow gold (*huangjin*) piled on them and the yellow earth (*huangtu*) which holds them. Due to the large amount of loess in North China, earth is idiomatically yellow. Zhu: "Yellow gold was piled on the dead (*wanggu*) nations' kings and empresses' open graves (*muxue* 墓穴, grave hole)" (Zhu *FR*: 212). Deng is very close to the original, and Yilin is not far off, but Zhu seems to turn the whole image downwards, filling up a hole rather than making a mound over a coffin.

Boat burials are not traditional in China. However, those who have died at sea receive special assistance through the performance of *shuilu* ("water-road") memorial services, intended to send comfort and material goods to the sea-dead. The sea-dead have a particularly difficult time because their descendants cannot make offerings to their remains. Graves and the rituals associated with them locate the dead, and discourage them from roaming, but the remains of the sea-dead (or river-buried) are lost. An additional aspect of Denethor's grief might be his inability to place Boromir in a tomb. Though he calms somewhat at the end, Boromir's mental agitation, violent death, and lack of a proper grave make him a prime candidate for a troublesome ghost.

Before heroes can "sleep" with noble ancestors or fellow warriors, they have to "go" there. The afterlife is frequently presented as a journey, a basic metaphor in English as in Chinese with little need of interpretation: "But now Boromir has taken his road" (*TT* III, i, 408), straightforwardly translated as road (*lu*) (Deng *TT*: 12; Yilin *TT*: 10; Zhu *TT*: 24). From the elves' point of view, human beings are in a sense always on a road to death, and beyond death to an unknown immortality (McBride 2020: 197–202). Hence, "they are called the Guests, or the Strangers" (*S*: 36). There are several variations in the Chinese: "guests" (*guoke*; passing traveler, transient) or "people on the road" (*luren*, passerby, stranger) (Yilin *S*: 35), "guest" (*fangke*, visitor) or "strangers" (*yixiangren*, people from a different native place) (Deng *S* 2015: 64), "the world's visitors" (*kelü*, a variant of *lüke*, guest, traveller), or "migrants" (*liulangzhe*, vagrant, wanderer) (Deng *S* 2002: 46).

As the Fellowship is about to leave Lothlórien, Galadriel tells Aragorn about a road of the future, beyond death. "For darkness will flow between us, and it may be that we shall not meet again, unless it be far hence upon a road that has no returning" (*FR* II, viii, 365). The "road that has no returning" is some version of the road to the Undying Lands, and the Halls of Mandos. Galadriel will one day go back to the Western Undying Lands, either by her own death or (as actually happens later) by sea. Yilin: "darkness will separate us, maybe it will be hard for us to meet each other, unless in the distant future, on a non-returning road (*buguilu*)" (Yilin *FR*: 457). The poetic metaphor of darkness as a sundering river is replaced by a functional "separate us," a flattening of the image which I also see in Zhu's retelling: "the path of the future still has many dangers and darkness ... In the future we might not again have the opportunity to see each other, unless on a route (*lücheng*) from which there is no way to look back (*wufa huitou*, no way to turn your head back/repent)" (Zhu *FR*: 578). Deng retains some of the flood but is more static than the original: "Because darkness will fill up (*miman*) between us, maybe we will not meet again, unless it is on that road (which) as soon as (one) goes from this point (*jiuci yiqu*), (one does) not again return"(Deng *FR*: 469).

There are several terms for returning in Chinese, and the Yilin translator has chosen *gui*, which has a slight connotation of dying. So, *buguilu* means primarily not-return-road, but can also hint at not-die-road. But Zhu has: a route on which you can't look back (*huitou*, literally turn the head back). Coming back into English, this evokes an image of Orpheus and Eurydice—except with some of the symbolic syntax inverted. An additional Chinese meaning of *huitou* is repent or recant—to be walking away from some evil, and then turn back to admit it. *Wufa huitou de lücheng* means then, the road on which you cannot repent your past deeds. This is perhaps a little grim compared to the notion that arrival in the Halls of Mandos would be joyous, or at least comforting for a mortal, before they go onwards to an unknown fate. But based on my reading of how the Chinese texts depict the afterlife, this phrase is consistent with an assumption, deep in the language, that the afterlife obeys moral rules. The Halls of Mandos are described as a place where people sit and ruminate on the good and bad deeds of their mortal lives. (See Chapter 9.)

Deng's phrasing, "that road (which) as soon as (one) goes from this point (*jiuci yiqu*), (one does) not again return"(Deng *FR*: 469) specifies the sense that as soon as you've started on that road, you can't come back. The original line, "a road that has no returning," leaves this detail unspecified, so what is added in Deng's retelling? Galadriel is not only saying, we'll meet again after you're dead, she is also suggesting this particular time and place is the starting point of their divergence, as if their steps from this point on lead inexorably to death (for him) and the Undying Lands (for her), consistent with her view that, win or lose, this war is the beginning of the end for Lothlórien.

The idea that the afterlife would take the form of a journey is by no means new to Chinese readers. Buddhist vocabulary tends to prefer *dao* (path, way) to *lu* (road). The "six paths" of Buddhism (the six broad categories of beings within samsara) is *liudao*, where *dao* means paths. Chinese funerals usually involve a journey, even if only from the home to the cemetery or crematorium. They take the dead person's body (with the strong sense of a soul still lingering nearby) and put it where, they hope, it will be at peace, and stay still, and slowly fade away into the spirit-realm. Beyond that physical journey, there is a spirit journey. Indeed in a Daoist funeral, the priest serves as a protector and guide and legal representative for the deceased in their negotiations with the first Court of Hell, where their punishment and reward are determined. The journey does not end there, of course, but continues to some other body, whether painfully in the hells, or blissfully as a god, or in the next human rebirth.

When Thorin is dying, he says to Bilbo: "Farewell, good thief ... I go now to the halls of waiting to sit beside my fathers, until the world is renewed" (*H*, xviii, 312; see also Hooker 2003: 95–100 on this passage in Russian). Zhu: "Farewell (*yongbiele*, literally we "forever part"), uniquely skilled thief ... Now I am going to my father's hall (*tingtang*) to be with him, until the time when the world is reborn (*lunhui*)" (Zhu *H*: 320). Wu's translation also uses *lunhui* (Wu *H*: 388). Here, as elsewhere, we see a hint of Buddhism in the use of *lunhui* 輪回/轮回 (transmigration, turning of the wheel). The "halls of waiting" lose their waiting-room quality here, and the near-future state of Thorin is primarily about hanging out with Dad (or Dads), in *his* hall. In *The Silmarillion*, a reference to elves going to the Halls of Mandos, "whence they may in time return" (*S*: 36) is straightforwardly "return to the human world" (Deng *S* 2002: 46) and "return to the world" (Deng *S* 2015: 64), but in the Yilin text we read, "die and are reborn (*si er fusheng*)" (Yilin *S* 35). Compare this also to the rumor that Beren and Lúthien "had returned from the Dead" (*UT*: 58), rendered as "from the domain of the dead (*wangzhe zhi jing*) had again returned to the human world (*chongfan renshi*)" (Shi and Deng *UT*: 78).

Whereas Zhu renders Thorin's "Farewell" as *yongbiele*, "(now we) forever part," the Yilin edition opts for the more casual *zaijian* (goodbye, literally "see [you] again"), which may or may not be true, depending on their respective afterlife fates. "Goodbye (*zaijian*), good person (*haorenr*), ... Now I will go to under the Nine Springs (*jiuquan*) to be companion to my ancestors (*xianren*), until this world gets a new birth (*xinsheng* 新生)" (Yilin *H*: 247). The term *jiuquan* 九泉 (nine springs) is a synonym of *huangquan* (yellow springs); nine here implies the deepest and hottest. This term dates from the Han dynasty. It has two principle meanings: the grave, and underground. Rather than using an ancestral image, the Yilin edition uses a more traditional myth. Whereas Zhu gave "the world is renewed" a Buddhist tone, here the *xinsheng* carries a vaguely Christian quality, but also echoes the *xinshenghuo yundong*, the New Life Movement, which was a more or less fascistic political campaign by the Nationalist government under Chiang Kai-shek, starting in 1934.

Ghosts

We do not see ghosts of elves or dwarves or hobbits, much less ghosts of orcs or ents. Ghosts in Tolkien are basically human. Most human spirits pass on to an afterlife and are not called ghosts. To be called a ghost, a soul must be still among the living, not "passed on" but somehow stuck without a body. The ghosts on the Paths of the Dead are the best example—they wish to die completely but are unable to, due to the magical power of their unfulfilled oath. But qualitatively, a ghost and a soul after death are the same thing; the difference is only in their social situations. This view is very familiar in

Chinese religions. If all is well, one's ancestors are not "ghosts" (*gui* 鬼)—because they are not problems, and to call them *gui* would be rude. They are small gods, family deities. But when things go wrong, they cause trouble. Graves function to locate ghosts and keep them there. When spirits possess the living, one common explanation in Chinese lore is that their graves were disturbed (Sinex 2005: 98; for a vivid example of the trauma of Chinese graves in chaos, see Jing 1997: 69–86).

All the emperors of China have had their tombs, but the best known are probably the "Terracotta Army" of Qin Shihuang near Xi'an, and the imperial tombs of the Ming and Qing rulers near Beijing. "Tomb of kings" (*RK* V, iii, 778) is "imperial tomb (*diwang lingqin* 帝王陵寝)" (Yilin *RK*: 62), "tomb (*muzhong* 墓冢) of kings" (Deng *RK*: 64), and a place "to let emperors and kings bury their bones (*diwang maigu*)" (Zhu *RK*: 90). "This is a tomb and memorial of Elendil the Faithful" (*UT*: 308) becomes "This is a [royal] tomb (*lingqin* 陵寝) and memorial place (*jinian zhidi*) of loyal and steadfast Elendil" (Shi and Deng *UT*: 403). Cirion identifies the tomb of Elendil (again *lingqin*), "and from it comes the awe that dwells on this hill and in the woods below" (*UT*: 304), which is rendered as "the reverent atmosphere (*jingwei fenwei*) which envelopes (*longzhao*, shrouds, covers) this hill and the woods below, comes from this tomb (*mu*)" (Shi and Deng *UT*: 398). Magical power emanating from a tomb and going downhill is good fengshui. The best location for a tomb is on a gentle hillside.

The most common general term is *fenmu* 墳墓/坟墓 or individually, *fen*, *mu*, and in various combinations. Isengard at night resembles a "graveyard" (*TT* III, viii, 541). All use *fenchang*, *fen* for grave and *chang* meaning a yard or field (Deng *TT*: 190; Yilin *TT*: 175; Zhu *TT*: 230). But we see many variations on *fenqiu* 坟丘 (grave mound, tomb), in which *qiu* is a mound or hill, but especially a grave mound. Hence, *shanqiu* 山丘, which combines mountain and hill, can mean hill, or tomb. Similarly there is *ling* 陵 (hill, mound, imperial tomb, mausoleum), and *zhong* 冢， 塚 (tomb, grave, burial mound). There are many instances of small hills assumed to be tombs, in English and Chinese. Lamenting their miserable lot, Sador comments, "Happier are those in the Great Mound" (*UT*: 106). "Those people who lie (*tang*) under the big hill (*daqiu*) are happier (*xingfu*, more fortunately blessed) than I" (Shi and Deng *UT*: 139). Of Finduilas, "She lies in a mound beside Teiglin" (*UT*: 111): "She lies under a tomb-mound (*fenqiu*) next to Teiglin" (Shi and Deng *UT*: 146). The Mound of the Elfmaid (*UT*: 112) is the elf young-woman's grave (*fen*) (Shi and Deng *UT*: 147). The mass burial mound of dead orcs near Helm's Deep is called the Death Down (*TT* III, viii, 540): *sigang* 死岗, death mound/ridge (Deng *TT*: 188); *siqiu*, death hill/mound (Yilin *TT*: 173); *siwangqiu*, death hill/mound (Zhu *TT*: 228).

For "the Dead," all three use *wangzhe* 亡者, a fairly plain term for ones who have died; *wang* also having the meanings of run away, gone, and lost (*RK* V, ii, 768; Yilin *RK*: 51; Zhu *RK*: 77; Deng *RK*: 53). We might translate *wangzhe* as "the departed." When the locals cry out, "The King of the Dead!" (*RK* V, ii, 771), Zhu and Deng use *wangzhe zhiwang*, king of the dead (Zhu *RK*: 81; Deng *RK*: 57), but Yilin uses *youlingwang* 幽灵王, king of dim spirits (Yilin *RK*: 55). All feared to go through the door into the mountain of the Dead except Legolas, "for whom the ghosts of Men have no terror" (*RK* V, ii, 769): "dim spirits and ghosts (*youling guihun*)" (Yilin *RK*: 52); "humans' dead spirits (*wangling*)" (Zhu *RK*: 77); "human ghosts (*guihun*)" (Deng *RK*: 53). Note the "of

Men," implying that there are ghosts of other beings. Zhu and Deng include that descriptor, but Yilin ignores it. And almost immediately they see animal ghosts. Once they go in, they are followed by "shapes of Men and of horses" (*RK* V, ii, 771). For "shapes," all three use *shenying* 身影 or *yingzi* 影子, a shadow or reflection of a body, hence silhouettes, which is both more specific and perhaps more ghostly than "shapes" (Yilin *RK*: 54; Zhu *RK*: 80–81; Deng *RK*: 56). Horse-ghosts feels like an undeveloped plot idea.

Deng and Yilin reasonably treat Butterbur's "spooks" (*FR* I, x, 166) as "ghosts (*gui*)" (Deng *FR*: 213; Yilin *FR*: 207). But Zhu reads the term more generally with the phrase "whatever kind of thing" (*shenme laitou*) (Zhu *FR*: 269). *Laitou* is a broad term meaning background, motives, cause, or force, and I have rendered it here as "thing." "Phantom" is treated mostly as a magical illusion. Gimli speculates about seeing "an evil phantom of Saruman" (*TT* III, v, 477), but surely meaning a magical projection, not in the sense that Gimli thinks Saruman is dead yet. Deng and Zhu opt for more of a magical manifestation: *huanying*, illusory shadow (Deng *TT*: 103), and *yingxiang*, shadow-image (Zhu *TT*: 131). Yilin gives the term its most ghostly form, with *gui yingr*, ghost shadow (Yilin *TT*: 95). But elsewhere in Yilin, "phantom" is illusion: one of the guards at Edoras asks if Gandalf and friends are "phantoms of [Saruman's] craft" (*TT* III, vi, 497), or "dark souls created by magic (*mofa huacheng de youling*)" (Yilin *TT*: 120). Deng has, "an illusory shadow (*huanying*) created by his evil techniques (*xieshu*)" (Deng *TT*: 131; and Zhu is very similar, Zhu *TT*: 163).

We learn something about the afterlife from the creepy death scene of Saruman, when the spirit departing the body is visible and witnessed by many. After Grima has killed him, "about the body of Saruman a grey mist gathered, and rising slowly to a great height like smoke from a fire, as a pale shrouded figure it loomed over the Hill. For a moment it wavered, looking to the West; but out of the West came a cold wind, and it bent away, and with a sigh dissolved into nothing" (*RK*, VI, viii, 996–997). The "body" of Saruman is a corpse, and Yilin and Deng make that explicit with *shiti* (corpse). Deng has the grey fog "gather (*ningju*, accumulate, condense)," in Yilin it "appeared," but Zhu specifies that it was "emitted (*mao*)" from the corpse (Zhu *RK*: 420; Yilin *RK*: 340; Deng *RK*: 348). The "pale shrouded figure" is in Zhu's version "grey figure (*cangbai shenying*, green-white body-shadow) wearing corpse's clothes (*shiyi*)"; Deng's translation is similar except that "shrouded" is "wearing long-life clothes (*shouyi* 寿衣, a euphemism for grave clothes)." Yilin ignores "shrouded." "Shrouded" can mean covered in a shroud (as a corpse), or obscured (as by a mist). Zhu and Deng side for the literal first meaning. The gaseous Saruman "wavered, looking to the West," as if hoping he might still return to the Undying Lands, or *huitou*—turn his head back to repent. This wavering is interpreted as "shook/swayed (*yaohuang*)" by Zhu, "leaned (*qingxie*, tilted) and flickered (*yaoye*, swayed)" by Yilin, and "swayed in the wind (*piaoyao*)" by Deng. Then the Valar blow him off Eastwards. Yilin condenses the two references to the West into one, which can only be a loss—In the original, Saruman's spirit first looks to the West, but the West rebuffs him. Here, we get only the wind. Where did he go? The *Untold Tales* unhelpfully tells us, "his spirit went whithersoever it was doomed to go" (*UT*: 391). Or, "his spirit (*linghun*) went to an unknown place it was decided (*zhuding*) he would return to" (Shi and Deng *UT*: 507).

Another word Tolkien likes for the dead is wight. The earliest uses of wight (e.g. *wiht* in *Beowulf*) have a general meaning of a living being, but quickly assume the sense of supernatural or unearthly beings. For example, the Lindisfarne Gospels (8th century) uses *wiht* to translate φάντασμά (*phantasma*) in Mark 6:49, where the disciples see Jesus walking on water and think he is a *phantasma*. It was subsequently translated as "spirit" in the King James Version of 1611, and "ghost" in most other translations. Among the various Chinese translations of this verse that I have found, the most common words are *guiguai, gui*, and *youling* 幽靈/灵. The word "wight" seems to have petered out by the nineteenth century.

Early in their story, the Hobbits have an extended encounter with a barrow-wight. For barrow-wight, Deng and Zhu have slight variants: *guzhong shiyao*, ancient tomb corpse *yao* (Deng *FR*: 164), and *gumu shiyao*, ancient grave corpse *yao* (Zhu *FR*: 212). Zhu's earlier translation has *muxue zhong de shigu*, dead bones or skeleton in the grave-pit (Zhu *FR* 2001: 198). Yilin has *guzhong yinhun*, ancient tomb *yin*-spirit (Yilin *FR*: 161). Bombadil opposes them with a song that starts, "Get out, you old Wight!" (*FR* I, viii, 139). For "you old wight," Deng gives us the vivid "rotting corpse *yao*" (*fuxiu shiyao*) (Deng *FR*: 178), Zhu "old corpse *yao*" (*laoshiyao*) (Zhu *FR*: 229), and Yilin the less grotesque "old *yin hun*-soul" (*laoyinhun*, with *yin* here the opposite of *yang*, implying dead) (Yilin *FR*: 174).

The description of the wights would fit into thousands of ghost stories: moans and groans, cold and dread. We hear the barrow-wights' ghostly voices, which "seemed far away and immeasurably dreary" (*FR* I, viii, 137). The usual meaning of dreary might have been a little puzzling in this context, with its sense of boring and dull. But Deng sees it correctly: "incomparably gloomy (*yinyu*)" (Deng *FR*: 176). Zhu's translation of this passage verges into paraphrase, so it is hard to see what he did with "dreary." But Yilin really cranks it up with "making peoples' body-hair and bones terror-stricken (*maogu songran*, be blood-curdling)" (Yilin *FR*: 172). From those voices came "strings of words" (*FR* I, viii, 137). Reasonably enough, the translators interpret the strings of words as songs (*ge*) (Zhu *FR*: 226) or song lyrics (*geci*) (Deng *FR*: 176; Yilin *FR*: 172).

Then we come to a very interesting and difficult line, descriptive of the bitter consciousness emerging from the barrow: "The night was railing against the morning of which it was bereaved, and the cold was cursing the warmth for which it hungered" (*FR* I, viii, 137). Deng follows the relatively abstract phrasing: "The black night was taunting/sneering at (*xiluo*) the dawn it was deprived of (*boduo* 剥夺), the cold was cursing (*zuzhou*) the warmth it was thirsting for (*kewang*)" (Deng *FR*: 176). Here, the "curse" in Chinese is clearly of the hostile ritual kind, not the mere utterance of profanities (see Chapter 12). The Yilin edition rather garbles the night cursing the morning. Yilin: "it was like the black night, because of mistaking (*cuoguo*, missing, faulting) the star light, abused (*gouli*, berated) it, the cold, because it could not get warmth, cursed (*zuzhou*) it" (Yilin *FR*: 172). Here, the black night is hostile to the *starlight*—a very different metaphor, though one that connects to the theme of starlight in the novel. The dawn ends the night—the night can never co-exist with the day, whereas stars permeate the night itself. Rather than implying the wights desire and hate life as an impossible goal, here the life they desire and hate is twinkling down at them all the time—like the residual "life" that persists in their ghostly state (in the form of their continued if muddled consciousness).

Zhu significantly reworks the night cursing the morning, producing a rather mixed set of metaphors. "The night's dimness (*yese*, night's dim light) under that mournful wail (*tonghao*) was like a wave making ripples, the cold life (*shengming*) cursed the warm thought (*nuanyi*) it never had an opportunity to get" (Zhu *FR*: 226). Tolkien and the translations shift from a description of the wailing song to a line which personifies night and cold, as if night/cold was singing the song. The emotion here is desire and also hatred, the combination of emotions so characteristic of Gollum's feelings for the Ring. We see it again in the case of the ring-wraith's feelings towards blood, noted below.

We are given the text of the wight's "incantation"—*zhouwen* (Deng), *zhouhua* (Yilin), *zuzhou* (Zhu) (see Chapter 12): "Cold be hand and heart and bone,/ and cold be sleep under stone / never more to wake on stony bed" (*FR* I, viii, 138). Deng's collaborator Shi writes: "The four limbs (*siti*) numb/stiff with cold (*jiangleng*), cuts into bone and enters heart, the rock-cave (*yandong*) long sleep is cold like ice, now in the open grave (*muxue*) suspended in long sleep" (Deng *FR*: 176). The original's "stone" references the grave (sleep under stone = lie in a grave; stony bed = grave), but now the tomb becomes a grotto-tomb and the grave is explicitly open. Hand, heart and bone certainly imply the whole body; as does Shi's four limbs (*siti*); Yilin goes for a bland "whole body" but adds vital organs: "Whole body (*tongti*) cold pervading my vital organs (*gaohuang*), / Insensate (*wan*, obstinate) stone serves as a bed, the earth serves as a house (*fang*)" (Yilin *FR*: 173).

Close to wights are wraiths. Frodo says, "or I shall become a wraith" (*FR* I, xi, 180). Deng and Zhu use *youling*, dark soul (Deng *FR*: 231; Zhu *FR*: 291). Yilin uses the more generic term *gui* (ghost) (Yilin *FR*: 226), but inconsistently, elsewhere using *youling*, such as translating "Ringwraith" (*RK* V, iv, 800) as "*mo*-ring-dark-soul (*mojie youling*)" (Yilin *RK*: 91). The Ringwraiths are semi-ghosts. These were originally human kings, whom Sauron gave rings of power, which gave them longevity and supernatural perceptions. But gradually their physical forms vanished and they became ghostly figures in Sauron's service. The term ringwraith is *jieling* (ring-soul) in Zhu and Deng, and *mojie youling* (*mo*-ring dark soul) in Yilin (*RK*, Appendix A, I, iii, 1016; Deng *RK*: 379; Yilin *RK* 366; Zhu *RK* Appendix: 13). Their leader is called the Witch-king (e.g., *RK* Appendix A, I, iii, 1016), though this term is a little odd in contemporary English—witches are female, whereas the Nine are all kings. In the Chinese there is no such issue with "witch" (*wu*) but the term is gendered with "king" (*wang*). In Deng's and Zhu's translations the term is *wuwang*, wizard-king, *wu*-shaman-king (Deng *RK*: 379; Zhu *RK* Appendix: 13). Yilin uses the less specific term *mowang*, *mo*-king (Yilin *RK*: 366), which is a bit confusing, as this term is more often used for Sauron.

Aragorn describes their enhanced sense of smell: "they smell the blood of living things, desiring and hating it" (*FR* I, xi, 185). Deng: "they can smell the scent of blood of living beings (*xianhuo shengling* 鲜活生灵), and desire and hate this scent" (Deng *FR*: 237). Deng is close, though it's an intriguing phrase, "*xianhuo shengling*, fresh or vivid living souls," as *xianhuo* is a phrase often used for seafood kept alive in the restaurant until just before cooking. Yilin: "they are able to smell out all animals (*dongwu*)'s blood-smell, they crave blood (*shixue* 嗜血, addicted to blood) and hate blood" (Yilin *FR*: 232). For the original, it is clear that the thing they desire and hate is blood, but Yilin makes the line bloodier still with repetition. Yilin has them smell animals' blood—are humans also animals?—though literally *dongwu* means "moving things" which would include us. Zhu: "they can smell (*wen*) living beings' blood and meat (*xuerou*), this makes them both desiring and hateful" (Zhu *FR*: 298–299). Zhu adds meat to the blood, hinting at our heroes as meat. For "smell," whereas Deng and Yilin use *xiu* 嗅 (smell, sniff), Zhu uses *wen* 聞, a word which means both smell and hear, suggesting an extra-creepy sense that perhaps the ringwraiths can *hear* our blood pumping.

Conclusions

Whether in English or Chinese, we find a broad spectrum of images of death and the afterlife, not always with logical consistency. A rebirth in some other place (blissful or miserable or transitional), a rebirth in or return to this world, existence in some collective (ancestral or tribal or other), a hell underground, an ongoing relation with the living, a vague sort of coma or sleep, a journey. Sometimes the afterlife is connected to a moral quality. The Halls of Mandos is sometimes just a waiting room, sometimes a confessional. Oblique suggestions of miserable (but non-supernatural) underground places shift towards the supernatural, towards hells rather than merely hellish places; towards places of the dead rather than mere dungeons in deep pits. There is a pervasive sense of ancestry, of going to be with one's ancestors, albeit entirely male, which is well suited to China's ancestral discourse and practice.

In the next chapter, we take a closer look at the afterlife and dwindling fate of the elves.

9

White Shores and Beyond

The Halls of Mandos

Increasing embodiment correlates with gradual disempowerment: first is Ilúvatar, formless and eternal; it created beings known as Ainur, made of sound alone—single-note at first, later forming chords; the sounds induced Ilúvatar to make light to match the melodies, and eventually this vision assumed material form. Then, a group of Ainur went to Arda and were known as the Valar. They could take form as needed. The elves were the first "race" of beings created or "awoken" by Ilúvatar. Hence they are known as the first-born. Their proximity to the Creator is reflected in their relative immortality, whereas the life-spans of dwarves and humans are commensurately shorter. "Men" also includes the Dúnedain, whose long life is due to their closeness to the elves and the Undying Lands. Various others appear—giant spiders, balrogs, ents, goblins, trolls, orcs, and uruk-hai. Not bothering to keep track of their short, miserable lives, orcs don't have birthday parties. And of course mammals, birds, insects, plant life, bacteria, and so on, more or less irrelevant to the story. The sense of an emergence from formless, powerful, and eternal towards embodied, limited, and mortal accords with the schema known as the Great Chain of Being (Chandler and Fry 2017: 103–104; Fimi 2009: 141), but also, as it happens, with the cosmogony of the *Daodejing* (see Chapter 12).

Perhaps the definitive statement on the immortality of the elves in contrast to human mortality is in *The Silmarillion*. "Their bodies indeed were of the stuff of Earth, and could be destroyed" (S: 118). By the phrase "of the stuff of Earth," presumably Tolkien had in mind the notion that elves and fairies are bound to the natural world. In "On Fairy-stories," he rejects the notion that fairies can be called supernatural: "they are natural, far more natural than he ['man']. Such is their doom. The road to fairyland is not the road to Heaven; nor even to Hell" (*OFS*: 28). We recall the traditional Western idea of fairies, that they may live a long time but they are creatures of the creation—they don't have souls; they are outside the possibility of salvation (Ostling 2018a: 32–33). Shippey asks, "Did elves have souls, for instance? Could they be saved? Anyone who had read Hans Christian Andersen's 'The Little Mermaid' would know that they did not and could not—not unless they married a mortal, as with Lúthien" (2003: 238). Yet, within an animistic framework, such a question is almost meaningless. Everything sentient (and even non-sentient) has a spirit.

The elves' spirits live on, for an extremely long time, until the very Earth is gone. Deng expresses this in the two versions of her translation: "Their bodies (*quti* 軀體)

really were made of the substance (*wuzhi*) of the Earth (*diqiu*, the planet)" (Deng S 2002: 147); her 2015 version is similar, except that for "bodies" she uses "flesh-bodies (*routi* 肉体)" (Deng S 2015: 141). The difference in nuance between *quti* and *routi* is notable: *quti* is fairly neutrally "body" but *routi*, "flesh"- or "meat"-body, emphasizes their physicality more bluntly. The Yilin translation also treats the phrase "of the stuff of Earth" as implying anatomical substance: "Their bodies (*shenti*) were the bodies (*qu*) of blood and flesh (*xuerou*) which could be destroyed" (Yilin S: 109).

The immortality of elves is frequently contrasted with human mortality. The passage goes on. Men are more frail, and die; "What may befall their spirits after death the Elves know not. Some say that they too go to the halls of Mandos; but their place of waiting there is not that of the Elves, and Mandos under Ilúvatar alone save Manwë knows whither they go after the time of recollection in those silent halls beside the Outer Sea" (S: 118). Despite being "immortal," elves are capable of dying physically. When their bodies die their spirits go to the halls of the Vala Mandos, and from there they are reborn in the Undying Lands. The post-mortem fate of humans is initially the same as the elves—they go to the same halls, on the North-Western edge of the Undying Lands. But humans are forever barred from these elysian fields, and even as they "wait" they are kept separate from the elves. They move on eventually but to an unknown fate.

The Yilin edition renders this passage: "The elves did not know afterwards what kind of a return home (*guisu*) their own deaths would be." The word "own" (*ziji*) suggests that the elves are talking about elf-souls rather than human souls, which muddies the picture. "Some elves said, their spirits (*linghun*) returned again to the halls of Mandos. But the place of their waiting for transmigration (*lunhui* 轮回) is not the elves' own domain. Under Ilúvatar, except for Manwë, there is only Mandos who knows where these spirits (*linghun*) gathered to the side of the outer sea in the silent halls (*diantang*) go" (Yilin S: 109). "What may befall" becomes "what kind of return home (*guisu* 归宿)." *Gui* means return, and is sometimes used as a synonym for death and/or afterlife. Whatever we came from, to that we return. *Su* means long-standing, lodging, home. The home we return to is an afterlife. For "Death is their fate" (S: 36) (speaking of humans), Yilin gives us: "Death is their *guisu*" (Yilin S: 35).

If those certain elves are right, and human spirits go to the Halls of Mandos to wait, their waiting seems to be a "time of recollection"—although it's not known what happens to them at that point. The Yilin text more or less gets this, except for the insertion of the idea of transmigration: "the place of their waiting *for transmigration* (*lunhui*)." *Lunhui* means "turning around, rotating back," and refers to samsara, the turning wheel of endless rebirths. But in Buddhism, the rebirth is not just once, as when the elves are reincarnated and live in the Undying Land; and not just an unknown fate beyond the world, as with humans. Deng's two versions are almost identical, though "what befalls" is interpreted as *jiyu*, fortune, usually good fortune. And for "the time of recollection," Deng gives two close synonyms for mental reflection: *huiyi* 回憶 and *fansi* 反思, both involving "thinking back," neither of which evoke reincarnation (Deng S 2002: 147; Deng S 2015: 141). Is there a moral dimension of this bardo state?

The *Silmarillion* passage goes on to mention the unusual case of Beren. He was a human who died and found himself in the Halls of Mandos. "None have ever come back from the mansions of the dead, save only Beren son of Barahir, whose hand had touched a Silmaril; but he never spoke afterward to mortal Men. The fate of Men after death, maybe, is not in the hands of the Valar, nor was all foretold in the Music of the Ainur" (S: 118).

Yilin:

In fact, except for Barahir's son Beren, there has not been a dead spirit (*siqu de jingling*) who has returned from those halls of the dead. Beren's hand once stroked a Silmaril. After he had been reborn (*fusheng*) he never spoke with anyone again. As for after the death of humans, their fate (*mingyun*) perhaps is no more held in the Valar's hands. In the music of the Ainur there has never been any hint. (Yilin S: 109)

The original has "none have ever come back"; the Yilin edition wants to specify, none of what? And answers, *siqu de jingling*. *Siqu* is dead-and-gone; but *jingling* is in all other cases a translation of "elf." The text would then appear to read, except for Beren (a mortal human), no dead *elves* have returned. I read this as a simple error, derived from the fact that dead spirits and elves are very close in Chinese, in a way they are not in English.

Deng's two versions have some interesting variations. Her 2015 version deals with the key phrase plainly: "humans who returned (*guilai*) from the halls (*diantang*) of the dead (*wangzhe*)" (Deng S 2015: 141). But her earlier version uses a more idiomatic and suggestive phrase: "there has never been a human able to return to life from the dark mansion" (Deng S 2002: 147). The phrase is *cong mingfu huanyang* 從冥府還陽, literally from the *ming* (dark/dim/deep) *fu* (mansion, government office), hence the underworld, netherworld; and *huanyang* (return to *yang*, revive, return to the living) in contrast with the use of *yin* for the dead, such as in the term *yinjian*, the *yin* world (of the dead), as we saw in the previous chapter. The phrase relies on a common perception of the afterlife as having juridical qualities: you go to hell, but not necessarily for punishment. Rather, your life is reviewed by a judge (usually Yama or Yanluo). Hell is imagined as a series of ten "courts" (*dian*). Some thus consider Mandos a judge. After the elf Saeros dies, Túrin says: "May Mandos judge him justly" (UT: 82). "I wish Mandos to fairly judge (*caijue*) him" (Shi and Deng UT: 108). Certainly Mandos has a bureaucratic role: "He is the keeper of the Houses of the Dead, and the summoner of the spirits of the slain" (S: 19). "Keeper" is a little vague: we get variations on his bureaucratic role: he "administers" (*zhangguan*) (Yilin S: 18; Deng S 2015: 47), or he is the "supervisor" or "controller" (*jiandu*) (Deng S 2002: 22).

Beren waits in the Halls of Mandos to bid farewell to Lúthien, before going "whence Men that die set out never to return" (S: 221). Yilin: "can never again be reborn (*fusheng*)" (Yilin S: 206). On the same page, the Yilin edition, inserting a stealth gloss on the Halls of Mandos, says the elves' *linghun* (spirits) wait there for *zhuansheng* (rebirth, another term for transmigration since *zhuan* means literally turning like a wheel) (Yilin S: 206). Then, in the original: "There those that wait sit in the shadow of their thought" (S: 221). But the Chinese adds a moral reflection: "Many elves sit there turning over in their thoughts the wrong and right and gain and loss (*cuodui deshi*) of their own whole lives (*ziji de yisheng*)" (Yilin S: 206). Generally speaking, in Chinese religious thought, transmigration isn't a morally neutral event, but a moment of reflection on one's past sins and virtues, which in turn determine the nature of one's next rebirth.

Tolkien seems to be setting aside postmortem judgment (such as might direct our spirits to heaven or to hell), perhaps because he was setting his tales in a pre-Christian or Pagan world, or because he did not want Ilúvatar to be quite Yahweh. But in the Chinese, there seems to be a tendency to understand the Halls of Mandos as a bardo state between rebirths—in which a moral judgment determines one's next birth. The terms also suggest multiple rebirths. While Tolkien apparently considered the possibility of multiple rebirths, he rejected this idea early on (Fornet-Ponse 2010: 70–71).

Mandos granted Lúthien the choice of staying elven (so she could be alive again in the Undying Lands, but without Beren) or becoming mortal, which she chose, in order to be reborn with Beren in Middle-earth, where eventually both of them died. Lúthien "chose mortality, and to die from the world, . . . and after a brief time [they] walked alive once more in the green woods, together they passed, long ago, beyond the confines of this world" (*FR* I, xi, 189). For "choose mortality," Zhu switches her embrace of mortality with her abandoning immortality: "Thereupon, she cast aside (*sheqi*) immortality (*yongsheng*)" (Zhu *FR*: 306). For "walked alive once more," Deng emphasizes the death and rebirth more explicitly with the phrase *si er fusheng*, died and born again (Deng *FR*: 243). Zhu also uses *fusheng* (Zhu *FR*: 306). Deng gives "passed" beyond the world a somewhat more spiritual "transcended" (*chaoguo*), along with an added embellishing phrase "once gone not returned" (Deng *FR*: 243). For "passed," Yilin uses *xianshi* 仙逝, sylph-died; died and became *xian* (Yilin *FR*: 238). Zhu and Yilin elaborate on "the confines of this world" by making the world more explicitly negative. Yilin: "the fetters (*jiban*, shackles, yoke) of the dusty world (*chenshi*)" (Yilin *FR*: 238) and "this world's fetters (*shufu*)" (Zhu *FR*: 306).

Elrond fears that his daughter is losing immortality for the sake of a passing fancy. Arwen choses Aragorn, the same choice that Adam and Eve made when they traded their immortality for a quickening of the pulse. But of course, eventually Aragorn dies (Amendt-Raduege 2018: 28–29). On his deathbed, he tells her: "But let us not be overthrown at the final test, who of old renounced the Shadow and the Ring. In sorrow we must go, but not in despair. Behold! We are not bound for ever to the circles of the world, and beyond them is more than memory. Farewell!" (*RK* Appendix A, I, v, 1038). The first line presumably means that despairing of death would be unworthy of those who resisted great evil. Zhu's translation makes this more explicit: "But, don't let us fail in the last test, we defeated the temptation (*youhuo*, seduction, lure) of the *mo*-shadow and the *mo*-ring, did we not?" (Zhu *RK* Appendix: 44). And then, he posits the continued life of the spirits of humans beyond the Halls of Mandos, where the two of them might be together again. As in all the translations, "the Ring" is given more specification by the prefix *mo*. Deng: "But, we in the past abandoned (*bingqi*) the *mo*-shadow and the *mo*-ring, and don't want to fail the last test. We must part—sad, but not in despair (*juewang*, without hope). Look! We are not forever confined (*jingu*) in the scope (*fanwei*) of the world, and outside of the limits (*xianzhi*) is absolutely not only memory. Farewell (*biele*)" (Deng *RK*: 410). The other translations are more or less the same (Zhu *RK* Appendix: 44; Yilin *RK*: 396). Presumably the idea that there will be more than memory implies that human spirits in that unknown state will be capable not only of remembering the past but also of having new experiences.

Our ability to die is called "the Gift of Men (or the Doom of Men, as it was afterwards called)" (*RK* Appendix A, I, i, 1011). The ambiguity of "doom" will be treated in the next chapter, but here "gift" also divides as it moves into Chinese. Deng (or, as this is an Appendix, Shi) puts the phrase in quotation marks: "'the human gift' (*renlei de zengli*) (later was called 'the human fate' (*suming*)" (Deng *RK*: 372). Though we can appreciate the meaning, clearly the ability to die does not feel like much of a "gift" to we mortals. The use of quotation marks suggests that irony. The Yilin translator shifts the meaning significantly: "their human endowment (*fuxing*, endowed nature, like *tianxing*) or . . . the grasp of fate (*mingyun zhi zhang*)" (Yilin *RK*: 360). Zhu: "'the gift of humans' (*renlei de liwu*) (afterwards, this was called 'bad luck of humans' (*renlei de eyun*)" (Zhu *RK* Appendix: 6). Similarly, when in the *Silmarillion*, a passage refers to both death and "freedom" as gifts to human beings (*S*: 36), Yilin uses a kind of genetic language: "their natural nature (*tianxing*, heaven-given nature) of liking freedom" (Yilin *S*: 34), which Yilin also calls a "gift" (*kuizeng* 馈赠) and a "natural endowment" (*bingfu* 禀赋) (Yilin *S*: 35). Deng's earlier translation uses the phrase "natural endowment (*tianfu*, heaven endowed) of freedom" (Deng *S* 2002: 45) and "gift bestowed (*suoci de liwu*)" (Deng *S* 2002: 46); her later version cleans this up with the simpler "gift (*liwu*)" (Deng *S* 2015: 64). The notion of Ilúvatar giving a "gift" seems oddly trivializing, like saying, "a present from God." So, one change we see in the Chinese is a language more appropriate, the verb *ci*, equivalent to the English "bestow." But the other change derives from the way in which, in Chinese, what is natural is from *tian* (heaven, sky, hence nature), contrasted with *renzao* 人造, human-made. Hence the "gift" of God is a natural endowment, like hair color or differences in height.

Hints of Chinese soteriology appear also in the Yilin text, for example when a certain dwarf "returns to the West." Glóin says no dwarf has entered the long-abandoned Moria recently, "save Thror only, and he perished" (*FR* II, ii, 234). The Yilin has: "except for Thror, and already his one life has returned to the West (*yimingguixi* 一命归西)" (Yilin *FR*: 292). The other translations make no such hint of the Pure Land, but add a little each in their own ways: Deng says Thror "already was murdered (*yuhai*, encountered harm)" (Deng *FR*: 301). And Zhu says, "died in battle (*zhansi*)" (Zhu *FR*: 375). Dwarves are long-lived but ultimately just as mortal as humans and hobbits. The Elves apparently believe dwarves will return to the earth, but according to the dwarves' own lore, after death, their spirits may also go to the Halls of Mandos—and after that, to an unknown fate—but in any case, since they did not come from the West, this is no actual "return" (Sterling 1997:17).

Yet, this line about Thror is not the only hint of the Pure Land. Aragorn asks how dangerous the world would be "if the Dúnedain were asleep, or were all gone into the grave?" (*FR* II, vi, 242). Zhu translates "asleep" very closely, but moves to an idiom for death: "if all the Dúnedain people were in a deep sleep (*chenshui*), or changed into a piece of yellow earth (*huangtu*)" (Zhu *FR*: 388). By contrast, Deng translates the grave very directly, but moves away from sleep: "If Dúnedain people sat and watched without getting involved (*zuoshi buguan*), or all entered the grave (*fenmu*)" (Deng *FR*: 311). Most interestingly, Yilin has: "If the Dúnedain sat and watched without getting involved, or all returned to the Western heaven (*guixitian*)" (Yilin *FR*: 302).

In Chinese Buddhism, the verb *gui* 歸/归 (return) has the sense of to die. It can also mean, more simply, "return" as in "I went to the library and returned," although *hui* 回

is more common. But when combined with "the West" or "the Western heaven," it indicates a reference to the Pure Land of the Buddha Amitabha. One of the key developments of Mahayana Buddhism was the notion that we can create a karmic connection to Amitabha so that in our next life we are born in his presence, in his *jingtu* ("pure land"; from the Sanskrit *sukhavati,* "land of bliss"). Devotion to Amitabha is therefore particularly associated with the setting sun, being both in the West and a natural metaphor for the end of life.

Throughout *The Lord of the Rings,* as part of the "thinning" of magic in Middle Earth, the elves are indeed heading into the sunset, "returning to the West"—either by marching slowly to the Grey Havens to board ships, or by dying. True, Gimli, Bilbo, Frodo and Sam are allowed to set food on the Undying Lands while they are still in their mortal bodies, but these are exceptions, in which one suspects Tolkien of a *deus ex machina* tinkering at the end of his story—by all the logic, these four should not set foot in that land, but in a moment of sentiment the author bends the rules so his beloved mortals don't quite go the way of all flesh. Tolkien said that they still eventually die, when they feel ready (Sterling 1997: 18).

On the subject of death, we find a complex negotiation of meaning, where "returning to the West" has implications of the Buddha Amitabha as well as the Halls of Mandos, each with their distinct logic. A Chinese reader might well think of the Halls of Mandos as the Buddhist Pure Land, or some kind of modified Pure Land, but a Western reader might assume it to be a version of limbo or purgatory.

The rare inter-breeding of elves and humans produces a problem of hybridity, which Tolkien and the Valar resolve with the choice of the half-elven. Their choice determines which "kindred" they would be, and hence their post-mortem fate. Tolkien's thinking about elf-human offspring was inconsistent (Fimi 2009: 152–153). The best known elf-human is Elrond, who "was granted the same grace as to those of the High Elves that still lingered in Middle-earth: that when weary at last of the mortal lands they would take ship from the Grey havens and pass into the Uttermost West" (*RK* Appendix A,I, i, 1010). Deng: "he also received the same grace (*endian*) as those high elves still roaming (*changyang*) in Middle-earth: when they at last are weary of the place of the dusty world (*chenshi zhidi*), then they can take a boat from the grey harbor and leave, go towards the land of the extreme West" (Deng *RK*: 371). Deng makes the high elves "roam" or "stroll" in Middle-earth rather than "linger," a word translated more literally by Yilin and Zhu. In translating "the mortal lands," Deng gives us a slightly Buddhist-inflected phrase, "the dusty life (*chenshi,* world of dust)." No doubt "grace" had a particular resonance for Deng, as a Christian and as a translator given to reading these works with a Christian eye, but in fact all three translations use the same term, *endian* 恩典 (Zhu *RK* Appendix 5; Yilin *RK*: 359).

Gandalf's Death and Resurrection

In the category of unusual post-mortem fates, we should include the resurrection of Gandalf. He says he "has returned from death" (*TT* III, x, 569). Zhu, "died and was again born (*si er fusheng*" (Zhu *TT*: 272). Aragorn says that Gandalf "has passed through the fire and the abyss" (*TT* III, v, 490). Deng: "He has passed through blazing fire and deep pool (*shenyuan*)" (Deng *TT*: 119–120). Zhu: "He has passed through a trial of flame and deep pool" (Zhu *TT*: 151). This is Aragorn speaking in the third person about Gandalf who is physically present, so Yilin adjusts the pronouns: "You have passed through the trial of a sea of fire (*huohai*) and deep pool" (Yilin *TT*: 111). Despite Gandalf saying the deepest point was "the uttermost foundations of stone" (*TT* III, v, 490), all three have decided that the abyss is filled with water. The original says, he fell through fire and a very deep hole; the translations sustain the previous parallelism of fire and water (Also *TT* III, v, 490; Deng *TT*: 120; Yilin *TT*: 111; Zhu *TT*: 152). Gandalf says to Wormtongue that he had "passed through fire and death" (*TT* III, vi, 503; Deng *TT*: 138). Zhu adds that the flame and death were a test (Zhu *TT*: 171). But Yilin: "I went through hot water and fire (*futang daohuo*) nine deaths one life (*jiusi yisheng*, narrow escape from death)" (Yilin *TT*: 127). Here, we see the dominance of the four-character habit in Chinese: "fire" becomes a four-character phrase which includes hot water, and to "death" we add a notion of death stacked heavily against life. The *chengyu* phrase *jiusi yisheng* might also suggest how much death he had to endure until being reborn.

So, Gandalf finally kills the balrog, and enters a liminal state between life and death. "Then darkness took me, and I strayed out of thought and time, and I wandered far on roads that I will not tell" (*TT* III, v, 491). Deng: "Then, I fell into darkness. I drifted away (*youli*, roamed away) outside of thought (*shenzhi* 神志, consciousness, mind) and time, on many roads I cannot proclaim with my mouth (*xuanzhiyukou*) slowly roamed for a long time" (Deng *TT*: 121). Yilin: "Later the sky went dark and the earth went dark (*tianhun di-an*), I was also dazed (*hunhun chenchen*), not knowing what evening that evening was (*jinxi hexi*, not knowing what day it was). One road came out into the world (*yilu chuangdang*). As for what road, I cannot say" (Yilin *TT*: 112). Zhu: "Next, I lost consciousness, I wandered away (*youli*) from time and consciousness, and slowly wandered on a road I am not willing to mention" (Zhu *TT*: 153).

For "darkness took me" we have three distinct views: I fell into darkness, everything went dark, and I lost consciousness. The original phrasing evokes Gandalf's utter passivity as he lies exhausted and dying, and makes "darkness" into the agent, if only grammatically. Deng retains Gandalf's helplessness but darkness becomes a thing he falls into; her choice is closer to the original than Yilin's weather-report and Zhu's rather clinical psychology. "Out of thought" is not quite clear: Deng's use of *shenzhi* for "thought" has a strong sense of consciousness, mind, as does Zhu's version; Yilin interprets it as, "I was dazed (*hunhun chenchen*)," where the *hun* echoes the *hun* in the previous phrase "heaven went dark" (*tianhun*). The semantic meaning seems lessened, but there is an added poetic effect of connecting the darkness of the world with the darkness of the mind.

"Naked I was sent back—for a brief time, until my task is done" (*TT* III, v, 491). Gandalf avoids saying who sent him back, and Deng and Zhu likewise use the passive voice. It seems clear that being "sent back" means returning to the world of the living, to Middle-earth and the world's ongoing crisis. Deng: "I nakedly (*chiluoluo*) was chosen (*bei . . . xuan*) to come back—this time only to stay for a very short period of time, until my responsibility (*renwu*) is completed" (Deng *TT*: 121; similar at Zhu *TT*: 153). But the Yilin translator made the assumption that this returning is more physical: "The wind king (*fengwang*, i.e., Gwaihir the eagle) took my unclothed body (*yibuzheti*) to come back, that was a task [undertaken] a brief time after my mission (*shiming*) was completed" (Yilin *TT*: 112–113). The eagle *brings* him, whereas in the original he was *sent* by unknown forces. If the giant eagle can fly into the realm of death and back, it might indeed be considered more angelic. It's also clear the Yilin translator saw the "task" as completed (killing the balrog) rather than referring to the mission still ahead.

Dwindling away to the Undying Lands

Not only do we have an (almost) undying "race," we have the Undying Lands, also known as Aman and the Blessed Realm. What kind of a place is this? The name "Undying Lands" (*RK* Appendix A I, i, 1011) is apparently of human origin. It is not that the place grants immortality to those who live there, but that the undying elves have exclusive access to it. Humans, even the Númenorians, were banned from setting foot on this continent. When some misguided Númenorians tried to sail there, the Valar cut off access entirely. Deng and the Yilin translators use the plain phrase *busi zhidi*, the not-dying place (Deng *RK*: 372, Yilin *RK*: 359). But Zhu interprets the place in more positive terms: *haiwai xianjing*, the sylph-domain beyond the sea (Zhu *RK* Appendix: 6).

Aman is also called "the Blessed Realm" (*FR* II, i, 216), capitalized with its definite article. Deng: "blessed (*mengfu*) place" (Deng *FR*: 276). Yilin interprets the Blessed Realm as the kingdom of heaven, *tianguo* 天國 (Yilin *FR*: 270). *Tianguo* has an association specifically with Christianity as a translation of "kingdom of heaven," but also, historically, with the *Taiping tianguo*, the aspirational domain of the Taiping (Great Peace), one side of the massive civil war of 1850–1864. Consistent with previous choices, Zhu implies the elves are *xian*: "the sylph domain over the seas (*haiwai xianjing*)" (Zhu *FR*: 345). Where Yilin Christianizes Aman, Zhu places Aman in the camp of the loosely Daoist island of the immortals, Penglai.

Penglai is an almost-unreachable island on which immortal beings live. It is cited in the *Shanhaijing* (Classic of Mountains and Seas), a fantastic travelogue dating from the Han, though based on earlier versions as old as the fourth century BCE. Immortals live on five islands in the Eastern sea (Pacific): Fangzhang, Yingzhou, Daiyu, Yuanjiao, and the best-known, Penglai 蓬萊. The Eight Immortals (*baxian*) live there, a group of Daoists the most famous of which is their leader Lü Dongbin (9th century CE). Qin Shihuang, the famous "first emperor" of the short-lived Qin dynasty, obsessed with immortality, supposedly sent several expeditions to find Penglai, all of which failed. Penglai belongs to a larger tradition of hard-to-reach places of immortality or longevity, including the hidden land in Tao Qian's "Peach Blossom Spring," various Daoist grotto-heavens, the land of the Queen Mother of the West (*Xiwangmu*), and Shambhala. And one might add the Buddhist Pure Land, since one has to die in order to get there.

Frodo receives a vision of Aman, as the "curtain" is drawn and "a far green country opened before him under a swift sunrise" (*FR* I, viii, 132). It is like rain stopping on a bright Spring morning in rural England, Edenic rather than heavenly (Kelly and Livingstone 2009: 88). Deng: "the sun suddenly rose, an expanse (*pian*) of distant verdant (*qingcui*) plains-wild fields (*yuanye*) spread out before him" (Deng *FR*: 169). Yilin: "the rising sun rose in the East (*xuri dongsheng*), vast green wild fields opened out before him" (Yilin *FR*: 166). Zhu: "in a blink up came the sun shining down, before him was an expanse of open verdant (*qingcui*) plains-wild fields" (Zhu *FR*: 218). The "green country" in all of these translations becomes *ye* (open country, wild uncultivated lands) or *yuanye* (a relatively flat, uncultivated, open country like a meadow). *Yuanye* does not have the polysemy of "country" with its meanings of countryside but also nation, but in any case presumably Aman is verdant countryside rather than a nation.

Frodo has the opportunity to verify this vision. Approaching Aman, he smells a sweet fragrance and hears singing, "And then it seemed to him that as in his dream in the house of Bombadil, the grey rain-curtain turned all to silver glass and was rolled back, and he beheld white shores and beyond them a far green country under a swift sunrise" (*RK* VI, ix, 1007). He remembers and confirms his earlier vision. Deng's translation is straightforward and consistent with the earlier episode. Zhu adjusts his language without much consequence. But the Yilin edition changes things: "At this time, Frodo felt himself like he had returned to the house of Bombadil in a dream, a grey rain curtain made everything change into silver-colored glass, also rolled back. He saw a white sea-coast (*hai-an*), also saw under a slowly rising sun, beyond the sea-coast an expanse of green homeland (*retu*)" (Yilin *RK*: 354). Instead of remembering a dream he had in Bombadil's house, Frodo now feels as though he was dreaming of being there. For some reason the sunrise changes from swift to slow. And the land he sees is described as a homeland (*retu*). Perhaps for Frodo it is a new homeland, since he has become alienated from the Shire.

The elves, for whom the Undying Land is their natural home, are drawn to it but in a mesmeric and fatalistic way. Galadriel says that with Celeborn, "together through ages of the world we have fought the long defeat" (*FR* II, vii, 348). This poignant phrase expresses Tolkien's conservative nostalgia. In "On Fairy-stories," he defends fantasy from the charge of escapism by simply admitting it: such escape "may ... proceed from a considered disgust for so typical a product of the Robot Age, that combines elaboration and ingenuity of means with ugliness, and (often) with inferiority of result" (*OFS*: 70). The elven aristocracy show us the pinnacle of his desires, and then we learn their struggle to preserve their moral beauty is as futile as resisting the construction of train stations or street lights. What do the translations make of this phrase? Yilin's translation is complicated: "With him together stubbornly and forcefully resisted (*wanqiang kangzheng*), passed full long lofty/outstanding (*zhengrong*) years and months" (Yilin *FR*: 434–435). Here, the sense is: together we are obstinately fighting back, for many noble years. We've lost the notion of their migration to the West as a defeat; she could be talking about tenaciously resisting Sauron. Zhu's first translation has the underwhelming "together shoulder to shoulder (*yiqi bingjian*) resist this world's darkness" (Zhu *FR*: 2001 520), which he wisely changed to: "We together shoulder to shoulder fight this for-long-years all-lost fight (*shibai de zhang*)" (Zhu *FR*: 551). Or: "fought this many-year lost fight." I like the addition of shoulder-to-shoulder which when talking about wife and husband is more vivid than "together." Zhu also captures the futility of resistance. Deng comes much closer: "We together have spent (*duguo*, passed) every age of this world, resisted (*kangzheng*) without rest in the long defeat (*changjiu de shibai*)" (Deng *FR*: 446). The beauty of the phrase "fought the long defeat" is surely going to be hard to reproduce in translation. Yilin says, stubbornly resisted. Zhu says, fought a fight that has been lost. Deng gets close to the heart of it, but nonetheless has to say, resisted "in" the long defeat (*zai . . . zhong*). To actually *fight a defeat* (distinct from fighting and losing, or fighting without hope) eludes all three of the translations. Actually, it barely makes logical sense in the English! Certainly the struggle with Sauron is part of that, but ultimately their defeat is larger than Sauron—indeed, even with the happy ending of Sauron's final destruction, the elves have lost.

Even so, for the elves the defeat is a relocation, not an end to their lives. It is an end of the beautiful Lothlórien, which cannot be moved. Frodo threatens Lothlórien and the elven power in Middle-earth. Though the One Ring is evil, all the rings are connected to it. Galadriel says that if Frodo succeeds, "Lothlórien will fade, and the tides of Time will sweep it away" (*FR* II, vii, 356). Regarding "the tides of Time," Zhu gives the metaphor more force with a torrent or flood of history. Tolkien has the tides "sweep away" (like a broom?), whereas the translators see that tides "wash away."

"We must depart into the West, or dwindle to a rustic folk of dell and cave, slowly to forget and to be forgotten" (*FR* II, vii, 356). Yilin: "We would be unable not to leave our native place (*lixiang beijing*) and go to the West" (Yilin *FR*: 445). Yilin uses a folksy idiom for "depart," *lixiang beijing*, literally "leave the native country and turn our backs on the well." The original says they must "depart," and surely they think of Lothlórien as their home, and some of them were perhaps even born there, but still, the Undying Lands should represent their truly native place. Zhu turns "depart" into "flee (*dun*)" and Deng gives the closest match, with a simple "depart (*likai*)" (Zhu *FR*: 564; Deng *FR*: 456).

As for the other option, if they stay, they will "dwindle to a rustic folk of dell and cave." If they stay, they will be "rationalized" like the fairies of Victorian times, dwindling down to folklore and butterflies. They will even forget who they are (Magliocco 2018: 343). "This physical waning was Tolkien's solution to reconcile the modern ideas of slender ghostlike elves with the true nature of the Eldar. It would explain why Men of later days perceived them as mere phantoms of their former might, and invented stories of invisible elves, or elves so tiny that they could not be seen" (de Rosario Martínez 2010: 74; cf. Fimi 2009: 56–57). Surely Tolkien had in mind the fate of fairies who had been rationalized into "flower and butterfly" creatures. Pre-Christian magic and the "small gods" throughout the world were demonized or exorcised or trivialized by Christianity (Ostling 2018a: 9–13). The use of "rustic" suggests more than merely "in the countryside," but rather "unsophisticated," or at least perceived to be so by city folk. Yilin: "or decline (*lunluo*, also: become homeless) to be cave-dwelling barren mountains wild people (*xueju huangshan de yeren*)" (Yilin *FR*: 445). Zhu: "we will diminish (*tuihua*, regress) to become primitive people (*yuanshiren*) living in mountain caves or in valleys" (Zhu *FR*: 564). Deng: "otherwise we will diminish and become a primitive ethnic group (*yuanshi zuqun*) in mountain valleys and caves" (Deng *FR*: 456). Yilin gives the elves' hypothetical possibility more power—wild people of the barren mountains living in caves, more like the Drúedain or Wild Men who are already much diminished by the time Théoden asked for their help. Or like whoever the Púkel-Men were modeled on, already long gone by the time of Aragorn. Zhu anthropologizes the scenario—primitive people living in a valley; Deng increases the anthropological feeling by making the "people" (*ren*) into an ethnic group (*zuqun*). A vanished ethnic group: a grim image, given our history of colonial genocide.

We get a further elaboration of the fate of elves in modernity. After Galadriel is offered the Ring, she has her megalomaniac fantasy of godhood, but wisely decides not to take the Ring. Then, "Already she seemed to him, as by men of later days Elves still at times are seen: present and yet remote, a living vision of that which has already been left far behind by the flowing streams of Time" (*FR* II, viii, 364; Ostling 2018a: 13–15). "Later days" means the Fourth Age of Middle-earth (dominated by humans), but surely also means our own modern world. For a moment, Frodo witnesses Galadriel becoming visibly irrelevant. Deng: "He felt, she already seemed like the impression (*yinxiang*) of elves by later humans sometimes: close before one's eyes, yet also far on the horizon, a living vision already far left behind by time's long river" (Deng *FR*: 467). The phrase "close before one's eyes, yet also far on the horizon" (*jin zai yanqian, queyou yuan zai tianbian*) is a lovely rhyming parallel phrasing. "Present and yet remote" has brevity and plainness, but Deng manages a beautiful parallel phrase, and adds rhyme. Yilin goes for a similar parallelism, though not in rhyme:

> It is just like the kind of feeling later humans often have when seeing little elves, he felt she is very close (*jinzai zhichi*, close as *zhi* and *chi*, i.e., short measures of distance, "inches and feet"), yet also far away (*yuanzai tianya*, far as heaven's limit, or ends of the earth; i.e. the horizon). She had long since been carried away in the long river of time which flows without ceasing, yet also vividly lifelike (*xuxu rusheng*) still appeared before one's face. (Yilin *FR*: 455)

Both of these versions refer to the horizon, evoking the Undying Lands. Zhu's version of this passage contains nothing of note (Zhu *FR*: 576).

Conclusions

As with images of death, for the afterlife we find a blurring of mythologies, and occasionally some explicitly Buddhist and Daoist images: the Halls of Mandos and the Pure Land, the Undying Land and Penglai. Human mortality becomes refigured as less imposed but more inherent—a heaven-endowed human nature, rather than a "gift."

In Tolkien's world, as in biblical and Daoist texts, we find a common narrative of our present condition being the result of a descent or fall—from abstract to concrete, from immaterial to material. As part of this unstoppable fall from a sacred world to a scientific one, the elves are fading away—a cultural history retold as a migration myth, or perhaps a sanitized vision of ethnicities erased, no longer floating with us here, downstream in the long river of time.

One area of conceptual divergence is around the nature of souls, in Tolkien's vision and in the animism of popular Chinese religious culture. The afterlives are different, especially around rebirth and the moral logic of rebirth. The notion that a being as obviously sentient as an orc would not have a soul or an afterlife is inconsistent with

Buddhism which would see orc souls as less fortunate but qualitatively the same as elf souls—an orc might one day be reborn as an elf. Certainly we could imagine Wormtongue's next life as an orc. Beren might have been mum on the issue but Gandalf tells us something of the state between transmigrations. Humans have a special fate—reborn briefly in the Halls of Mandos but then moving to an unknown but greater fate beyond the world. But this unique trajectory now feels arbitrary, especially since elves bear some strong resemblance to *xian*. Imagining all the life-forms of Middle-earth as moments of transformation in the great wheel of samsara reduces the sense of each life-form having a separate fate.

10

Fate and Doom

"Fate," from Latin *fatum*, "that which has been spoken," is a quasi-legal judgment pronounced by the gods, which is therefore unchangeable. Still, if we know our fate, we might change our course—though if we can change our course, was it actually our fate? The gods can be in error, or change their minds, or be open to negotiation. The gods can speak obscurely. Fate is also seen as impersonal, like a natural law. Some related words imply a fixed path: destiny, karma, predestination, providence, lot; and some fate-adjacent words imply randomness: chance, luck, fortune, hap.

Tolkien used the ambiguities of fate, chance, and luck to preserve the dramatic functions of free will, especially to resist some terrible force or inevitable end (Shippey 2003: 150–154). It is a common narrative device, in Tolkien and elsewhere, to have characters or the narrator name some looming ruin as a matter of fate. *The Lord of the Rings* is full of pessimistic predictions, and yet in the end it turns out (mostly) fine. This is Tolkien's eucatastrophe: there is no way the heroes can escape death, and then right at the last moment they do. To achieve this effect, the pessimism has to counteract our default assumption that the heroes will survive. If the book's title was *The Tragedy of Frodo*, we might be more nervous as the last battle approaches, but otherwise our genre expectations suggest only minor, flawed, or evil characters will die. We know the *King* is going to *Return*, after all. Indeed, all the "bad guys" die, and on the "good" side we have Boromir, Théoden (admittedly, not minor characters) and a smattering of good guys we scarcely know (Théodred offstage, Isildur and Déagol long ago). And nameless hordes.

Making fate a character or plot device in the story requires similar deception. If we're told something is fated (inevitably going to happen) by a credible source or by the narrator, then it must happen, but not necessarily as expected. We accept the prophecies Macbeth receives from the conjured apparitions, since someone who knows how the story will end has put those words into their mouths. As it turns out, the apparitions' prophecies had an invisible asterisk, similar to the one at the end of Glorfindel's "not by the hand of man will he fall" (see Shippey 2003: 182; see also Bob-Waksberg 2010). Galadriel reveals the small print when she says of the visions in her mirror, "not all have yet come to pass. Some never come to be" (*FR* II, vii, 354).

Brian Attebery comments:

> Some of the devices Tolkien uses to turn a simple story into temporal counterpoint are available to the writer of realistic fiction. Yet, we are uncomfortable when a

primarily mimetic story calls too often upon coincidence, foreshadowing, oracular pronouncements, or repetition of patterns. We see the author's hand too plainly at work, the card up the sleeve. But when Tolkien and [Diana Wynne] Jones set up prophecies or parallel events, they do so within the context of a magical world, in which coincidence and correspondence have the force of natural law. (1992: 59)

Or, as Terry Pratchett remarked, "Million-to-one chances . . . crop up nine times out of ten" (Pratchett 1987: 218). Is fate unchangeable, or can it be negotiated with? Is it a divine command or a good guess? Is fate impersonal and pervasive, like gravity, or inherent and individual, like DNA? And how does all of this sound in Chinese?

Fate in Chinese

A starting point in the Chinese lexicon is the term *mingyun* 命運/命运 with its key parts, *ming* and *yun*. First, words involving *yun*. By itself, *yun* means to carry or transport, to use or operate, to move (as in *yundong*, "movement") or function, and also fortune and fate. We might think of the English phrase, "that's how it goes." *Yundao* 運道 (the way of *yun*) might be given literally and figuratively as "the way it goes." *Shiyun* 時運 ("fortune, luck") combines time or occasion (*shi*) with *yun*. "When the time comes, your *yun* will change" (*shilai yunzhuan* 時來運轉). *Yunqi* 運氣 gives the "movement" a kind of atmosphere (*qi*)—*yunqi* is the energy of how things go, usually translated as "luck." In addition to *zouyun* 走運 (to "make *yun* go," i.e. have good luck) one can also *jiaoyun* 交運 (make *yun* intersect—with oneself, for good effect). One's *yun* can be overturned (*daoyun* 倒運) which isn't good. One can even complain enviously about other people's dog-shit *yun* (*goushiyun* 狗屎運)—meaning their "dumb luck."

Where *yun* is basically about change, *ming* suggests destiny, command, lifespan, or lot. And often it has the more specific sense of one's allotted years. *Tianming* 天命, "the mandate or command of heaven," endorses the rule of emperors, but more broadly whatever has been ordained by "heaven" or the natural order. The notion of one's fated life-span being what is commanded fits well with the usage that something "is decided" (*zhuding* 注定) and "is decided within one's *ming*" (*mingzhong zhuding* 命中注定), abbreviated to *mingding* 命定. In the polysemy of "doom" we will see the same sense—a thing decided or commanded by the highest power is naturally an inevitable fact. Predestination is *mingli* 命理, the pattern or principle of *ming*. If your *ming* is big (*mingda* 命大)—that's good. If your *ming* returns to the Yellow Springs (*minggui huangquan* 命歸黃泉), you're dead—you've got "no more *ming*" (*meimingle* 沒命了). An expert in seeing your *ming* in the stars (*xingmingjia* 星命家)—astrologer—can "calculate your *ming*" (*suanming* 算命). Hopefully, you won't "die when it's not your *ming*" (*siyufeiming* 死於非命)—die before your time.

There are various words using *shu* 數, literally "number, amount." Fate can be *qishu* 氣數 (the number of *qi*, which has a wide range of meanings, probably here meaning vital breath), also *yunshu* 運數 and *mingshu* 命數. Along with *fen* 分 (portion), this usage seems to correlate to the English notion of "lot," or what has been allotted to you, especially in terms of lifespan. Fate is also *dingshu* 定數, fixed number. It is a common notion in Chinese religion that we all have a set lifespan, but sometimes it is ended before it should be—as when we say "died too soon," but perhaps invoking the Chinese storytelling tradition of people who find themselves in the first court of the underworld only to discover there was a clerical error. The notion of each species' lifespan being destined is common in Tolkien's works: "each race begins with a 'fixed quantity' of life, and if life is somehow extended beyond this the result is that the individual feels 'stretched,' as Bilbo complains" (Sterling 1997: 18).

Another term is *yuanfen* 緣分 and the similar term *yinyuan* 因緣. *Yuan* is used for predestined relationships; if two people "have *yuan*" (*youyuan* 有緣), it means they have probably met before, in a previous life, and so are destined to meet again. Karmic connection is a very useful plot device in traditional Chinese fiction. If you have marriage-*yuan* (*yinyuan* 姻緣) or emotion-*yuan* (*qingyuan* 情緣), you'll find your true love—even stronger would be a marriage-*yuan* from a past lifetime (*qianshi yinyuan* 前世姻緣). It's said that if you have *yuan*, you could be a thousand miles apart and you'll still meet; but if you don't have *yuan*, you could be facing each other and not meet. This term tends to refer to what is outside of our control in the complexities of interpersonal relationships, closely related to karma, about which more below.

Gandalf says, "fortune or fate have helped you" (*FR* II, i, 216). What's the difference? Perhaps: fortune is luck, whereas fate means it had to happen? The translations clearly support this interpretation, all agreeing on *yunqi* for fortune and *mingyun* for fate (Deng *FR*: 275; Yilin *FR*: 269; Zhu *FR*: 344). *Yunqi* implies a temporary state; you might hope for good *yunqi* as you sit down to play mah-jong. But *mingyun* is a more permanent fact about your life and your lifespan. However, "fortune" is sometimes treated as good luck, and sometimes as fate: in the *Unfinished Tales*, Annael says, "if our fortune is good" (*UT*: 18), which becomes: "If [we have] good luck (*xingyun*)" (Shi and Deng *UT*: 31); but elsewhere, Tuor notes that "fortune still favoured him" (*UT*: 19), which becomes "his own fate (*mingyun*) still cared for him" (Shi and Deng *UT*: 32). When the fortune is named as bad, such as, "What an evil fortune!" (*FR* II, v, 321), Yilin says *eyun* (bad luck) approaches, Deng has *yunqi* (luck) is bad, but Zhu invokes a more supernatural agency: "Could it be this is heaven's will (*tianming*)?" (Yilin *FR*: 402; Deng *FR*: 412; Zhu *FR*: 510). Compare the various luck-related renditions of Aragorn's, "Alas! An ill fate is on me this day" (*TT* III, i, 403). "Ai! Today my bad luck hits me head-on (*eyun dangtou*)" (Deng *TT*: 6). Yilin: "Old Heaven (*laotian*)! Today I have really inverse luck (*daoyun*)" (Yilin *TT*: 3). "Ought to die! (*gaisi*; "damn it") Luck (*yunqi*) today is really bad" (Zhu *TT*: 16).

By Whom is Fate Fated?

Tolkien wavers within the twilight between free will and a providential pattern (Whitt 2010: 115–116). One of the basic strategies is grammatical ambiguity, especially in the use of the passive voice to avoid actually naming the subject. These examples might refer to divine intervention (McBride 2020: 101) but are "deliberately vague and obscure" (Flieger 2009: 165). For example, Gandalf says to Frodo: "you have been chosen" (*FR* I, ii, 60). And the translators replicate this construction: Deng, "you were chosen (*xuanzhong*)." And Zhu's version is similar (Deng *FR* 75–76; Zhu *FR* 109). Yilin: "because chosen [were] you," *jiran xuanze le ni*—not exactly passive voice as such, but without specifying the subject (Yilin *FR*: 75).

In a famous line, Gandalf addresses the limits of the individual's power. Frodo laments the perilous times, and Gandalf agrees: "so do all who live to see such times. But that is not for them to decide. All we have to decide is what to do with the time that is given us" (*FR* I, ii, 50). The key phrase here is the time "that is given us," a passive construction which avoids the question of agency. Who gave us this time? Deng renders this line as: "All common people under heaven who happen to be present at the time (*shifeng qihui*) have this wish, but this does not go according to their deciding. What we must decide, is only what kind of response [we should] make to the time that we confront (*mianlin*, face)" (Deng *FR*: 63). Deng removes the question of "given," making the time (i.e., situation) simply something they are facing. Zhu has a similar solution: "what we decide is only how to use the precious time in our hands to prepare well" (Zhu *FR*: 94). From the various nuances of "given us" Yilin isolates the sense of limitation: "what we should do in the limited time" (Yilin *FR*: 62). The original text is evasive. The translations give us no more information but do not provoke the obvious question.

Gandalf comments on Bilbo acquiring the Ring: "Behind that there was something else at work, beyond any design of the Ring-maker. I can put it no plainer than by saying that Bilbo was *meant* to find the Ring, and *not* by its maker. In which case you also were *meant* to have it" (*FR* I, ii, 54–55). Again the passive voice—*who* meant it? To *mean* (intend, desire) is an attribute of sentience. I do think Gandalf could have put it plainer if he'd wanted to. This is a rare instance when the most literal translation is by Zhu. "Behind this is something in action which exceeds the power of the maker of the magic ring. I can only say, Bilbo was decided/fated (*zhuding* 注定) to get the *mo*-ring, and this was not the maker of the ring's idea; in the same way, you were also decided (*zhuding*) to possess the *mo*-ring" (Zhu *FR*: 100). We have the same "something" and the same passive voice. But Deng is slightly more explicit than the original. "Behind that, there was still a certain kind of power (*liliang*) working, overriding (*lingjia*) the magic ring's maker's plan. I could say it no more clearly, Bilbo was **decided** (*zhuding*) to find this magic ring, and furthermore this **is not** the magic ring's maker's idea. According to this analogy, you were also **decided** (*zhuding*) to get it" (Deng *FR*: 69). We still have the passive voice, but in place of "something else," we have a "certain kind of power"; *liliang* is used to translate lines such as "there are many powers in this world" (*FR* II, i, 214; Deng *FR* 273). Even the verb "overriding" gives that power more agency than the indirect "beyond any design." For "meant to," Yilin gives "decided within fate (*mingzhong zhuding*)," a passive construction, and for "something else at work," gives us *zuosui* 作祟 (to haunt, to have an evil influence), a considerable increase in malevolent intention over the neutral "at work" (Yilin *FR*: 68). It increases the sense of danger to think that an evil power has chosen Frodo, rather than Ilúvatar.

Along with "meant" we also have "ordained" and "appointed," but still without a subject. Aragorn to Frodo: "but it has been ordained that you should hold it for a while" (*FR* II, ii, 240). Instead of the passive voice, Yilin adds a subject, "But now fate (*mingyun*) has decided temporarily that it is yours to take care of" (Yilin *FR*: 300). Zhu also supplies a subject, less abstract: "The prediction (*yuyan*) already said, you should continue to hold it" (Zhu *FR*: 385). Deng indicates that the subject of "ordained" is unspecified members of the Council of Elrond (presumably): "But we have decided" (Deng *FR*: 309). As mentioned in Chapter 2, the passive voice is possible in Chinese but is used much less than in English. Here, is a case where all three translations turn passive to active.

In addition to the passive voice, another way to avoid naming the supernatural agent is simply to omit it, especially in phrases where the omission is already idiomatic. In English, the phrase "bless you" frequently omits the subject of the verb (God), so that when Gandalf says, "Well, well, bless my beard!" (*FR* I, ii, 62), we might wonder who he is asking to do this. In the Chinese, we get some ideas. Deng specifies: "Heaven protect my beard!" (*tianyou wuxu*) (Deng *FR*: 78). Yilin and Zhu approach the utterance non-literally, but with widely varied interpretations: "scoundrel thing! (*hunzhang dongxi*)" (indicating Sam) (Yilin *FR*: 77), and, "Luck is really not bad!" (Zhu *FR*: 111). Deng's use of *tian* (heaven) sounds somewhat theological, yet we understand it as a mere rhetorical flourish, not a fragment of liturgy. Sam uses the same verb, preceded by "Lor," presumably a dialect word for Lord, i.e. God; the abbreviation and dialect seem to soften the theology. "Lor bless you" and "Lor bless me" (*FR* I, ii, 62). All three translations use "old heaven" (*laotian*) which can also mean "God" in a general or casual way (Deng *FR*: 78; Yilin *FR*: 77; Zhu *FR*: 112). On another occasion, when Sam says, "But bless you!" (*FR* I, v, 103), Deng again uses "old heaven" (Deng *FR*: 132), and Zhu uses *shangtian* (heaven above) (Zhu *FR* 175), but Yilin goes abruptly more theological, using the most common word for (a loosely Christian) God: "I ask *shangdi* to protect you!" (Yilin *FR* 131). The same tendency to supply the missing subject (God) of the verb in idioms appears in some parts of Ledoux's French translation (Ferré et al 2011: 55; see also Turner 2006: 175).

When the idioms are more obscure, the translations become more mixed. One of the trolls says "Blimey" (*H*, ii, 39, 41). This oath is an abbreviation of "God blind (or blame) me!" or "May God blind (or blame) me if I (do something bad or speak a lie)." Yilin invokes a supernatural power in a general way: "heaven (*tian-a*)!" and "*Ai-ya! Tian-a!*" (Yilin *H*: 31, 33). Zhu: "Mother! (*Maya*)" (Zhu *H*: 44, 45). Wu: "grandma (*nainaide*)" and then *tian-a* (Wu *H*: 50, 53). Interestingly, Wu uses "mother" (*mamade*) to translate "What the 'ell" in the same exchange (*H*, ii, 39; Wu *H*: 50). One troll asks another to identify Bilbo, and the troll says, "Lumme, if I know!" (*H*, ii, 41), i.e. God love me if I know. Wu: "*ai-ya-ya* 哎呀呀, I couldn't know him!" (Wu *H*: 53). *Ai-ya-ya* is just as it sounds, an elaborated form of *ai*, an expression of surprise. Zhu reads it as "*Bendan*! How would I know?" *Bendan* is stupid egg, stupid "bastard" or just "idiot" (Zhu *H*: 45). Yilin, even less meaningfully, just uses an interjection of surprise: "Hai 嗨!" (Yilin *H*: 33). Here, the supernatural agency implied by these expressions is either made more explicit or ignored entirely.

Karma

One kind of "unpersonal governing force that predetermines events" (Fornet-Ponse 2010: 84) well known to Chinese readers is karma. It is particularly associated with Buddhism but also spread beyond Buddhism into popular religion and general ways of thinking. Moving from Sanskrit to Chinese, karma was translated as either *ye* 業 (action, work) or *yinguo* 因果, cause and effect. A related term is *yebao* 業報, karmic reward or retribution. Boromir admits to trying to seize the Ring, and thus, "I am sorry. I have paid"—presumably for that moral failing (*TT* III, i, 404). The translations vary here. Deng makes the phrase as much an accounting as the original, if anything emphasizing the economic analogy: "I have paid the price for this (*wo weici fuchu daijia*)" (Deng *TT*: 6). Yilin and Zhu place the payment in more karmic terms: "[it is] retribution (*baoying* 報应)" (Yilin *TT*: 4). And "my crime has its retribution (karmic response, just deserts) (*wozui you yingde* 應得)!" (Zhu *TT*: 16).

The idea of karma shows up explicitly. Frodo says it's a "pity" that Bilbo did not kill Gollum, and Gandalf says that the pity in Bilbo's heart stayed his hand. "And he has been well rewarded, Frodo" (*FR* I, ii, 58). Frodo meant "it's a pity" only idiomatically—"I regret that ..."—whereas Gandalf takes "pity" literally, similar to the exchange with Bilbo over the meaning of "good morning" in *The Hobbit* (*H*, i, 6–7). Gandalf's point is that the virtue of mercy in Bilbo was a protection from the evil in the Ring. Yilin gives this as: "Bilbo's good has a good reward (*shan you shanbao*)" (Yilin *FR*: 72). Here is explicit use of karma, in its basic and popular form of *shan you shanbao*. The phrase is sometimes combined with its logical partner, *e you ebao* (evil has an evil reward). This is a saying (though not quite a *chengyu*) of popular morality, derived from but no longer exclusive to Buddhism. The original contains the gist of it, "he has been well rewarded," the passive voice avoiding any specific agency, although "reward" seems to imply an outside agent. Zhu does not supply the full phrase, but nonetheless uses *shanbao*: "this gave him a good reward (*shanbao*)" (Zhu *FR*: 106). Deng's "And he got ample reward (*huibao*)" (Deng *FR*: 73) is similar, with the *hui* 回 of *huibao* 回報 meaning "return"—as in his goodness returning to him. Yilin's translation puts the agency most firmly in the realm of karma rather than any divine reward. I suspect Chinese readers, seeing the word *bao* (reward), think first of karma rather than divine action.

It's worth staying with this conversation for its elaboration of fate. Apparently none the wiser from Gandalf's rebuke, Frodo says, "He deserves death" (*FR* I, ii, 58). All three translations resort to idioms. Deng gives us, "He should die (*gaisi*)" (Deng *FR*: 73). Though this back-translation sounds very close to the original, *gaisi* has a somewhat richer resonance in Chinese, often used for hostile emphasis in the way that we say "damned" or "bloody" (or stronger words). I will say more about *gaisi* in Chapter 12. In English "he deserves death" is not particularly idiomatic, distinct from its simple meaning. Hence in the Chinese, there is less of a sense that Frodo is really asserting a specific judgment, and more that he is just saying "curse him." Still, Gandalf taking literally the merely idiomatic *gaisi* fits with his pattern of taking idioms literally, also seen in "pity" and "good morning."

For Frodo's, "He deserves death," Yilin gives us a significant expansion of *gaisi*: "Guilty so [he] should die ten thousand times (*zuigai wansi*)" (Yilin *FR*: 73). A bit of hyperbole, fairly typical of the use of the number ten thousand (*wan*) in Chinese. Yet this harsher phrase is still basically idiomatic or rhetorical. Taken literally, it makes Frodo more demented and sadistic, so it makes more sense that (the Chinese) Gandalf upbraids him on the literal meaning of his words. Zhu takes the line in a totally different direction: "His being killed is a punishment that fits the crime (*zuiyou yingde*)." Literally, "the crime or sin has a response" (Zhu *FR*: 106). His death would be a case of his sins having a (natural, morally balanced) response—again an implication of karma.

Chance

In English, chance isn't quite the same as luck or fate. Chance contains the idea of coincidence and randomness. It is closer to probability than magic. Chance comes from Latin, cognate of "cadence" (in the sense of what "falls" or befalls one); the *OED*'s first listing starts with "the falling out or happening of events." Perhaps it arose from the observation that when things fall, you can't always predict where they will land, and it must surely be related to sortilege—divination by dropping things.

I cannot forebear to note first a rather picturesque set phrase related to chance. Gelmir says, "And think not that our meeting was by chance" (*UT*: 22). "Don't consider we are [clumps of] duckweed in a river meeting each other (*pingshui xiangfeng* 萍水相逢, i.e., strangers meeting by chance)" (Shi and Deng *UT*: 36). Gandalf uses the same idiom in reference to running into Thorin in Bree (*UT*: 326; Shi and Deng *UT*: 424).

However, the key word in translations of chance is *qiao* 巧, which covers a range of meanings including ingenious, deft, cunning, coincidental, and just in time. It is found in the translations, in various combinations. In translating "was it just chance that brought you"? (*FR* I, vii, 123), Yilin has, "was it chance (*zhengqiao* 正巧)" (Yilin *FR*: 155). *Zheng* can mean many things, the relevant sense here is rightness or exactness. Zhu: "chance meeting (*qiaohe* 巧合)" (Zhu *FR*: 205). Deng: "Or was it only chance (*pengqiao* 碰巧) that we met that time?" (Deng *FR*: 158). *Peng* means to bump into; the image of chance as "bumping into" something. Of Túrin and Melian, we read, "often she met him there, as it were by chance" (*UT*: 76). "She often met (*yudao*) him there, as if only by chance (*pengqiao*)" (Shi and Deng *UT*: 101). In the original, "met" can mean by chance or by arrangement; the Chinese *yudao* implies ran into. Sam agrees with Frodo that the road ahead of them is grim, but "We must take it and chance our luck, if there is any luck in Mordor" (*RK* VI, ii, 907). Yilin: "We must go from there, take a chance (*pengpeng yunqi*, bump-bump into luck), if luck can be bumped into in Mordor" (Yilin *RK* 224). Deng uses the same idiom (Deng *RK*: 230). It is a natural metaphor. Perhaps the most commonly experienced form of accident is the bump. Zhu comes at it in another way: "We must gamble luck (*duyidu yunqi*), and hope this thing luck is still effective (*guanyong*) in Mordor" (Zhu *RK*: 285).

When Elrond explains that the Ring has emerged and must be dealt with, we see the term *qiao* and the use of the passive voice. He makes explicit his rejection of pure chance without ever naming another explanation. Their fortuitous gathering is more than merely coincidental:

> "That is the purpose for which you are called hither. Called, I say, though I have not called you to me, strangers from distant lands. You have come and are here met, in this very nick of time, by chance as it may seem. Yet it is not so. Believe rather that it is so ordered that we, who sit here, and none others, must now find counsel for the peril of the world." (*FR* II, ii, 236; see McBride 2020: 104)

Here, Elrond implies some higher plan to their various paths, but he does not say whose plan it is—if it is not "by chance," then someone must have "ordered" precisely this line-up at this moment. Through the use of the passive voice, Elrond avoids any attribution of agency.

Deng renders this as,

> You were called (*bei zhaohuan*) here, for precisely this matter. I say 'were called' but you strangers (*moshengren*) from distant lands, I did not call you. You have come, meeting at this time and this moment, it looks like coming together by chance (*couqiao*), really it is not so. We should rather believe, this *xi* [a count noun for things tied together or coming together] of fate (*mingyun*)'s arranging: we in these seats, and not other people, must now find a method to respond to the crisis this world faces. (Deng *FR*: 303).

Though Deng (like Zhu) begins by reproducing the passive voice, she names the agent as "fate (*mingyun*)." For "by chance," Deng uses *couqiao* (*cou* = gather). Yilin and Zhu use the similar phrase *qiaohe*, chance meeting (Yilin *FR*: 293; Zhu *FR*: 377). Zhu however uses *yinyuan* 因緣, a term laden with Buddhist meaning: causal predestination or past-life connections. "Meeting according to (karmic) causes (*yinyuan jihui*), you came here at the critical moment (*guanjian shike*, door-key or door-bolt moment; hinge or crux)" (Zhu *FR*: 377). The implication is that something deep in the past lives of those assembled bound them together even from before they were born, and this "cause" (*yin* 因) is now manifesting its "fruit" (*guo* 果) according to the workings of karma (*yinguo* 因果).

Yilin also attributes supernatural agency: "I consider it is more like the calling of the will of heaven (*tianming de zhaoji*)" (Yilin *FR*: 293). Certainly, *tian* (heavens, sky, natural order) can be used in the sense of fate, but *tianming* has specific political meanings: typically, "heaven" determines who should be emperor. Zhu also uses the term *tianming*, saying that they are "receiving what the will of heaven has commissioned/ entrusted (*shou tianming suotuo*)" (Zhu *FR* 378). Whoever Elrond is being coy about in English is named in Chinese as "fate" (*mingyun*) by Deng, and heaven's will (*tianming*) by the other two. In this context, Deng seems to be closer to Elrond's evasion: whatever "fate" is, it means they gathered there not by Elrond's or any of their own intentions. Fate is grammatically an external force, yet one's fate is also innate. With Yilin and Zhu, however, we inch closer to an external force, even if it is "heaven," not a specific god but rather a diffuse and collective will. We see a pattern of naming what is avoided in passive voice constructions, though the newly named agent may range from abstract to specific, from impersonal karma to God's orders.

Doom

"Doom" is one of the most difficult words to translate, due to its range of meanings and its ambiguity. From its earliest uses in the tenth century, the word "doom" meant legal judgment by a ruler, probably involving a bad sentence. Or it was used as a general term for laws. But by the fifteenth century, usage had developed to include more abstract senses of fate and destiny, as if the legal judgment was now imputed to the universe or fate or God. Doom was something decided about you, which could not easily be appealed. And since we are mortal, we are all under a death sentence. Hence, doom came to mean inevitable ruin, ultimate destruction. It was sometimes applied to the final judgment day predicted in the Bible (see Whitt 2010: 116–118).

The meanings follow a clear sequence, but range over several distinct concepts. Very often, writes Shippey, "the reader cannot make a clear decision as to the word's meaning" (2003: 255). The translators have to judge in each particular case whether they will give it the sense of judgment, inevitable ruin, the "last days," fate, or bad luck. Chinese does not have a term which matches the same semantic spectrum as "doom," and the translations are therefore obliged to be more precise and explicit. If we were to reverse the order—to imagine that Tolkien's text was the translation of any one of the Chinese texts (or a digest of the three)—then we would see "doom" as a loss. Here are several distinct things in the "original" Chinese, which are now rendered in English as only one word. English would seem to have an impoverished lexicon.

Doom as Judgment

The oldest sense of doom as judgment is well represented in the texts. The court case of Túrin's semi-accidental killing of Saeros features multiple uses of the word, all very clearly related to judicial utterances. For example, his elf friends tell him to let the king judge, but instead he says, "I will go now where his doom cannot find me" (*UT*: 82). "Now I will go to a place his judgement jurisdiction (*panjue guanxia*) does not reach" (Shi and Deng *UT*: 108). *The Silmarillion* refers to a divine court of judgment called the "Ring of Doom" (*S*: 49). Where Deng gives two variants of the literal concept: *panjue quan*, a circle/group of judgment, and *shenpan zhi huan*, ring of trial (Deng *S* 2002: 63; Deng *S* 2015: 76), Yilin gives the distinctly bureaucratic *huanxing yishi tai*, ring-shaped platform of discussing official business (Yilin *S*: 46).

These are all closely tied to the oldest sense of the word, the utterance of a judicial decision. But in some cases, the speech-act is merged with the effect it brings about, namely the state of being under judgment, and the punishment. Faramir, for example, speaking formally in his capacity as son of the Steward of Gondor, says he will consider the situation with Frodo, Sam, and Gollum. "Then I will declare my doom" (*TT* IV, vi, 675). Here, doom is *panjue* (judgment) (Zhu *TT*: 433, Deng *TT*: 366), and a near synonym *jueding* (decision) (Yilin *TT*: 339). Part of his decision is a provisional death sentence on Gollum, should he betray Frodo. In this case the judgment is considered not only an utterance but a sentence. He says, "This doom shall stand for a year and a day" (*TT* IV, vi, 675). Here, Deng is consistent, with *panjue* (Deng *TT*: 367); Zhu goes with *mingling* (order) (Zhu *TT*: 434); and Yilin is a little more bureaucratic with *guiding* 规定, rule, stipulation, regulation (Yilin *TT*: 339). Faramir says to Gollum, "You are under doom of death," and if you betray Frodo, "the doom shall fall" (*TT* IV, vi, 675). For the latter idiom, Yilin explains, "then [you] can't not die (*feisi buke*)" (Yilin *TT*: 340). Zhu has Faramir invoke his extended authority: "Any person can immediately put you to death (*zhusha*)" (Zhu *TT*: 434). And Deng gives it the most legal sound: "The death-guilt judgement (*sizui panjue*) will go into effect (*shengxiao*)" (Deng *TT*: 367).

The frayed edge of the semantics of "doom" becomes visible in the translations. King Aragorn judges Beregond. "Now therefore I must pronounce your doom" (*RK* VI, v, 947). This is clearly a judicial pronouncement, but interpreted in several ways. Zhu has the juridical "pronounce the judgement (*panjue*)" (Zhu *RK*: 344). But, using the overlap of doom and fate, Deng has "pronounce your fate (*mingyun*)" (Deng *RK*: 284), while Yilin combines the senses of doom as judgment and as end: "your sentence to death (*sixing*)" (Yilin *RK*: 275). Similarly, the pronouncement and the execution are blurred when Boromir asks Gandalf, regarding Gollum, "To what doom did you put him?" (*FR* II, ii, 248). Does this mean judgment, sentence, or punishment? Two translations make the decision: Deng and Zhu both ask, "How did you punish him?" (Zhu *FR*: 398; Deng *FR*: 319), whereas Yilin settles for a bland, "How did he end up?" (Yilin *FR*: 310).

Doom as Fate

The word "doom" is often interpreted in the translations as related to fate (*mingyun* or similar terms). Doom as a verb is usually in the passive voice: to be doomed is to be fated, for example with "the journey of Boromir was doomed" (*TT* IV, v, 655–656; Deng *TT*: 341; Zhu *TT*: 403; Yilin *TT*: 316). "Yet she was doomed to wait upon an old man" (*RK* V, viii, 849; Deng *RK*: 154; Yilin *RK*: 150; Zhu *RK*: 198). When Mandos says, "So it is doomed" (*S*: 49–50), Yilin has, "It is decided like this (*jiu zheyang jueding leba*)" (Yilin *S*: 47). Deng's earlier version is almost the same (Deng *S* 2002: 64), but her later translation supplies a subject: "fate (or, the order) is like this (*mingdang ruci*)" (Deng *S* 2015: 77).

There are relatively few uses of "doom" as a transitive verb. Pippin is horrified "when he heard Gandalf reject the terms and doom Frodo to the torment of the Tower" (*RK* V, x, 873). Gandalf *dooms Frodo*. However, the translations are mixed on this point: Yilin and Deng retain Gandalf as the cause of Frodo's torture: "Pippin heard Gandalf refuse the terms, making Frodo fated (*zhuding*) to receive the evil black tower's torment" (Deng *RK*: 185; almost identical at Yilin *RK*: 180). But Zhu distances Gandalf with a euphemistic passive voice: "Frodo was fated (*mingding*) to forever endure a painful time in the black tower" (Zhu *RK*: 234).

In many cases, "doom" as "fate" is a noun. Close variants include *mingzhong zhuding*, *zhuding*, *mingzhong jueding*, *mingding*, and *suming*. While doom-as-fate can be an impersonal force, it can be attached to or belong to a person—*my* fate. Frodo says, "It's my doom, I think, to go to that Shadow yonder" (*TT* IV, i, 590). Deng gives this as "my fate (*ming*) decides (*zhuding*) [me] to go . . ." (Deng *TT*: 254, similar at Yilin *TT*: 234, Zhu *TT*: 302). There are many similar cases, reading doom as fate and preserving the possessive. Théoden to Aragorn: "It is your doom, maybe, to tread strange paths" (*RK* V, ii, 762); all read it as "your fate" (Yilin *RK*: 43; Zhu *RK*: 66; Deng *RK*: 45).

Arwen says of Lúthien, "Yet her name is not mine. Though maybe my doom will be not unlike hers" (*RK* Appendix A, I, v, 1033). Here we have my doom, her doom. Deng uses a similar double-negative: "my fate (*mingyun*) may not necessarily be unlike hers"

(Deng *RK*: 404). But the others stumble on Arwen's grammar. Yilin simplifies the thought: "my fate (*mingyun*) might be the same as hers" (Yilin *RK*: 390). And Zhu gets it wrong: "my fate (*mingyun*) might be different to hers" (Zhu *RK* Appendix: 37). Though this is an error, it is interesting to think of Arwen resisting the obvious analogy to Lúthien, the lens through which everyone is viewing her situation.

Denethor petulantly cries, "But if doom denies this to me, then I will have *naught*" (*RK* V, vii, 836). All translators take this "doom" as "fate" (*mingyun*, *mingzhong zhuding*, or *suming*). Deng and Yilin read the second half of his utterance straightforwardly, but Zhu adds a striking idiom: "If fate (*mingyun*) does not allow me to do this, then I can only burn jade and stone together (*yushi jufen*, i.e. destruction of good and bad alike)" (Zhu *RK*: 180; cf. Deng *RK*: 138; Yilin *RK*: 136). (If this idiom seems strange, consider its equivalent, "throwing the baby out with the bathwater"!) In a testy exchange with Gandalf, Denethor reveals the "Stone" (i.e., the palantir) which was glowing "with an inner flame, so that the lean face of the Lord was lit as with a red fire" (*RK* V, vii, 835). Then he sets light to himself, and as he burns he clasps the Stone. It would be hard to say that Denethor represents the jade here, and the palantir is not actually destroyed, yet Zhu's idiom prefigures the flames that engulf them.

Doom as Bad Luck

You generally don't read that anyone was doomed to a happy ending. Hence a natural reading of doom is bad luck (*eyun*). For example, things are depressing in Edoras: "Doom hung over them" (*RK* V, iii, 785). Yilin: "bad luck approached (*eyun lintou*)" (Yilin *RK*: 71). Deng: "bad luck hung above their heads" (Deng *RK*: 73). Zhu's reading differs: "They knew clearly that they themselves would encounter the last day (*mori*)" (Zhu *RK*: 101). Or later, "right in their path stood a single mighty stone like a finger of doom" (*RK* V, ii, 768). Deng elaborates the simile, with "like a finger symbolizing bad luck (*xiangzheng eyun*)" (Deng *RK*: 53). And Yilin adds the magic/demonic preface: "like a bad luck *mo*-finger (*eyun de mozhi*)" (Yilin *RK*: 51). Zhu makes the stone far more threatening: "like a death-god's finger (*sishen de shouzhi*)" (Zhu *RK*: 77).

A variation on the theme of doom as fate and bad luck is the use of the word "star" (*xing*). Gandalf says of the witch-king. "hidden from the Wise is the doom that awaits him" (*RK* V, iv, 801). Here, his fated death is given an astrological certainty. Zhu: "his overcoming star (*kexing*, jinx, bane) is a riddle even the wise can't know" (Zhu *RK*: 126). Though Yilin takes "hidden from the Wise" to mean the witch-king *is actually hiding from* the Wise, the fateful star is there: "only the wise ones he does his utmost to avoid await his death-door-star (*sangmenxing*, star of losing or dying)" (Yilin *RK*: 91). Deng reads doom here as fate (*mingyun*) (Deng *RK*: 93).

Doom as the End/Last Days

Galadriel says to Frodo, "Do you not see now wherefore your coming is to us as the footstep of Doom?" (*FR* II, vii, 356). Capital-d Doom, a proper noun. One might consider what Frodo brings as a kind of judgment or unavoidable fate, but the meaning of ruin is foremost. All three translations focus on this aspect. Yilin: "disaster we can't avoid (*zaijie nantao*)" (Yilin *FR*: 445). Zhu: "like the last days are approaching" (Zhu *FR*: 564). Deng keeps the footstep in there: "the sound of footsteps of the last days (*mori de zuyin*)" (Deng *FR*: 456). In some cases, the word is unambiguous: "The Lord of the Ringwraiths had met his doom" (*RK* VI, ii, 898). Zhu: "has been destroyed" (Zhu *RK*: 272). Deng: "run into his disaster-fate (*jieshu* 劫数, disaster-lot)" (Deng *RK*: 219). Yilin: "encountered his death-door-star (*sangmenxing*)" (Yilin *RK*: 213).

The sense of doom as inevitable end is also foremost in the ents' marching song. Perhaps they mean to pass judgment on Saruman or consider their march in accordance with the workings of the universe, but mainly they want to destroy Isengard. "To Isengard with doom we come!" (*TT* III, iv, 474). Deng: "Our goal is Isengard, we bring the final ending (*zuihou de jieju*)!" (Deng *TT*: 99). Zhu: "Isengard's last days are before our eyes!" (Zhu *TT*: 126). But Yilin takes it all in a different direction: "Approaching Isengard, we stick out our chests (*tingqi xiongtang*)! Facing death, we stick out our chests!" (Yilin *TT*: 92). The doom is now simply death; but instead of bringing death to Saruman, here their own death is something to be faced proudly.

"Doom" appears in one of the most critical texts of the story, Boromir's dream-prophecy. He hears a voice, telling him to go to Imladris to find Aragorn's sword, counsel, and the Ring. "There shall be shown a token / That Doom is near at hand" (*FR* II, ii, 240). In context, "Doom" might not mean inevitable end, for the rest of the verse is somewhat optimistic, relating to restored kingship and powerful counsel, though also to the Ring waking. It might mean, ruin is close, but we can avoid it. It might also mean, a judgment will soon be made, or the manifestation of some fated event. Zhu: "At that place a matter must manifest (*jixian*, traces appear), / The last days will approach without doubt" (Zhu *FR*: 384). Consistent with his frequent usage, Zhu reads doom as last days. But Deng and Yilin read it as misfortune. "the fated end (*mingshu jieju*) is in the fingers' grasp" (Deng *FR*: 308). Here, Deng adds a footnote specifically on her translation of "Doom": "It can refer to fortune (*mingshu*) or to bad luck (*eyun*), it is a double meaning" (Deng *FR*: 308). Yilin: "bad luck (*eyun*) is before our eyes" (Yilin *FR*: 299).

As often happens in Tolkien's works, characters in the story interrogate the story itself. Regarding this line about Doom, there is an exchange between Boromir and Aragorn. Boromir asks, "Is then the doom of Minas Tirith come at last?" (*FR* II, ii, 241). Deng and Yilin have him ask if Minas Tirith's *bad luck* has come, whereas Zhu asks if the city's *last days* have come (Deng *FR*: 309; Yilin *FR*: 300; Zhu *FR*: 386). Since he is naturally obsessed with Gondor, Boromir assumes the prophecy refers to Minas Tirith. Perhaps Boromir merely follows his father's Gondorcentric assumptions, as when Denethor speaks of signs of the impending "doom of Gondor" (*RK* V, i, 738). "Gondor will encounter calamity (*jienan*)" (Yilin *RK*: 12). "Gondor's last days approaching" (Zhu *RK*: 30). "Gondor's great trouble (*dajie*) approaching" (Deng *RK*: 15). But Aragorn challenges this idea: "The words were not *the doom of Minas Tirith* ... But doom and great deeds are indeed at hand" (*FR* II, ii, 241). An odd combination—great deeds and doom—judgment? Inevitable ruin? The three translations each remain consistent with the previous usages: bad luck (Deng *FR*: 309–310; Yilin *FR*: 300) and last days (Zhu *FR*: 386).

Perhaps the most famous use of the word is the name of the great volcano in Mordor, Mount Doom (e.g., *FR* II, ii, 239), given as "last-days mountain" (*morishan*) in Deng and Zhu (Deng *FR*: 307; Zhu *FR*: 383), and "bad luck mountain" (*eyunshan*) in Yilin (Yilin *FR*: 298; see Hooker 2003: 251–253 on Russian translations of Mount Doom). Similarly, the Cracks of Doom (*FR* I, ii, 59; Deng *FR*: 75; Zhu *FR*: 108; Yilin *FR*: 75) and Gulf of Doom (*TT* IV, v, 666; Yilin *TT*: 329; Zhu *TT*: 420; Deng *TT*: 355). Why *morishan* rather than *eyunshan*, I asked Deng:

> Because it decides the fate of the elves, humans, hobbits. If they fail, if Frodo fails, that's everybody's last days. Also, the term *morishan* is from Zhu Xueheng's edition, he used it. So when I was doing the translation, what we thought about was, when it's possible for us not to change the terminology that everyone is used to, we didn't change it. Of course we also had to consider when translating a name, its textual context (*shangxiawen*, text above and below), namely, a sentence and this [name] inserted into it, and how it is changed into Chinese so that it has meaning, or how you can express the meaning more—then we can make a choice. (2017)

Conclusions

Doom in translation wavers among various meanings, and the translators read the word in different ways. In theory, any word can be subject to the same splitting of hairs, but "doom" is particularly potent, blurring the idea that whatever happens to the characters has been somehow *decided*, and also is probably going to be bad. We find different concepts of what is beyond our control, and how even so we can influence or negotiate with the inevitable future. There are overlaps of meaning, such as a decision made which cannot be appealed, or more broadly: that some things are said to be destined yet in fact turn out differently. There is a tension of pessimistic fatalism and the sudden irruptions of free will, and occupying a middle ground is luck. We also see the shared view of chance as not in fact truly random. To the pervasive passive voice for fated and doomed, the translations frequently add a subject, occasionally something specific such as *Shangdi* or a prediction or the Council, but more often relatively abstract agents such as heaven or fate. The basic feeling of fate is fairly consistent however, that in this fictional world, coincidence is rarely mere coincidence, and there is no such thing as an accident.

The semantic spectrum of "doom," and the narrative tricks of fate, are available in English as in Chinese, though with some redistribution of meanings and many distinct idioms for expressing them. We can see karma in the original—if not the term, then certainly the idea—indeed, it runs through the entire "sacramental" aspect of the works, the sense that everything is meaningful. It is a world filled with omens, in which words have consequences. Even speaking of chance (*qiao*), the text refutes it—it seems to be chance, but it isn't. This feeling of universal significance produces the story's premodern aura perhaps more deeply than its Medieval trappings and feudal social world.

We have seen how the unique features of one language force translators to make hard choices, and also how in Tolkien's world words have a magical potency. The next two chapters address these aspects of language.

11

Language

Questions about language arise directly and pervasively from Tolkien's works. The stories themselves feature many translations of inscriptions and utterances—on the Ring itself, on the great door of Moria, and so on. There are various dialects of Elvish, the "Black Speech," Valarin, Old Entish, Khuzdul, the Drúadan language, "the dreadful language of the Wargs" (*H*, vi, 111) and presumably others, such as used by the Eagles, or the giant spiders of Mirkwood.

Perhaps the strangest language is the one which is invisible: the Common Speech (also called Westron). Whereas we have many opportunities to actually read elvish words (transcribed or in their original script), we never read any examples of the common speech, because it has already been "translated" into English, by Tolkien. He claims that *The Hobbit* is actually the Red Book of Westmarch (*FR* Prologue, 1), which began as Bilbo's diary:

> Tolkien developed an elaborate line of reasoning, according to which Modern English (in which the book was written) was not the language spoken by ... the hobbits, who were speaking in the 'Common Speech' referred to many times in *The Lord of the Rings*. On the contrary, Tolkien indicated that he had 'translated' the 'real' 'Common Speech' of Middle-earth of the Third Age into Modern English, while he had left the languages that were unrelated to it—like the different languages of the Elves, Quenya, Sindarin, Dwarves, including Khuzdul and the Black Speech—in their original form. (Fimi 2009: 190–191, see also 128–129; Shippey 2003: 117)

The insertion of elven fragments in an English (or Chinese) text serves as a foreignizing effect. For example, Frodo says *Elen síla lúmenn' omentielvo* (Quenya, transliterated in Roman letters), then translates it, "A star shines on the hour of our meeting" (*FR* I, iii, 79). All three translations give the elven in Roman letters (Deng *FR*: 101; Yilin *FR*: 100; Zhu *FR*: 138). The insertion of elven into the text (when context allows us to understand it) resembles the common convention of putting "s'il vous plait" into a French character's speech which is otherwise in English. This "foreign-soundingness" works on the assumption that the readers know what that French phrase means (Bellos 2013: 37). But this is not the case here, since we find long strings of elvish, intelligible only to the uttermost nerdiest fans who have learned Tolkien's pseudo-language. Quenya's relation to English is so tenuous that it goes beyond having a character say "merci beaucoup."

The Problem of G for Gandalf

When Gandalf arrives in the Shire just before Bilbo's birthday party, he brings a cargo of fireworks, "each labelled with a large red G"; the G is followed by letters from Tolkien's invented or adapted scripts, a Tengwar rune representing g, and a Sindarin or Cirth rune representing g (*FR* I, I, 25; see *RK* Appendix E, II, i, 1098–1099). Here, we have an English sentence featuring a capitalized initial letter (G) and two samples of other scripts. However, Gandalf's name could not possibly be represented by "G," because G is a Roman letter, so the runes stand in for it—the letter G here represents a translation of both the Tengwar and Sindarin runes. Presumably the fireworks are labeled only with runes, which our narrator has specified as equivalent to G. All of the translations use the Roman letter G here (plus the runes), even though Gandalf's Chinese name does not begin with G, or with any "letter," but rather with the syllable *gan* 甘 (Deng *FR*: 30; Zhu *FR*: 53) or *gang* 刚 (Yilin *FR*: 28) They could have said that the fireworks were each marked with the character *gan* 甘 (or *gang* 刚), but then the runes that follow would have been incorrect, only representing the g- of *gan* or *gang*.

But the Hobbit children make the problem a little more complicated, when they see the runes and shout, "G for Grand!" (*FR* I, i, 25). Such precocious Hobbit children, they can read runes already! But how did the children see the runes representing the hard g sound and make the connection that it might also stand for *the English word* "grand"?— unless the Common Speech word translated into English as "grand" by coincidence also starts with a g- sound? Deng says the letter G "represents *goubang*!" a colloquial phrase meaning "pretty good" and which retains the hard g sound (Deng *FR*: 30). As if the Common Speech word for *goubang* happens also to start with g. Yilin has the children ignore "Grand" and say, "that G is Gandalf!" (Yilin *FR*: 28) retaining the Roman letter G in the sentence. Modern Chinese readers are all very accustomed to *pinyin*, so this is an easily understandable remark. Zhu skips the letter G entirely and has the children say, "this abbreviation means grand (*zhuangyan*)!" (Zhu *FR*: 53). Why exactly the runes would signify the term *zhuangyan*, is not clear. They could have tried: *gan* (甘) is the *gan* of *gandaofu* (Gandalf), except that *gan* is not the first character of any word meaning "grand." They might have had the children say, "*Gan* 甘 is also the *gan* of *ganyuan* 甘願 (ready and willing)!" though you'd still be stuck with runes that are still not pronounced *gan*.

Later we have the same problem, when Galadriel gives Sam a box with a rune. "Here is set G for Galadriel ... but also it may stand for garden in your tongue" (*FR* II,viii, 366). Deng, "This inlaid character G represents Galadriel.... But in your language, G can also represent flower garden" (Deng *FR*: 469). She adds a footnote explaining that "Galadriel" and "garden" both start with g (in English). Yilin, "This character G is an abbreviation (*suozi*) for Galadriel, but, in your language it also represents flower garden" (Yilin *FR*: 458)—it is not clear why. Zhu seems a little more cautious: "Carved here on this is an abbreviation (*suoxie*) of my name, but in your language it also represents the meaning of flower garden" (Zhu *FR*: 579). Perhaps Zhu is evasive here because he has transliterated Galadriel as Kai-lan-cui-er 凱蘭崔爾, and so it couldn't be G in any case, it would be K. Deng uses Jia-la-de-rui-er 加拉德瑞尔, same problem, but in her footnote she specifies [Roman letters:] "Galadriel" after the Chinese name.

The problem reoccurs, with an S-rune on the goblins' shield, and Aragorn remarks, "S is for Saruman, I guess" (*TT* III, i, 406). Deng and Yilin use "S," but Zhu has only, "I guess this represents Saruman" (Deng *TT*: 9; Yilin *TT*: 6; Zhu *TT*: 20).

By way of comparison, Neil Gaiman's *M is for Magic* becomes *mo shi mofa de mo* 魔是魔法的魔. *Mo-* is the *Mo-* of *Mofa* (magic). The English title suggests "m" might stand for any number of things (million, Mycroft, magnesium), but this particular letter "m" is an abbreviation of "magic." Or another interpretation: we are going through a whole alphabet: a is for amulet, b is for blasphemy, etc. It does evoke Sue Grafton's *M is for Malice* and suchlike books. But the Chinese title cannot quite work that way, since "m" is a minimal phonetic unit and *mo* 魔 is a character representing a syllable. There is no Chinese character that only represents the *m-* of any syllable. To be sure, *mo* might be the *mo* of other terms with the same character: *mogui, mowang, mofang*, etc., but it's a pretty small list compared to the letter 'm.' And all of this small list would have something to do with the meaning of *mo*. In the Chinese title, *mo* (魔) could not for example be the *mo* of *moxing* 模型 (model) or *mori* 末日 (doomsday).

The Word *the*

After three decades of grading term papers written by students whose native language is not English, I can say with confidence that the single most problematic word in English is the word *the*. Though it is possible to rationally deduce when "the" should be used, or "a" or no article at all, usually I correct it and move on, hoping that the student will gradually develop an intuitive feel for the word. And in fact, sometimes I am not sure either. But generally, the definite article implies a known and specific object. "To be or not to be" is "a" question, but we know that for Hamlet it's "the" question—the decisive, specific, and essential question.

Gandalf at one point glosses his use of italicized "*the*" with a helpful note. He says, "And here is our little Bilbo Baggins, *the* burglar, the chosen and selected burglar" (*H*, i, 25). He implies that there are lots of burglars, but here is the specific one I have chosen. Yilin says, "This person is 'burglar' I took great pains to pick (*jingxin tiaoxuan*)" (Yilin *H*: 20). Burglar = *yedaozhe*, night-thief. Zhu however delves into the treasury of *chengyu* to render "chosen and selected," using *queping zhongxuan* 雀屏中選—which usually refers to careful selection of a son-in-law, from a story about the Tang emperor Gaozu choosing (*zhongxuan*) a man for his daughter to marry by hitting with an arrow the eye of a peacock (*kongque*) on a folding screen (*ping*). Zhu: "I found this *queping zhongxuan* burglar (*feizei*)" (Zhu *H*: 29). No mention of "*the*," except in so far as "*the*" implies specifically chosen. Wu: "So, I found our little Bilbo Baggins, **that** burglar, that one-picked-out-of-a-hundred (*baili tiaoyi*) burglar" (Wu *H*: 32).

When Bilbo is preparing for his 111st birthday party, "Days passed and The Day drew nearer" (*FR* I, i, 24). Deng uses the closely related *na*, "that,": "Days passed day by day, that day came closer and closer" (Deng *FR*: 30). From the context it is clear which day she means. Yilin explains, "[the] day of the party" (Yilin *FR*: 27). And Zhu, "[the] big day" (Zhu *FR*: 52). Similarly, after Bilbo has gone, Frodo enjoys being "*the* Mr. Baggins of Bag End" (*FR* I, ii, 42). Deng has, "becoming **that** Bag End Mr. Baggins" (Deng *FR*: 52), whereas the others explain: "being the owner (*zhuren*) of Bag End" (Yilin *FR*: 51), and "inheriting Bag End Cave to become Mr Baggins" (Zhu *FR*: 80).

But the question of *the* intrudes into the story itself. "And why do you call him Dúnadan?" asked Frodo. "*The* Dúnadan," said Bilbo (*FR*, II, i, 226). Frodo is unfamiliar with the word, and with the linguistic category it belongs to. Deng has Frodo ask, "and why call him dúnadan?" with Bilbo answering that he "is **a certain** (*mou*) dúnadan" (Deng *FR*: 287–288). Deng adds a footnote, "a certain dúnadan (the Dúnadan) here is to emphasize that Dúnadan is not a person's name, but is a title; *the* in English functions as a definite article (*dingguanci*), demonstrating a specific thing" (Deng *FR*: 288). *Mou* 某 is usually translated as "a certain" as in "a certain Mr. Wang" or in *mouzhong* 某種 "a certain kind of" (clothes, say). So, Bilbo is saying, this ranger belongs to a particular *category* called Dúnadan (plural Dúnedain). Zhu uses a similar although vaguer solution: "Why do you call him dúnadan?" "**That (nawei**, that person) **dúnadan**" (Zhu *FR*: 360). Yilin's translation shifts the meaning: "Then why do you call [him] dúnadan?" "The people here commonly call him dúnadan" (Yilin *FR*: 281). Bilbo seems to be saying, "I don't know, that's what people call him."

The same problem arises from Radagast's unfamiliarity with Hobbits. He says, "the Riders ask for news of a land called Shire." Gandalf corrects him: "*The* Shire" (*FR*, II, ii, 250). Yet this is odd. "Dúnadan" of the previous example is after all not an English nor a Westron word, but a Sindarin word unfamiliar even to the relatively bookish Frodo. But "shire" is a common noun in English, *sûza* in the Common Tongue (*RK* Appendix F, II, 1108), for a certain area of land, like a borough or county—or *jun* 郡 (Wang 2020: 79–80). Radagast is being obtuse here: news of a land called County? Surely, if he was unaware of the Hobbits' home, he might have said, "the Riders ask for news of their shire." Gandalf then treats the word as a proper noun with "the" and a capital S. It is not surprising that the Hobbits are so insular that they name their shire the Shire, along with the Water and the Hill. If the dwarves had named their homeland "the shire" using their Khuzdul language, Radagast might have been justifiably confused, but then Gandalf wouldn't have been able to simply put "the" before it. So, what happens when we move this exchange into Chinese?

Deng has, "Another person told me, no matter where the black riders go, they all ask after a place called *Xia-er* 夏尔." "**This** *Xia-er*" (Deng *FR*: 322; see also Hooker 2003: 272–274 on the Russian for Shire). So "shire" is transliterated, not translated: for Chinese readers, it might as well be "a place called XYZ." In which case, why does Gandalf say "this"? Zhu has almost the same solution: "a place called *xia-er*." "It's this *xia-er*." (*jiushi zheige xia-er*) (Zhu *FR*: 401). It makes sense if we translate "shire": Gandalf is thus saying, it's not a place called Shire, it's this shire right here (except that this conversation with Radagast takes place near Bree, which is not in the Shire). Yilin completely changes the whole exchange: "they ask about news from *Xia-er* 霞尔." "*Xia-er*!" (Yilin *FR*: 313)—as if Gandalf is startled or upset to hear the name.

A similar muddle results when Treebeard declares, "I am an Ent ... *The* Ent, I am" (*TT* III, iv, 453; Deng *TT*: 71; Yilin *TT*: 66; Zhu *TT*: 92), when Beorn calls a rock in the river nearby "the Carrock" (*H*, vii, 126; Yilin *H*: 100; Zhu *H*: 135; Wu *H*: 159–160; see also Shippey 2003: 101), and when Bilbo sees a mountain and asks, "Is that *The* Mountain?" (*H*, iii, 51; Yilin *H*: 41; Zhu *H*: 56; Wu *H*: 66). How many novels spend so much time instructing us on the definite article?

Capital Letters

As we have seen, "the" is frequently connected to capital letters. In early drafts, Shippey notes, "A common practice for Tolkien at this stage was simply to make names out of capital letters." Hence, The Hill, The Water (2003: 96). There is a road near Bree called "the Road" (*FR* I, ix, 147), which all three translations convert to *dadao* (big road) (Deng *FR*: 188; Yilin *FR*: 184; Zhu *FR*: 241).

Bag End is dug into "the hill—The Hill, as all the people for many miles round called it" (*H*, i, 3). Here Tolkien shifts from ordinary generic noun "hill" to proper noun "The Hill." Yilin: "the big mountain (*dashan*) there. People of many miles around all called this mountain big mountain" (Yilin *H* 1). Zhu: "the hill (*shanqiu*), many people nearby called this hill 'little hill (*xiaoqiu*)'" (Zhu *H*: 5; Wu *H*: 6 is almost the same). As for "The Water, the small river that ran at the foot of The Hill" (*H*, i, 4–5), Zhu attaches smallness to the Water and uses quotation marks to help clarify that "little river" is a name: "the 'little river' (*xiaohe*) ... this river was a little river that wound past the foot of the little hill (*xiaoqiu*)" (Zhu *H*: 7; Wu's version is similar, Wu *H*: 8). Yilin does an interesting thing here: "the big river (*dahe*). The so-called big river was no more than a small stream under the foot of the big mountain" (Yilin *H*: 2). Because of the capital W, the Water must be big, but then the text explains this is a grandiose name, because in fact it was just a little river. Typical hobbits—they think this trickle is a great River!

But in the case of a term like "the Enemy," in addition to specificity, capitalization also signifies a weight and menace, a euphemistic avoidance of a name which also serves to dichotomize good and evil. Their enemies are now *the Enemy*. When we read that, we are tempted to use a deep, throaty voice, as in a movie trailer voice-over. Indeed, the Dwarves "spoke in whispers of the Enemy" (*FR* I, ii, 42). Deng, "the great enemy (*dadi*)" (Deng *FR*: 53). Yilin, "the enemy (*diren*)" (Yilin *FR*: 52). Zhu, "the *mo*-king" (Zhu *FR*: 81). Deng turns the capital E into "great," but Yilin leaves the term more generic, and Zhu names the enemy by title.

Garbled Language

One of the fundamental differences between English and Chinese is that written English is phonetic (albeit unreliably so), and written Chinese is only in a very limited sense phonetic. English spoken words are constructed of phonemes which can be assembled and disassembled: ent = the three sounds e, n, and t; and represented by graphemes (the letters e, n, and t). Words can easily be fragmented. So, for example, as Gandalf is reading the damaged *Book of Mazarbul* in Moria, he narrates his reconstruction of a partial text: "The first clear word is *sorrow*, but the rest of the line is lost, unless it ends in *estre*. Yes, it must be *yestre* followed by *day* . . ." (*FR* II, v, 314). It's a little odd because "yesterday" is not spelled "yestreday." Archaism, or poor spelling? In any case, here the text he is reading cannot of course *actually* say "sorrow" or "yestreday" because it is written in the runic writing system Cirth. Gandalf is translating Khuzdul (presumably) into Westron, and Tolkien is translating Westron into English. Gandalf reconstructs a full word from a few letters. Zhu handles this problem by taking "yester" and "day" as equivalent of the two Chinese characters of the term for yesterday, *zuotian* 昨天. "I can discern the first word is sorrow, but the characters of the line after that are all blurred away, at the end it seems like it is *zuo* 昨 . . . that's right, that should be *zuotian* 昨天 (yesterday)" (Zhu *FR* 499). *Zuotian* means yesterday, and if we divide it, the *zuo* refers to yester-, and *tian* means day. This is a very reasonable solution to the translation of a fragment of a word. But Deng and Yilin do something more ingenious. Deng, "only at the end of the line [is] the incomplete character '*zha* 乍.' Yes, for sure it is the character '*zuo* 昨'" (yester-)" (Deng *FR*: 403). *Zha* 乍 is a word which means first or suddenly, but it is also the right half of *zuo* 昨, yester-, and clearly this is what is intended. Yilin does the same thing (Yilin *FR*: 392). They manage to actually fragment the word beyond merely splitting the two-word phrase in half. They thereby imply damage to the manuscript not only after "yestre-" or *zuo-* (obscuring the "-day" or *tian*), but also damage to the character *zuo*, on its left side so that only the 乍 of 昨 is still visible. After all, Gandalf could only read "-estre-" and needed to add both the y- and the -day. This is ingenious translation work!

A somewhat different problem presents itself with the representation of mispronunciation. When Bilbo had a cold, he said, "thag you very buch" (*FR* I, i, 30). Deng changes what is obviously *feichang ganxie nimen* (very much thank you all), to *huichang ganhei nimen* (Deng *FR*: 37). The changed syllables have their own meaning (*hui* = grey, *hei* = black), but clearly the reader does not try to read the meaning, but recognizes mispronunciation. Yilin has a similar solution, *feiqiang ganxi nimen* (Yilin *FR*: 35). Zhu's solution is similar, though using a different set phrase: assuming *duoxie dajia* 多謝大家 (much thanks everyone), Bilbo makes the sound *douxie dadia* 都謝大嗲, switching *duo* to *dou* (converting "much thanks" to the unidiomatic "all thanks") and using the rare syllable *dia* (flirtatious, self-indulgent) to alter what would normally be *dajia* (everyone) (Zhu *FR*: 61). There is no such word in English as "thag," but as English uses a phonetic script, the representation of the sound is no problem, and we easily interpret it as "thank" with your nose stopped up. The Chinese script on the other hand is not phonetic. While it is possible to fabricate new characters (for ludic effect), they would be very hard to read. So the translators instead use alternate existing characters with different sounds, changing *feichang* to *huichang* and so on. Again, these changes to well-known set phrases are easily understood as distorted pronunciations. But surely, these do not accurately represent the sound of speaking with a cold. Those of you who know Chinese, pinch your nose shut and try saying *feichang ganxie nimen*. It sounds more like *feichag gadxie dibed*—the n- and m-sounds either gone or sounding like d- and b-sounds. But such sounds (*chag, gad, bed*) do not exist in Mandarin Chinese. Mispronunciation is possible in any language, but a phonetic script may have the advantage in *sounding* like gibberish.

One of Tolkien's most famous bits of garbled speech is when the trolls capture Bilbo, and ask him what he is. Bilbo starts to say "burglar," but corrects himself. "Bilbo Baggins, a bur—a hobbit" and the trolls say, "A burrahobbit?" (*H*, ii, 41). Yilin drops the ball on this one: "Bilbo Baggins, a 'burgler' ... no, a hobbit." ... "hobbit?" (Yilin *H*: 33). True, the trolls might not have heard of hobbits, but they also ignore the admission of burglary. Zhu comes up with something good: "Bilbo Baggins, I am *fei*—*e*—hobbit." ... "not-hungry (*fei-e*) hobbit?" (Zhu *H*: 45). *Fei* 飛 is the first half of a common term for burglar (*feizei*); combined with a hesitation syllable *e* 呃, this fragmentary utterance is mistaken for a different *fei-e* 非餓, "not hungry." It does not reproduce the non-word "burrahobbit," but it gives us Bilbo's nervous blurt and the trolls' misunderstanding. Especially as the trolls are contemplating eating Bilbo. They are hungry for hobbit. Wu tries the same trick with less effect: "Bilbo Baggins, I am a *fei*—*e*—hobbit" (Wu *H*: 53). "*fei-e* 飞蛾 hobbit?" Instead of "not hungry," the *fei-e* here means "flying moth." Indeed perplexing for the trolls.

When a stranger having a pint in The Ivy Bush refers to "jools" (jewels) (*FR* I, i, 23), Deng substitutes the expected translation 珠宝 (*zhubao*, jewels, pearls and gems) with 猪宝 (pig-treasure), uses a homophonic *cuozi* (mistaken character) to substitute for a non-standard pronunciation (Deng *FR* 28). As a spoken line, since the two *zhu* are the same tone, there would be no discernable mispronunciation or accent; we see it only in the written form—just as in English, we only see the spelling "jools" when it is written. Zhu and Yilin make no attempt to mimic "jools" (Zhu *FR*: 51; Yilin *FR*: 26). The point of spelling it "jools" is to evoke rustic speech, far from the Queen's English—in which "jewels" is a two-syllable word. One of the rustic hobbits says, "No thank 'ee" (*FR* I, ii, 43), but none of the translators attempt such a specific class or dialect marker (Deng *FR*: 54; Yilin *FR*: 53; Zhu *FR*: 82). The Gaffer's "drownded" (*FR* I, ii, 22) becomes merely *yansi*, (drowned) (Deng *FR*: 27; Zhu *FR*: 49; Yilin *FR*: 25; see also Savelli 2020: 6). In the Chinese, the rural hobbits are slightly less rustic and non-standard. Stopfel notes a similar reduction in the differences of tone in a German translation (2005: 12).

The worst speech patterns belong to Gollum, who has particular weaknesses in subject-verb agreements, plurals, and verb tenses. Gollum's "I wants it" (*FR* I, ii, 52) is also translated in correct grammar, equivalent to "I want it" (Deng *FR*: 65; Yilin *FR*: 65; Zhu *FR*: 97). Similarly, the excessive pluralization is ignored for "pocketses" (*FR* I, ii, 56; Deng *FR*: 71; Yilin *FR*: 70; Zhu *FR*: 103), and "goblinses" (*H*, v, 94; Zhu *H*: 103; Yilin *H*: 76; Wu *H*: 121). Certainly, if Chinese readers follow Gollum's meandering thoughts, morbid obsessions, and schizophrenic monologues, there is no doubt his mind is long since ruined. But the Chinese Gollum has better grammar.

Difficulty over verbs is partly due to the fundamental feature of Chinese as a non-conjugated language. Treebeard is talking about Saruman, using past tenses. Gandalf says, "I observe ... that with great care you say *dwelt, was, grew*. What about *is*?" (*RK* VI, vi, 958). His point is made by the contrast of "was" and "is." Yilin ignores the verb tense details, entirely skipping *dwelt, was, grew*. "I notice you always talk about past circumstances, now how is he? Is he dead?" (Yilin *RK*: 288). Zhu and Deng have very similar solutions. Deng also emphasizes the contrast with the use of bold font: "when you speak of him you are very careful to use the **past tense** (*guoqushi*). And **now**? Did he die?" (Deng *RK*: 299; cf. Zhu *RK*: 360).

Finally, we find something close to pure nonsense, such as Tom Bombadil's song with its mixture of meaningful words (hey, merry, ring, hop), conventional sing-song words (fal la), and more or less non-existent words (dol, don dillo, dong) (*FR* I, vi, 116). Each translator makes a game attempt to render the line freely, with a mixture of semantic and non-semantic words such as: "Hei hei dong! Happy dong! Strike (*qiao*) ah ding ding dong!" (Deng *FR*: 149), and "Happy ah! Ha-ha-py-py (*kuaikuai huohuo*) strike a copper gong ah!" (Yilin *FR*: 146; cf. Zhu *FR*: 195). We see a similar playfulness with Treebeard's "roomty toom tum" (*TT* III, iv, 453; Deng *TT*: 72; Yilin *TT*: 67; Zhu *TT*: 94).

Archaisms

Gandalf reads Isildur's note on the Ring. Isildur died in the year 2 of the Third Age. So Gandalf (reading this in 3018 of the Third Age) is quoting words written more than three thousand years before. Perhaps this justified the archaisms here: its use of a very obscure English word ("glede"), and the use of the -eth verb endings: seemeth, loseth, fadeth, saith (*FR* II, ii, 246). Such "foreignizing" words naturally stand out, though as Turner argued, Tolkien sustained the archaic effect more by avoiding modern words than inserting old ones (Turner 2006: 170–173). There is simply no way for any of the translators to reproduce the archaic verb endings (Deng *FR*: 316–317; Yilin *FR*: 307–308; Zhu *FR*: 395). There are archaic features in Chinese, but the translators do not make use of them, reducing the sense that three millennia have passed since Isildur died. The -eth ending, for third person present indicative, was replaced by -s (hence, I *seem*, but it *seems*.) These uses were already close to gone by the nineteenth century, but survived in poetry along with Thee and Thou. Still, for "If thou art in haste" (*RK* V, ii, 758) Zhu and Deng use *ru* 汝 ("you," archaic or at least literary) (Zhu *RK*: 60; Deng *RK*: 40; cf. Yilin *RK*: 38).

I asked Deng about the archaism of verbs and syntax in the original, and the relative lack of this archaism in the translations:

> When we were translating the Wenjing edition, we particularly considered this problem. Namely, what kind of language should we use to translate? Also, what level do we want to reach? A very real problem was: who are our readers? Our readers, what kind of language do they want to read? Of course we can influence them. I'd say we decided we absolutely didn't want *dabaihua* (colloquial speech)—that's what we didn't want. But did we want to reach into such ancient Chinese? That couldn't be, because there were very many readers who couldn't understand it. Under these circumstances we could use modern Chinese, but within this modern Chinese, we could make it relatively elegant and literary, not a colloquial style. We could try hard to let whatever kind of person speak whatever kind of words, which is to say, the "tone" of their speaking, or their "style." Which is to say, when we were translating Gandalf's language, when he was speaking, his manner of speaking can't be Pippin's or Merry's manner of speaking....

Now as for what you just asked, the grammar problem, my own view is, first you have to ask, who is reading it? What kind of language are modern people used to? You can slightly change their reading level, but you can't completely ignore their level. If you use something too hard, they absolutely won't accept it. It's a process of making choices, and self-control. Because my view is, I'm a person of this time, what I do is to serve this time's readers. (2017)

There are a great many examples of changes from archaic to modern colloquial tone. "Nay, stay your wrath!" (*RK* V, iv, 796) becomes, "OK, don't be angry!" (Yilin *RK*: 85; Zhu and Deng are very similar: Zhu *RK*: 118; Deng *RK*: 87). Or, "trothplighted" (*RK* VI, vi, 955) becomes in all three translations *dinghun* 订婚, the ordinary word for engagement (Yilin *RK*: 285; Zhu *RK*: 356; Deng *RK*: 295). "Go not to the Elves for counsel" (*FR* I, iii, 83) becomes "Don't go ..." (Deng *FR* 105; Zhu *FR*: 143; Yilin *FR*: 104).

Obscure words are treated in different ways. What about objects given as gifts called "old *mathoms* of forgotten uses" (*FR* I, i, 37)? Deng transliterates it, *masong* ("horse pine") (Deng *FR*: 46), Yilin has *lao wanyir*, old playthings (Yilin *FR*: 44), and Zhu, *liwu*, gifts (Zhu *FR*: 73). What of cram? (*FR* II, viii, 360), Deng transliterates it as *kelamu*, with a footnote, explaining it's a type of cake or biscuit (Deng *FR*: 462; similar to Yilin *FR*: 451). Zhu translates it as *ganliang*, dry provisions (Zhu *FR*: 570). Arwen answers Aragorn with a "linnod" (*RK* Appendix A, I, v, 1036). Shi transliterates "linnod" with a footnote saying it's a kind of elven poetic form (Deng *RK*: 408). Yilin and Zhu make no reference to a linnod (Yilin *RK*: 394–395; Zhu *RK* Appendix: 42). Isildur says, "This I will have as weregild for my father, and my brother" (*FR* II, ii, 237; the term also appears in *RK* Appendix A, II, 1040). Deng, "I will have this ring as compensation (*peichang*) against my father and younger brother's death" (Deng *FR*: 305). And in the Appendixes, *shushajin*, atone-for-killing money (Deng *RK*: 415). Zhu names it "treasure to commemorate (*jinian*) my father and younger brother" (Zhu *FR*: 380), but later, paraphrases it as "you now owe me a lot" (Zhu *RK* Appendix: 46). Yilin first uses "compensation (*peichang*)" (Yilin *FR*: 295) and later, *xuezhai*, debt of blood (Yilin *RK*: 400).

Idioms

Some of the idiomatic expressions used in Middle-earth do exist in English, or the English of Tolkien's time and place; but others were surely concocted, meant to sound like proverbs and sayings even if they were invented. Such as when Boromir and Aragorn start exchanging proverbs about wargs and orcs (*FR* II, iv, 290). Others, I'm not so sure of—I've never heard them, and web searches don't get me any hits other than their appearance in Tolkien's works, but they might have been in circulation in his time. There are of course many fairly well-known expressions in English. "It never rains but it pours" proved a little slippery (*FR* I, ix, 150). Deng and Yilin, "If it's not dying of drought then it's dying of a flood" (Deng *FR*: 192; Yilin *FR*: 187). Zhu is a bit closer with, "If it doesn't rain, then it floods" (Zhu *FR*: 244).

"You have put your foot in it!" (*FR*, I, ix, 157). Deng, "This time you would consider your muddy foot deeply stuck (*suan nizu shenxian*)" (Deng *FR*: 202). Yilin, "you've lost your footing" (*shizu*) (Yilin *FR*: 197). Zhu, "This time you have extended your foot to jump into a heap of trouble!" (Zhu *FR*: 257). After all, what is the "it" you've put your foot in? Mud? Cow-dung? Or a pickle: "A nice pickle we have landed ourselves in" (*FR*, II, ii, 264). Deng and Zhu read "pickle" as trouble (Deng *FR*: 339, Zhu *FR*: 423), but Yilin tries to refer to something edible: "We brought bitterness upon ourselves (*zitao kuchi*, self-incurred bitterness to eat)" (Yilin *FR*: 331).

Two cases of the idiom, "the apple of (someone's) eye." In the first, Grishnákh, speaking of the Nazghul: "You ought to know that they're the apple of the Great Eye" (*TT* III, iii, 441–442). A curiously affectionate term, as if Sauron patted them on their heads. All the translators spotted the idiom, using phrases such as "the great *mo*-eye's darlings (*xingan baobei*, heart-and-liver precious)" (Deng *TT* 55; cf. Yilin *TT*: 53) and "favorite general (*aijiang*)" (Zhu *TT*: 75). But no one attempts to reproduce the pun on the apple of his Great Eye. Later, the horse Shadowfax is called "the apple of the king's eye" (*RK* V, i, 745), all translated as treasure (*zhenbao*) (Yilin *RK*: 21; Zhu *RK*: 40; Deng *RK*: 23).

Bilbo "had run off into the Blue" (*FR* I, ii, 41). Presumably, "the Blue" is the hazy distance, literally and metaphorically. Deng: "ran off to a non-existent country (*wuyouxiang* 乌有乡)" (Deng *FR*: 51). Yilin: "ran off to the blue mountain" (Yilin *FR*: 50). Zhu: "ran off to the wild wastes (*huangye*)" (Zhu *FR*: 79). The same phrase appears in *The Hobbit* with a little explanation: Gandalf is to blame for young people "going off into the Blue for mad adventures" (*H*, i, 8). Wu: the young people "suddenly lose their path (*shiqule zongji*), put themselves into a crazy adventure (*fengkuang maoxian*)" (Wu *H*: 12). Yilin similarly ignores the Blue: "go off on adventures (*maoxian*)" (Yilin *H*: 5). Zhu: "to have a dream (*fameng*) to go on adventures!" (Zhu *H*: 10).

In some cases, we see a well-known phrase only implied, such as to sleep like a log. "Sam slept through the night in deep content, if logs are contented" (*FR* I, vii, 126). Deng puts the log in there correctly, by inserting the stealth gloss "like a log": "All night like a log he slept dead-heavily (*sichen*, quiet as the dead), completely content—if a log can be content" (Deng *FR*: 161). Yilin gets the log in there but removes the elliptical humor. "Sam only remembered at night sleeping very deeply—like a log" (Yilin *FR*: 158). And finally Zhu goes off into the Blue a little: Sam slept without dreams, "because like a log, noise wouldn't wake him" (Zhu *FR*: 209).

Gandalf contrasts himself with Tom Bombadil. "He is a moss-gatherer, and I have been a stone doomed to rolling" (*RK* VI, vii, 974). Surely in English we unavoidably have an image of Mick Jagger as Gandalf—an intriguing casting idea! But "a rolling stone gathers no moss" is not a *chengyu*, so the translators have to improvise. Zhu: "He is a stay-at-home type of person (*jujiaxing de ren*), but I am fated to rush about all over (*dongben xipao*, east run west run)" (Zhu *RK*: 384). Yilin has a similar version (Yilin *RK*: 309). Deng tries her best but in this case I feel starts to over-explain: "He is an unshakable (*leida budong*, thunder strikes he doesn't move) moss growing all over (*changman qingtai*) person (of a certain type, *zhur* 主儿), and I all along have a rolling stone not growing moss fate (*ming*)" (Deng *RK*: 320).

Théoden: "But it has long been said: *oft evil will shall evil mar*" (*TT* III, xi, 581), which means something like: often, the desire to do evil shall harm the evil-doer. Deng is very close in meaning and certainly retains the musical quality: *hairen faner haiji*, harming people contrarily harms oneself (Deng *TT*: 242). It sounds very idiomatic to me, though I have not found it in any dictionary. Zhu, however, goes for the familiar idiom: evil has evil karmic retribution, *e you ebao* (Zhu *TT*: 288–289), as discussed in the previous chapter. This is loosely the same meaning, though karma does not necessarily work through will. Yilin on the other hand, is medicinal rather than moral: "this is called using poison to attack poison (*yidu gongdu*)" (Yilin *TT*: 222).

Conclusions

This chapter has been about aspects of the original that resist easy translation due to innate features of English that don't exist in Chinese, such as verb conjugation and phonetic script. These problems are not incidental but emphatic because of Tolkien's concerns with language which permeate the story. Certainly one could invert that analysis to see what the English "translation" of the Chinese "originals" made of features innate to Chinese. The need for English to be very specific about verb tense would seem to be a severe reduction in ambiguity, as would the compulsion to specify definite or indefinite articles alien to the "original" Chinese.

The following chapter continues the theme of language, but moving into its magical and sub-creative potency.

12

Magical Language

Magic is a reasonable metaphor for being lost in a novel, enchanted by a poem, under the spell of a play, but for Tolkien it was really, actually, magic; and more than magic—it was theology. As long as the story exemplifies virtue in some way, the author participates in divinity in the act of "sub-creating" a "Secondary world" which is a re-enactment of God's creation of the real or Primary world (*OFS*: 77). Language makes real things, both for Tolkien as an author and for the people in Middle-earth. The stories are riddled with worries about language: taboos, omens, prophecies, spells, curses, oaths, seductions, ambiguities, translations, and stories. If you say a thing, it might come true. Petty argues, for example, that Tolkien avoided a too-explicit description of the balrogs because it was dangerous to enter into the mind of evil in fiction—imagining evil too vividly opens a door best kept shut (Petty 2011: 57). And yet, "The Locked Door stands as an eternal Temptation" (*OFS*: 142).

Words have "magical" potency, for readers and characters. So, what kinds of magical language do we find in Tolkien's works? And how do the translations present these magical words? How do the stories' potent words interact with Chinese categories of magical language?

Bad Language

Of Khuzdul, the language of the Dwarves, Sam remarks, "A fair jaw-cracker dwarf-language must be!" (*FR* II, iii, 278). For "fair jaw-cracker," Deng has, "(it) twists the mouth and grinds the teeth (*aokou you moya*)!" (Deng *FR*: 358). Yilin uses the same *aokou* (Yilin *FR*: 349). Zhu comes from another angle: "They still really love to speak *ka-la-ka-la* dwarf language!" (Zhu *FR*: 445). *Ka* 喀 is a character often used for transliterating, or for a noise made in coughing or vomiting. *La* 啦 has various uses but is almost empty of semantic meaning. For hobbits, Khuzdul is a language made of mere noise, almost physically painful to speak. Yet it is certainly not in itself evil.

More crucially, there is the Black Speech, created by Sauron as the common tongue or semi-functional pidgin of his servants (Ashford 2018: 29). We have an example of it, spoken at the Counsel: *Ash nazg durbatulûk*, etc. (*FR*, II, ii, 247). Gandalf speaks the words on the Ring, and suddenly he is monstrous, the sky darkens, and "the Elves stopped their ears" (*FR* II, ii, 248). The line is given in a Romanization, reproduced by the translators (Deng *FR*: 318; Yilin *FR*: 309; Zhu *FR*: 397). Perhaps to pre-empt confusion in the readers, Deng adds a footnote: "This is the way of reading the magic ring's inscription in the Black Speech, its meaning is as in the translation given below in the text." Such a footnote suggests that some Chinese readers might not understand what English readers immediately know to be a text they should not attempt to understand. But the point is, the *meaning* of the inscription isn't the problem—when Gandalf speaks the Westron translation, everyone is fine—the mere *sound* of the Black Speech gives elves a migraine.

Another example of the Black Speech, specifically the dialect of Mordor, comes later. The orc Grishnákh says, "*Uglúk u bagronk sha pushdug Saruman-glob búbhosh skai*" (*TT* III, iii, 435). There are different versions of Tolkien's translation of this, such as: "Ugluk to the cesspool, sha! The dungfilth; the Saruman-fool, skai!" and "Ugluk to the dung-pit with stinking Saruman-filth—pig-guts gah!" (Ashford 2018: 30). Grishnákh is clearly just combining two proper nouns with various unpleasant meanings and noises. Deng and Yilin reproduce the text in Roman letters (Deng *TT*: 47; Yilin *TT*: 44), but Zhu breaks the language even further by arbitrarily transliterating the proper nouns into Chinese and retaining the rest in Roman letters, which gives us an odd mix: "烏骨陸 u bagronk sha pushdug 薩魯曼-glob búbhosh skai" (Zhu *TT*: 65). Presumably, all of this *ug* and *gronk* and *glob* is meant to sound bad to our ears, whereas "dungfilth" and "pig-guts" would no doubt sound lovely in Quenya.

Isildur describes the inscription on the Ring. "It is fashioned in an elven-script of Eregion, for they have no letters in Mordor for such subtle work; but the language is unknown to me. I deem it to be a tongue of the Black Land, since it is foul and uncouth. What evil it saith I do not know" (*FR* II, ii, 246). We are told that although the *script* is elven and subtle, the *sound* of the inscription is "foul and uncouth" (*FR* II, ii, 246), a phrase rendered as "hard to hear (*nanting*) and uncouth (*cuye*, rough and wild)" (Deng *FR*: 317), "course (*cubi*) and vulgar (*esu*, evil and common)" (Yilin *FR*: 307), and "evil and weird (*guguai*)" (Zhu *FR*: 395). Isildur could not know the meaning was "evil," since he could not understand it. We might accept he was sensing the nature of the Ring, but it is not by way of the semantic meaning of the words that he judges them evil. This inscription could be saying, "How do I love thee? Let me count the ways," and it would still sound horrible. "Tolkien refers to the 'beauty' of the 'word-form' independent of meaning as capable of giving aesthetic pleasure" (Fimi 2009: 77)—and presumably the reverse: a word can sound "ugly" even if its meaning is not. Some languages, such as French and Irish, Tolkien simply found ugly (ibid., 87). Even if we don't know the meaning we are affected by the word itself. When orcs speak, the "evil" is not only in their guttural voices, but in "their abominable tongue" (*TT* III, iii, 435): "their hateable (*kezeng*) language" (Zhu *TT*: 64), their "hard-to-listen-to (*nanting*) language" (Deng *TT*: 46), "their irritating (*taoyan*) local dialect (*tuhua*)" (Yilin *TT*: 44).

Tolkien moves easily from his fantasy world to political commentary, saying,

> their language was actually more degraded and filthy than I have shown it. I do not suppose that any will wish for a closer rendering, though models are easy to find. Much the same sort of talk can still be heard among the orc-minded; dreary and repetitive with hatred and contempt, too long removed from good to retain even

verbal vigour, save in the ears of those to whom only the squalid sounds strong. (*RK* Appendix F, II, 1108)

The degraded language of the orcs can "still" be heard—"still" as in: during Tolkien's time. This passage is from the Appendixes, where the authorial voice is less obviously in-character and the fourth wall can be broken. Where and when exactly can "models" of orc-speech be found? Tolkien uses "orc" to refer to people with the attributes of (in this passage:) degradation, filth, dreariness, repetition, hatred, contempt, distance from good, and impressed by the "squalid." More generally, the orc-minded have crudity, lust, lust for power, violence, and greed. Cody Jarman (2016: 153) may be right that Tolkien harks back to a premodernist conception of language, but in this passage I hear a much simpler explanation: the Tory intellectual recoiled from the dirty words of the urban working class.

There is also "the dreadful language of the Wargs," partially understood by Gandalf. Bilbo hears it, and "it sounded terrible to him, and as if all their talk was about cruel and wicked things, as it was" (*H*, vi, 111). No doubt, the wargs were indeed speaking of cruel things as they closed in on the hunt, but in another context their speech might be pleasant, as when curling up to sleep with the well-fed pack. But as it is presented to us, it is a language in which only cruel and wicked things can be said. Bilbo guesses this despite having no idea what they were saying, and the omniscient narrator confirms his suspicions.

Seductive Language

Saruman is famous for the evil in his voice. Which language he is speaking is not the issue here, but rather, the magical qualities of his arts of persuasion, described as enchantment, powerful, a spell, or enthralling. In contrast to the phonetically painful languages, Saruman's words are seductive: "its very sound an enchantment" (*TT* III, x, 564). Deng as usual comes closest to the original, "itself full of magic power (*moli*)" (Deng *TT*: 220), whereas Yilin simplifies slightly, "full of captivating power (*meili*)" (Yilin *TT*: 202), and Zhu elaborates, "its every word and every sentence (*meizi meiju*) like music captivated (*meihuo*) people's minds" (Zhu *TT*: 264). His speech is repeatedly described as a spell or as transmitting a spell, a term usually translated using variations of *zhou* 咒, about which more below (*TT* III, v, 481, Deng *TT*: 109, Yilin *TT*: 101, Zhu *TT*: 138; *TT* III, x, 563, Deng *TT*: 218, Yilin *TT*: 201). The Riders were silent "as men spell-bound" (*TT* III, x, 565), "like they were repressed (*zhenzhu*, pressed down, controlled) by a spell (*zhouyu*)" (Deng *TT*: 221), "like they received the spell (*zhouyu*)'s poison (*guhuo*, venom and puzzlement)" (Yilin *TT*: 203), "like they'd been struck by magic (*zhongle mofa*)" (Zhu *TT*: 266). His voice "was enough to hold them enthralled" (*TT* III, x, 564). "Enthralled" is *rumi*, entered an astray state (Deng *TT*: 220; Yilin *TT*: 202), or the more interesting "lost their sense of self (*mishi ziwo*)" (Zhu *TT*: 264).

Something in his voice induces both obedience and amnesia. "Those who listened unwarily to that voice could seldom report the words that they had heard; and if they did, they wondered, for little power remained in them" (*TT* III, x, 564). That last phrase clearly means that the semantic meaning of the words themselves were not the basis of the power, but Saruman's mind or personality or voice. Deng clarifies what was lost, "those words had no captivating power (*meili*)" (Deng *TT*: 220). Zhu elaborates, "those words were fundamentally ordinary talk with nothing strange (*pingtan wuqi*)" (Zhu *TT*: 264). And Yilin reads "them" to mean the listeners: "because they themselves had no power to control themselves" (Yilin *TT*: 202; see also Chisolm 2019: 94, 99).

The passage goes on to contrast real magic with mere tricks. "For some the spell lasted only while the voice spoke to them, and when it spoke to another they smiled, as men do who see through a juggler's trick while others gape at it" (*TT* III, x, 564). All three translate "spell" here as *moli*, magic power. In reference to gaping at a "juggler's trick," Zhu is succinct: "a magician's (*moshushi*)'s trick (*guiji*)" (Zhu *TT*: 264). Yilin has "a magic performance (*moshu biaoyan*)" (Yilin *TT*: 202). Both change juggling into conjuring, where Deng leaves the nature of the trick open: those watching "a variety show (*zashua*) cheap trick (*baxi*) are dumbstruck (*mudeng koudai*, eyes wide open and mouth blank)" (Deng *TT*: 220). The idea that you believe Saruman when he's speaking to you, but not when he speaks to another, might be comparable to how we "believe" (or at least, suspend disbelief) when absorbed in a story, but knowingly see it as just made up when we step back, or as Sam says, go from "inside" to "outside" a story (*TT* IV, viii, 696).

Curses

"Cursing" refers to a spectrum of practices, from the "expletive" meant to shock or just release stress, through to malevolent, magical speech-acts. The effect of a "dirty word" may be related to class, gender, and religion. How can we calibrate or assess the precise degree of offensiveness, especially in a time when it is increasingly difficult to predict what readers will find offensive? Is there a seismometer for shock value? Certainly we can't imagine Bilbo Baggins saying "fuck." Instead, for abuse, Tolkien uses a variety of euphemistic, dated, or quaint terms. For example, Sam castigates himself for not bringing along a rope. He says, "Well, if I don't deserve to be hung on the end of one as a warning to numbskulls! You're nowt but a ninnyhammer, Sam Gamgee" (*TT* IV, i, 594). The *OED* describes ninnyhammer as the same as ninny: a blockhead, fool, or braggart. There are examples from 1592 on, apparently fizzling out in the mid-nineteenth century, but the next citation is in 1954—as spoken by Sam Gamgee. Ninnyhammer is listed in *Life of Tristam Shandy* (1767) along with numskuls, doddypoles, and dunderheads. The *OED* cites an example from 1991 which puts it along with dunces, boobies, dingbats, rattlepates, wallies, and jobbernowls. Clearly these terms now belong to a register of obsolete affectations, humorously mild, almost mocking the person who says them as a fuddy-duddy, goody two-shoes, or old fart.

How do the translations deal with numbskull and ninnyhammer? For numbskull we get *shagua* 傻瓜, (stupid gourd) (Yilin *TT*: 239); *bennaogua*, (stupid brain-gourd) (Deng *TT*: 259); and Zhu paraphrases using *ben* (stupid) (Zhu *TT*: 309). For ninnyhammer, we get "very big (*tiandade*, as big as the sky) idiot (*shagua*, stupid gourd)" (Deng *TT*: 260), "stupid egg (*bendan*)" (Yilin *TT*: 239), and "brain bag thick porridge (*naodai zhuangjianghu*)" (Zhu *TT*: 309). In English, we sometimes call a head a gourd ("he's out of his gourd") but the usage is much more standard in Chinese. The lexicon also involves eggs—*bendan*, stupid egg. But surely the great payoff here is the magnificent idiom implying that Sam's brain-bag is full of thick porridge. These are all mild and picturesque, as appropriate for Sam to be speaking them, but not nearly as antiquated as "ninnyhammer."

Still in the category of mild curse-words, Otho Sackville-Baggins says "Fiddlesticks!" (*FR* I, i, 38). One would not expect anyone to have the word's oldest meaning in mind—a horse-hair bow for playing the fiddle. Deng renders this as "what joke is this? (*kai shenmo wanxiao*)" (Deng *FR*: 47). Yilin has "not worth a penny (*yiwen buzhi*)" (Yilin *FR*: 46). Zhu uses *huche* (nonsense, drivel) (Zhu *FR*: 75). Later, Sam expresses surprise with: "Snakes and adders!" (*TT* IV, i, 598), not in response to actual snakes, but surely a pun on Snakes and Ladders. For this, we get: "big snake little snake ah!" (Deng *TT*: 265), "these snakes and scorpions! (*shexie*)" (Yilin *TT*: 244–245), and "*yaoming*!" which is literally, "takes life," "it'll kill (me)," but functions like "holy cow!" (Zhu *TT*: 315).

It is not always possible to decide when the verb to "curse" (someone) is an actual speech-act, or just an expression of exasperation or anger. When Boromir calls after Frodo with, "Curse you and all halflings to death and darkness!" (*FR* II, x, 390), is he casting malevolent magic, or just angrily berating them? The three translations do not resolve this ambiguity, using *zhouzu* or *zuzhou* for "curse," with Yilin using a set phrase for the latter part of the line: "I want to curse you (*zuzhou*), curse you and all the little people with 10,000 calamities without recovery (*wanjie bufu*)!" (Yilin *FR*: 487; cf. Zhu *FR*: 614; Deng *FR*: 501).

When we hear the orcs, the tone is inevitably lower. Ugluk swears (in the sense of invoking a higher power): "By the White hand!" and adds, "Run, curse you!" (*TT* III, iii, 439). Zhu: "In the name of the white palm I curse (*zhouma*, curse and scold) you.... Stupid eggs (*hundan*), why don't you run!" (Zhu *TT*: 71). But we find a significant variation here. Deng has "White hand above! (*baishou zaishang*) ... *gaiside*, quickly run!" (Deng *TT*: 52). Yilin: "Needs a spanking (*qianzou* 欠揍)! Let us run (*geiwopao*), *gaiside*!" (Yilin *TT*: 49). Two of the three translations render "curse you" as *gaiside*, "ought to die." *Gaisi* is what you would say if you wanted to *zuzhou* someone, though in both languages, "I curse (*zuzhou*) you" is a speech-act which names the category of utterance and also actually *does* it.

This wavering continues throughout the corpus: Gollum says, "Curse them!" (*TT* IV, i, 599), Deng and Zhu have *zuzhou* (Deng *TT*: 266; Zhu *TT*: 317) but Yilin uses *gaisi* (Yilin *TT*: 246). Damrod says, "curse the Southrons!" (*TT* IV, iv, 645), Deng uses *zuzhou* (Deng *TT*: 327), Yilin uses *gaisi* (Yilin *TT*: 302), but Zhu covers both the bases: *zuzhou* those *gaisi* southern people!" (Zhu *TT*: 387). Zhu even uses *gaisi* for "Alas!" (*TT* III, i, 403, Zhu *TT*: 16). Legolas uses the form of a curse, though clearly not intending actual harm: "A plague on Dwarves and their stiff necks!" (*FR* II, vi, 338). Deng erases any sense of the curse: "Dwarves and their stubborn bad temper, really make people's heads ache!" (Deng *FR*: 434). But the others use *gaisi*. Yilin: "ought-to-die (*gaisi*) little dwarves, really are stubborn-headed asses (*toujianglü*)" (Yilin *FR*: 423). Zhu: "ought-to-die (*gaisi*) hard-headed (*yingtou*) dwarves!" (Zhu *FR*: 538). The translations confirm the sense that Legolas is not casting a spell to afflict the dwarves with plague, but is only using the idiom of the curse out of irritation.

As malevolent ritual speech-acts, curses generally take the form of "May something bad happen to you," or "May some powerful force do something bad to you." It is not just a prophecy, for a prophecy predicts but doesn't make it happen; here, the speaking of it is intended to make it happen. Those disloyal soldiers lingered on in ghostly form for thousands of years because Isildur laid upon them a curse, not just a prediction (*RK* V, ii, 765). Faramir says to Gollum: "And may death find you swiftly" if he fails Frodo (*TT* IV, vi, 675). The construction "May … (something happen)" is translated as "[I] wish/vow (*yuan* 願)" (Zhu *TT*: 434, Deng *TT*: 367), while Yilin changes it into a mere prediction: "your time of death will immediately come" (Yilin *TT*: 340). Sam later invokes Faramir's curse to make another curse: "May the curse of Faramir bite that Gollum and bite him quick!" (*TT* IV, ix, 706). Zhu: "I hope Faramir's curse (*zuzhou*) quickly repays (*baoying* 報應) on Gollum's body!" (Zhu *TT*: 480; and similar at Yilin *TT*: 377; Deng *TT*: 408). Again, the mere desire for and speaking of it changes the reality. Death did find Gollum after he turned against Frodo, though not swiftly.

The negative and hostile curse is mirrored by the positive and voluntary oath, a closely related magical speech-act. The oathbreakers (*RK* V, ii, 772) are *beiqi shiyan zhe* 背弃誓言者 ones who abandoned/renounced their oath (Yilin *RK*: 56, and similar at Deng *RK*: 57), with the key term *shi* 誓 (oath, vow, pledge); or the somewhat weaker *huinuozhemen*, ones who destroyed a promise (Zhu *RK*: 82). Yet for "Oaths ye have taken" (*RK* V, v, 818), all use *shi* (Yilin *RK*: 113; Zhu *RK*: 152; Deng *RK*: 115). The texts are riddled with prophetic oaths, such as Aragorn foreseeing that he and Éomer would meet again, which Aragorn formalizes as both oracle and oath with, "But I say to you …" (*RK* V, ii, 762; and *RK* V, vi, 830). The idea of an oath as ironclad is very familiar in Chinese fiction, especially *xia* fiction. In Buddhism, an oath (such as taking the precepts) is an event of body, speech, and mind which itself creates karmic causes.

Spells

Some said Túrin "was cast under a spell by the Dragon" (*UT*: 112). In case we might confuse a spell with something nice, Shi and Deng add the familiar prefix: "he was given a *mo*-spell (*mozhou*) by an evil dragon (*elong*)" (Shi and Deng *UT*: 147). Or, Glaurung "bewitched you both to your doom" (*UT*: 142). "Bewitched" does not sound benign, and again Shi and Deng clarify: "poisoned and bewitched (*guhuo* 蛊惑) the two of you until your ruin" (Shi and Deng *UT*: 184). *Guhuo* combines *gu* (poisonous insect, to drive insane, poison) with *huo* (puzzle, delude).

"Incantation" is generally treated as a synonym of "spell." Frodo hears the creepy song sung by the barrow-wights turn into an "incantation" (*FR* I, viii, 137), and we find three variants, all relying on the common term *zhou*. Zhu uses *zuzhou* 詛咒, where *zu* also has the meaning of cursing and malediction (Zhu *FR*: 226). Deng uses *zhou*-text (*zhouwen*) (Deng *FR*: 176). Yilin gives "*zhou*-word (or -language)" (*zhouyu*) (Yilin *FR*: 173). For, "Gandalf tried various incantations" (*H*, ii, 48), Zhu has, "recited (*niansong*) various kinds of *zhouyu*" (Zhu *H*: 53), and Wu also uses *zhouyu* (Wu *H*: 60), while Yilin generalizes the action with, "Gandalf did the best he could (*shichu hunshen xieshu*, came out with full-body skills)" (Yilin *H*: 38). For the knives "wound about with spells for the bane of Mordor" (*TT* III, i, 405), Deng and Yilin use *zhouyu* (Deng *TT*: 8; Yilin *TT*: 6) and Zhu, "spell text (*zhouwen*)" (Zhu *TT*: 19).

Zhou has noun and verb uses, a spectrum including incantation, spell, curse, malediction, to revile. The character indicates an oral act, indicated by the two mouths (*kou* 口) in both its variant forms, 呪 or 咒. The other part of zhou, *ji* 几, has the archaic meaning of a small table—words spoken over an altar? *Zhou* covers the same spectrum as "curse," both a magical speech-act and an expression of hostility; and as both utterance and written text.

In his notes on writing systems, Tolkien describes the distinction between letters and runes (*RK* Appendix E, II, 1091). Deng's collaborator Shi Zhongge transliterates "rune" as *runiwen*, rune-text (Deng *RK*: 495). But more interestingly, Zhu gives *fuwen* 符文, tally-text or talismanic writing (Zhu *RK* Appendix: 113). Similarly for the "plain runes" that Thorin sees on the map (*H*, iii, 59), Zhu gives "simple *fuwen*" (Zhu *H*: 65), Yilin gives "mysterious (*shenmi*) marks/symbols (*fuhao* 符号)" (Yilin *H*: 48). *Fu* derives from the practice of breaking an object (bamboo or ceramic, perhaps) in two, so that one half could be given as a marker of debt or deputed authority, demonstrated by rematching the two halves. It was used to credential envoys and officials. Aside from commercial and bureaucratic uses, it was by extension applied to talismans—in the sense that a Daoist talisman represents one half of a match in the spirit-world, and hence authority, control, or credit in the spirit world. An object which bears a tallying relationship with a spirit or demon would be a valuable means of control. Hence *fuban* 符板 (tally-plate or tally-board) and *fupai* 符牌 (tally-plate or -tablet), and *fulu* 符籙, tally-register, a text used by Daoists to ward off evil. Zhu gives the runes a much greater magical property.

Zhu seems particularly inventive around spells. Failing to open the Doors of Durin, Gandalf claims, "I once knew every spell in all the tongues of Elves or Men or Orcs" (*FR* II, iv, 299), Deng and Yilin both use *zhouyu* (Deng *FR*: 383; Yilin *FR*: 374), but Zhu takes a different route: "I once had a knowledge of this kind of password (*tongguan miyu*) used by all elves, humans and half-beast-persons" (Zhu *FR*: 476). *Tongguan miyu* is more literally pass-gate secret language/code/cypher. Similarly, when Gandalf says he "put a shutting-spell on the door" (*FR* II, v, 319), Deng uses "a shutting (*guanbi*) spell (*zhouyu*)" (Deng *FR*: 408) and Yilin merely "recited a spell (*zhouyu*) against the door" (Yilin *FR*: 398), but Zhu says Gandalf tried to "seal (*fengyin*) that door" (Zhu *FR*: 506). *Fengyin* is commonly used of sealing an envelope; among the meanings of *feng* are envelope and to seal (a letter); *yin* is stamp, engrave, or otherwise imprint a mark on another surface. Zhu strengthens the idea of sealing the door, like an envelope with a wax seal, imprinted with the words Gandalf spoke.

Gandalf goes on: "The counter-spell was terrible. It nearly broke me. For an instant the door left my control and began to open! I had to speak a word of Command" (*FR* II, v, 319). There are variants for "counter-spell," but the notable term here is a "word of Command," capital-C, clearly a kind of spell of a higher order than his shutting-spell or the counter-spell. Deng uses "recite (*nian*) a 'command' (*mingling*) word" (Deng *FR*: 409). And Yilin, "recite a command-talisman (*lingfu* 令符, order-tally)" (Yilin *FR*: 398).

But, again revealing his gamer roots, Zhu gives, "I was forced to display (*shichan*, display skill) a true-word technique (*zhenyanshu* 真言術)" (Zhu *FR*: 506). *Zhenyan*, "true or real word," is also a Buddhist term, the most common translation of mantra. The Japanese pronunciation of the term is Shingon which also denotes one of the major sects of Buddhism, but in Chinese lacks that sectarian meaning. Perhaps a mantra is greater than a spell (*zhou*), though the distinction is not absolute: the Buddhist text the *Dabeizhou* is usually translated as "the great compassion mantra." Romano notes a case of using *zhenyan* as a translation of *logos* in the Christian Bible (Romano 2013: 94), which however did not catch on—if it had, we might imagine the word Gandalf used to seal the door was the same Word of the first verse of the Gospel of John.

Cosmogonic Spells

At Rivendell, Frodo is lost in an experience far beyond an aesthetic rapture, when the songs begin to *make* what they describe, or at least "almost it seemed":

> At first the beauty of the melodies and of the interwoven words in elven-tongues, even though he understood them little, held him in a spell, as soon as he began to attend to them. Almost it seemed that the words took shape, and visions of far lands and bright things that he had never yet imagined opened out before him. (*FR* II, i, 227)

Is this magic, or a description of the way in which we all "almost" feel ourselves in the world of a vivid story or song? For Tolkien, with his view of fantasy storytelling as an "elvish craft," we can assume both (*OFS*: 61, 64). The notion that listening to the ballads of the elves might seem to actually break down the barriers and give one a vision of paradise fits perfectly with some of what Tolkien wrote about the magical or divine power of artistic creation. "An essential power of Faerie is thus the power of making immediately effective by the will the visions of 'fantasy'" (*OFS*: 42). In this particular moment, the Undying Lands seem to be not only a physical location far to the West, but a creative magic conjured by the elves, not even reliant on the listener's full understanding of the semantic meanings ("he understood them little"). The "words took shape," sound transmuting into light just as the visible (and, eventually, tangible) universe derived from the singing of the Ainur. Tolkien said that his stories arose out of a desire to create a world in which his invented languages could live, though this claim may be part of his "biographical legend" (Fimi 2009: 195, also 64–67). He viewed the storyteller's acts of "world-building" as echoes of God's creation of the real world. Here, we see: God created by narration the world (eventually including Tolkien); Tolkien sub-created by narration a vision of gods singing into being a world (eventually including elves); and the elves who inhabit it sub-sub-created in song a vision of paradise. This description of Frodo mesmerized and drifting into sleep is loaded with meaning.

Deng renders this first line as: "At first, the elegant lyrics in the elven language and the wonderful melody intertwined together, even though he could not understand much, but as soon as he began attentively listening, he then immediately entered a trance (*rule mi*, entered a 'lost' state)" (Deng *FR*: 288). Zhu uses the same term, "was lost in it" (Zhu *FR*: 361). Their use of the character *mi* (lost, astray) is interesting. Naturally it can simply mean lost, as in *milu*, "lose the road," when you're walking around and don't know where you are. As a translation of "held him in a spell," *mi* initially brings to mind *mixin* "lost or astray faith." But *mixin* is a modern term, coined specifically to translate "superstition." The older phrase it evokes is *mi er xin zhi*, "got lost [in something such as a story] and thereby believed it." Certainly we can say a certain story or song put a spell on you, and *mi* lacks that sense of magical technique from the original phrase "held him in a spell," but it gains a feeling of wandering. Here, Frodo is not "held," but "enters." With a rather different metaphor but still involving motion, Yilin says the music "immediately lured (*yin*, drew in) him" (Yilin *FR*: 282).

One interesting aspect of the three translations of this passage is in the image of words taking shape. Zhu is perhaps most literal around the phrase "took shape": "Soon those lyrics seemed to be like changing into a concrete form (*juxiang*)" (Zhu *FR*: 361). *Juxiang* is composed of *ju* 具, which has several meanings, but here: to have; cf. *juti* "having a body" another term for concreteness. And *xiang* 象, "image." This is contrasted with *chouxiang* 抽象 (abstract, literally removed-image). Deng adds a little: the words "seemed to change magically to assume form (*huanhua chengxing* 幻化成形)" (Deng *FR*: 288). But here, the Yilin edition dispenses with the abstraction and gives us a tangible and specifically Chinese image: "This singing was like a long-spool picture scroll (*changzhou huajuan*)." The most famous of all such works of art is *Qingming Shanghe Tu*, "Along the River During the Qingming Festival," by Zhang Zeduan (1085–1145), which is 5.25 meters long. Such scrolls were most often landscapes, which by their very length implied the viewer wandering a great distance. Yilin depicts Frodo listening to a song, and the music and words are so vivid he sees them painted, concretely in the form of a scroll. Frodo seeing a picture of endless roaming, rather than the more immersive experience of the original or the translations of Zhu and Deng.

Yilin continues, "before him manifested a thing he had never seen before (*jiansuo meijian*, see what was not yet seen), a thing he had never imagined before (*xiangsuo meixiang*) distant scenery and bright view" (Yilin *FR*: 282). Yilin does a clever thing here, taking the phrase "that he had never imagined" and elaborating it in two parallel four-character phrases, explicitly associating vision and imagination.

A vision of a world seeming to come into being from sound replicates the cosmogonic myth of Ilúvatar. The *Ainulindalë* begins with a disembodied unity creating a series of successively less powerful and more physical beings. The first generation of such beings manifests as musical notes, which form chords, and hence harmony, complexity, and inevitably discord. Vision is created to express that music, and then comes the materialization of that vision—the world. We are presented with a descent into materiality, multiplicity, and specificity.

Initially, thought alone made beings, comparable to our beginning the creative process by simply imagining things: "and he made first the Ainur, the Holy Ones, that were the offspring of his thought" (*S*: 3). Yilin: "He (*ta* 他) first made the 'holy worthies' [or sages, *shengxian* 圣贤] Ainur. These 'holy worthies' all were born from what his heart-mind thought" (Yilin S: 3). Deng, "He (*ta* 祂) first from His own thought made the many Ainur, 'the sacred envoys,' they were before the myriad things were made and were with Him" (Deng S 2002: 3). Deng uses a less common variant of the third person pronoun, *ta* 祂 rather than the more common *ta* 他 as Yilin uses. They are pronounced the same and both mean "he," but 祂 has a radical which indicates it is used for gods. In her later translation, she changed "sacred envoys" (*shensheng de shizhe* 神聖的使者)" to "sacred ones (*shenshengzhe* 神圣者)" (Deng S 2015: 31).

The world emerges from unity to multiplicity, from potential to actual, from a thought to ink on paper. We might compare several images: Ilúvatar's thinking the world into being, the emergence of ideas from the cauldron of soup, biblical narratives of creation, and Daoist ideas of order emerging from chaos. Genesis 1:1, from the *RSV* says: "In the beginning God created the heavens and the earth. The earth was without form and void …" The International Catholic Biblical Society translation has: "At the start of the original beginning, when the Lord of Heaven made heaven and earth, the great land was one expanse of *hundun* 混沌, without form and without pattern …" I have checked several Protestant translations and they also use *hundun* for "void."

Furthermore, "it seemed to him that Ilúvatar took no thought for the Void, and he was impatient of its emptiness" (S: 4). Li Yao's version for Yilin renders this as, "In his view, Ilúvatar basically had not thought of the *hundun* unmanifested world (*hundun weikai de shijie*). Facing an expanse of emptiness (*kongxu*), he was very impatient" (Yilin S: 4). *Hundun* is a term of Daoist origin, usually glossed as a chaotic potentiality, a seething foment which allows no divisions. It is *not* empty. Whereas in a void there is nothing, in *hundun* there is *no* (particular, individualizable) *thing*. Everything is there at least in potential, but this reality is indivisible, so we are unable to make subject-object distinctions, let alone distinctions such as chair-table-room-person. In this sense there is both everything and no *thing* in *hundun*. If an image of emptiness is a bowl with nothing in it, the image of *hundun* would a bowl with a gloppy, squishy soup in it—indeed, the term comes to us in its English pronunciation of its Cantonese pronunciation: wonton. A Chinese soup. *Hundun* does resemble the Buddhist idea of sunyata (emptiness), in that neither posits a simple absence (like an empty room). *Hundun* emphasizes the fertile chaos of infinite potential, whereas sunyata emphasizes absence (of any separate thing). In Genesis, God creates *ex nihilo*, or perhaps starts with "waters," but then needs to separate and structure this wonton soup of raw material. In Daoism there is no real sense of who created *hundun*, but otherwise the actualization of our world is somewhat comparable to the narratives in Genesis and the *Ainulinalë*.

There are other examples of the term *hundun* as Void. "But when they were come into the Void, Ilúvatar said to them: 'Behold your Music!' … and they saw a new World made visible before them, and it was globed amid the Void, and it was sustained therein, but was not of it" (S: 6). The Yilin edition: "Coming to the place of *hundun*, Ilúvatar said to them: 'Look at your music!' … Before the Ainur's eyes appeared a new world, that was a giant globe which formed in the midst of *hundun*. It seemed to be continuously suspended there, constant and not decreasing" (Yilin S: 6). Deng: They came to "the domain of emptiness", and "Before their eyes appeared (*chuxian*) a new universe (*yuzhou*, space and time), in the emptiness (*kongwu*) there was a globe (*qiuti*, sphere-body) manifested (*xianxian* 顯現), existing (*cunli*) and not falling in the emptiness (*kongxu*), yet not belonging to (*bu shuyu* 不屬于) emptiness" (Deng S 2002: 6; Deng S 2015: 34 is similar). Whereas Yilin breezes past it, the more theologically aware translator picks up on the notion of the world being "in" but not "of" the Void, very much analogous to John 17:13–14, with its contrast of Christ and Christians being "in" but not "of" (*shuyu* 屬于/属于) the world.

Conclusions

When Tolkien called storytelling "sub-creation," he made a direct parallel from God's creation of the real world through thought and speech to the author's creation of fictional worlds out of thought and speech. As MacDonald said of God, "He utters them into the visible" (MacDonald 1893: 4), which could as much describe an author's work. One can see Tolkien's creation story (from the *Silmarillion*) and the scene of elven music building a world around Frodo as variations on the theme.

All authors are by definition focused on words, but considering Tolkien's career in philology and his theology of sub-creation, we can assume an unusual intensity to that focus. Whether in his essay *On Fairy-stories* and other writings, or at various points in his fictional works, Tolkien constantly dabbles with the line between the imaginary and the empirical. With his metaphors of soup and divine creation and spells and singing and (in the Chinese) long-spool picture-scrolls, he seems to be be trying to sense the nature of that line, and hence (perhaps) the nature of God's creativity.

There is an inevitable overlay of meanings from Daoism, especially in the emergence of concrete particularity from the infinite potential of *hundun*. Daoism does not, however, posit a will acting in this fall. In Daoist philosophy, we often see a parallel between the cosmogony and our consciousness of "objects"—the emergence of ideas and categories, making the world multiple and fragmented. When, as babies, we start to multiply the "things" in the world (Mummy, Daddy, teddy bear, cookie ...), we are re-enacting the big bang. Though it is useful to have lots of categories to divide up the world, in Daoism it is also a loss, or a fall. We move further away from our own infinite potential when we treat the world as a multiplicity of separate objects. We mistake what we say as eternal truth when we fail to see how our language makes our world.

13

And Back Again

How does this exploration of translations reflect back on the original? What does suspending the hierarchy of original and translation tell us about this story, so familiar to English-language readers? This is a thought experiment, in which we consider the works as cultural circulation, independent of the intentions of the authors or any actual publication history. Looking back at the English from the Chinese or any other language emphasizes how Tolkien's work is a global school of storytelling, a diffuse mythos, and a folkloric tradition.

So, let us pretend Tolkien was the *translator* of a complex narrative tradition (and I don't mean the Red Book of Westmarch). We might imagine a paragraph from a book review:

> The Chinese narrative cycle known collectively as *Mojie* ("Magic Ring") consists of several versions of an extended set of interconnected narratives. These multiple mythologies present us with distinct voices, even if the plots are virtually identical. Professor Tolkien appears to have synthesized multiple examples of the original Chinese literary tradition into a single text. However, in the decision to publish only *one* English translation, he has reduced a great richness of storytelling diversity to a single voice. If we wish to read the story in all its true variety, we can only await translations of the many originals, but until then we must make do with this expedient digest. And we might ask, what was lost in translation?

Or at least, I might ask, how has this exercise changed *my* reading of *The Lord of the Rings*? Certain words and lines now stand out to me, because I hear something else behind them. A vivid image of Galadriel's eyes watching the movements of mountains and seas. Aragorn as a kung fu hero. Zen Master Gandalf. Sam's brain-bag full of thick porridge. Time being much more river-like than in the original. The possibility of entirely different costumes and architectures. A curious attention to the word "the." Middle-earth is no longer quite so European; the Shire is a little less Worcestershire. I have an inclination to see the story's many coincidences and intuitions as results of past-life karma or an impersonal, natural order, rather than the hidden influence of Ilúvatar, who is now a little less like a code for Yahweh. A stronger sense that the people of Middle-earth might pass through the Court of Hell.

The tension of the noble heathen unable to find Christian salvation is somewhat easier to reconcile in the context of traditional Chinese religions, without any assumption of a single life and a single God in a single Heaven forever. There are pervasive hints of Chinese soteriology, such as returning to the West (-ern Pure Land), or the Halls of Mandos as a place of judgment and repentance rather than mere reflection. In addition to many such specific details, there is an irreducible difference of atmosphere derived from the obvious fact of the "Chineseness" of the Chinese texts, so that even the most faithfully translated passage is still a different "form of life."

I can *imagine* the story differently, because I have access to other formulae, an alternative abracadabra, an unfamiliar alchemy. My head-canon has more potential. There are new flavors in my cauldron of soup. Gosetti-Ferencei defined the imagination as "the presentational capacity of consciousness which can meaningfully transform what is thereby given" (2018: 5). I would emphasize the word *transform*—not just consume. It is active more than passive. I am basically unconcerned with "staying faithful" to Tolkien—as if that were even possible. *Why not* put *LOTR* in an *wuxia* box? Especially if a new box promises a different gift within.

Though the original is not a simple, singular, fixed thing, it is, compared to the translations, *relatively* singular. Its meaning to a reader always remains open, but there is a much stronger sense that, even if you see a new thing in each re-reading, you are dealing with the exact same words (with a few frayed edges for earlier drafts, editing changes, authorial tinkering). Whereas, in Chinese or any other language, we can always look forward to a new *Mojie*, to the *next* one and the *next* one after that. Translation enlarges the franchise. Translation "may open your hoard" so that the meanings that had been "locked" in a single language may "fly away like cage-birds" (*OFS*: 84). After multiple re-readings, the original may become a little too cozy; but reading a translation, I might feel like Keats upon reading a new translation of Homer, "like some watcher of the skies / When a new planet swims into his ken." Or, in Zha Liangzheng's translation, like "an astronomical observer (*guanxiangjia*) discovered a new constellation (*xingzuo*)" (2002: 25). Or, per Ni Ching-hsi and Chou Yung-chi, "At this time I felt like a person keeping watch in the sky (*zai tiankong liaowang*), / A new planet suddenly flashed (*shan*) past his line of sight (*shixian*)" (Liu and Zhang 1992: 343).

Translation does not just overlay additional images onto the dominant image. The original and the translations talk to each other, and don't always agree. The dissonance between them makes the characters unstable, more ambiguous. My images of characters or events in a story are now more complicated, and less obvious. But rather than feeling that I've lost something—I used to have a crisp, specific image in mind, now it's gone—I would instead gamble that I'm seeing more. What I'm losing is simplicity, what now feels like a relatively flat single image. This is not entirely different from how you see more during each re-reading, but here, the new vistas are inherent to every word of a translation. Sometimes there is an increase of specificity, when one text gives us a general or ambiguous term and another text names names. Or vice versa, where two or more meanings are lumped together, which gives a sense of nuance lost, but ambiguity gained.

These new layers are comparable to, but not exactly the same as the way in which, having seen the films, we see particular images when we return to the books. One could certainly bring the films into the mix, not only by looking at subtitles or dubbing but also including aspects related to the change in medium: for example, audiences hear Viggo Mortensen's voice, and returning to the novels, we still hear his voice. "Our imaginations are permanently colonized by the visual and aural world of the films" (Hutcheon 2012: 122). How is this overlay of voice affected when the English *film* is speaking a different language from the Chinese *books*? Do Chinese readers *not* hear Viggo Mortensen? How does translation interact with adaptation?

Future explorations of translations of Tolkien could go in many different directions. I considered or wrote drafts of several chapters which were set aside for reasons of length. These included: class, hierarchy, and feudalism; cosmogony, especially in relation to the Bible and Daoist ideas (touched on in Chapter 12); cosmology, the basic shape of the universe, compared to the Buddhist world-system; the dragon/*long* in comparative terms; the overlay of Éowyn and Mulan; ideas of human nature and moral corruption (especially the effects of the Ring); and riddles, thinking of Adam Roberts' *The Riddles of the Hobbit*. The use of the translated perspective is a way to re-see any aspect of the texts. Indeed, one might take any of the themes from Tolkien scholarship— nature, war, theology, women—and in each case, imagine what could be suggested by the shift in perspective from one side of the glass to the other. Imagine what is before your very eyes and yet invisible, as long as you are viewing it from the perspective of only one language.

Bibliography

Chinese Translations of Tolkien

There have been multiple editions of the translations. Here I list the editions which I have used or referred to in this book, and a representative sample of other translations.

Translations by Zhu Xueheng 朱學恆

Habiren 哈比人 (Hobbit Person/People). Taipei: Linking, 2001.
Mojie Erbuqu: Shuangcheng qimou 魔戒二部曲：雙城奇謀 (The Second Book of Magic Ring: The Ingenious Plan of the Twin Walled-Cities). Taipei: Linking, 2001, revised 2012.
Mojie sanbuqu: Wangzhe zailin 魔戒三部曲：王者再臨 (The Third Book of Magic Ring: The King Again Approaches). Taipei: Linking, 2001, revised 2012.
Mojie shoubuqu: Mojie xianshen 魔戒首部曲：魔戒現身 (The First Book of Magic Ring: The Magic Ring Appears). Taipei: Linking, 2001, revised 2012.

The Yilin Press Edition

Mojie: Mojie zaixian 魔戒：魔戒再现 (The Magic Ring: The Magic Ring Re-appears.) [*The Fellowship of the Rings*], translated by Ding Di 丁棣. Nanjing: Yilin Press, 2001.
Mojie: Shuangta qibing 魔戒：双塔奇兵 (The Magic Ring: The Surprise Attack of the Twin Towers.) [*The Two Towers*], translated by Yao Jinrong 姚锦镕. Nanjing: Yilin Press, 2001.
Mojie: Wangzhe wudi 魔戒：王者无敌 (The Magic Ring: The King is Triumphant) [*The Return of the King*], translated by Tang Dingjiu 汤定九. Nanjing: Yilin Press, 2001.
Mojie qianzhuan: Huobite ren 魔戒前传：霍比特人 (The Prequel to The Magic Ring: Hobbit Person/People), translated by Li Yao. Nanjing: Yilin Press, 2001.
Mojie qiyuan: Jingling baozuan 魔戒起源：精灵宝钻 (The Beginning of The Magic Ring: The Elves' Jewel) [*The Silmarillion*], translated by Li Yao 李尧. Nanjing: Yilin Press, 2001.

Translations by Deng Jiawan 邓嘉宛/鄧嘉宛 and Collaborators

Beilun yu Luxi-en 貝倫與露西恩. (*Beren and Lúthien*) with Shi Zhongge 石中歌 and Du Yunci 杜蘊慈. Taipei: Linking, 2017.
Gangduolin de xianluo 刚多林的陷落, (*The Fall of Gondolin*) with Shi Zhongge 石中歌 and Du Yunci 杜蘊慈. Shanghai and Beijing: Shanghai People's Publishing House and Horizon Media, 2020.
Hulin de zinü 胡林的子女 (*The Children of Húrin*). Taipei: Linking, 2008.
Jingling baozuan 精灵宝钻 (The Elves' Jewels). Shanghai and Beijing: Shanghai People's Publishing House and Horizon Media, 2015.
Jingling baozuan 精靈寶鑽 (The Elves' Jewels) (*The Silmarillion*). Taipei: Linking, 2002.

Mojie: Mojie tongmeng 魔戒：魔戒同盟 (Magic Ring: Alliance/Fellowship of the Magic Ring) with Shi Zhongge 石中歌 and Du Yunci 杜蘊慈. Shanghai and Beijing: Shanghai People's Publishing House and Horizon Media, 2013.

Mojie: Shuangta shutu 魔戒：双塔殊途 (Magic Ring: Twin Towers Different Routes) with Shi Zhongge 石中歌 and Du Yunci 杜蘊慈. Shanghai and Beijing: Shanghai People's Publishing House and Horizon Media, 2013.

Mojie: Wangzhe Huilai 魔戒：王者归来 (Magic Ring: The King Returns) with Shi Zhongge 石中歌 and Du Yunci 杜蘊慈. Shanghai and Beijing: Shanghai People's Publishing House and Horizon Media, 2013.

Numennuo-er yu zhongzhou zhi weiwan de chuanshuo 努门诺尔与中洲之未完的传说 (Unfinished Legends of Numenor and Middle-earth) (*Unfinished Tales of Númenor and Middle-Earth*) with Shi Zhongge 石中歌. Shanghai and Beijing: Shanghai People's Publishing House and Horizon Media, 2016.

Translation by Wu Gang 吴刚

Huobite ren 霍比特人 (Hobbit Person/People). Shanghai and Beijing: Shanghai People's Publishing House and Horizon Media, 2013.

Other Translations (list is not exhaustive)

Hulin de ernü 胡林的儿女 (*The Children of Húrin*), translated by Ma Xiao 马骁. Nanjing: Yilin Press, 2009.

Mojie 魔戒 (Magic Ring), 6 volumes, including *Mojietuan* 魔戒團 (Mo-ring Group), *Shuangtaji* 爽塔記 (Record of the Twin Towers), and *Guiwang guilai* 國王歸來 (Nation's King Comes Back), translated by Zhang Li 張儷, Zheng Damin 鄭大民, Zhang Jianping 張建平, Wu Hong 吳洪, Yang Xinyi 楊心意. Taipei: Linking, 1998.

Mojie zhi zhu xilie 魔戒之主系列 (The Main Series of Magic Ring), 15 volumes, including *Huobite lixianji* 霍比特歷險記 (Record of the Adventures of the Hobbit), *Mojie tongmeng* 魔戒同盟 (*Mo*-ring Fellowship/Alliance), *Shuantaji* 雙塔記 (Record of the Twin Towers), and *Guowang guilai* 國王歸來 (Nation's King Comes Back), translated by by Hai Zhou 海舟 and Yang Xiaohong 楊小紅. Taipei: Variety Publishing, 1997–1998.

Xiaoairen chuanglongxue 小矮人闯龙穴 (Small Dwarves' Venture into the Dragon's Cave) (*The Hobbit*), translated by Xu Pu 徐 朴. Beijing: China Children's Publishing House 中国少年儿童文学出版社出版, 1993.

Xiaoairen lixianji 小矮人歷險紀 (Record of Small Dwarves' Adventure) (*The Hobbit*), translated by Liou Huey Yeou 劉會友. Taipei: Linking, 1996.

Xiaoairen lixianji 小矮人历险记 (Record of Small Dwarves' Adventure) (*The Hobbit*), translated by Xu Pu 徐 朴. Ji'nan: Tomorrow Publishing House 明天出版社, 2000.

Secondary Works

Abbott, Joe. "Tolkien's Monsters: Concept and Function in *The Lord of the Rings* (Part 1) The Balrog of Khazad-dum." *Mythlore* 16, no. 1 (Autumn 1989): 19–26, 33.

Alkier, Stefan and David M. Moffitt. "Miracles Revisited: A Short Theological and Historical Survey." In *Miracles Revisited: New Testament Miracle Stories and their Concepts of Reality*, edited by Stefan Alkier and David M. Moffitt, 315–335. Berlin: de Gruyter, 2013.

Amendt-Raduege, Amy. *'The Sweet and the Bitter': Death and Dying in J. R. R. Tolkien's* The Lord of the Rings. Kent, OH: Kent State University Press, 2018.

Ashford, David. "'Orc Talk'": Soviet Linguistics in Tolkien's Middle-earth." *Journal of the Fantastic in the Arts* 29, no. 1 (2018): 26–40.

Attebery, Brian. *Stories About Stories: Fantasy and the Remaking of Myth*. Oxford: Oxford University Press, 2014.

Attebery, Brian. *Strategies of Fantasy*. Bloomington, IN: Indiana University Press: 1992.

Baidu Tieba Zhihuanwang ba 百度贴吧指环王吧 (Baidu Post Bar Lord of the Rings forum). Available online: https://tieba.baidu.com/f?kw=%E6%8C%87%E7%8E%AF%E7%8E%8B&ie=utf-8 (accessed March 1, 2021–March 31, 2022).

Baker, Mona. *In Other Words: A Coursebook on Translation*. London and New York: Routledge, 1992.

Barrie, J. M. *Pan Bide* 潘彼得 (Peter Pan), translated by Liang Shiqiu 梁實秋. Taipei: Jiuge Publishing Co.: [1936] 1987.

Barrie, J. M. *The Annotated Peter Pan*, edited by Maria Tatar. New York and London: W. W. Norton, 2011.

Bassnett, Susan. "Translation." In *The Handbook of Creative Writing*, edited by Steven Earnshaw, 367–373. Edinburgh: Edinburgh University Press, 2007.

Bellos, David. "Fictions of the Foreign: The Paradox of 'Foreign-Soundingness.'" In *In Translation: Translators on Their Work and What It Means*, edited by Esther Allen and Susan Bernofsky, 31–43. New York: Columbia University Press, 2013.

Bellos, David. *Is That a Fish in Your Ear? Translation and the Meaning of Everything*. New York: Farrar, Straus and Giroux, 2011.

Benjamin, Walter. "The Task of the Translator." In *Walter Benjamin: Selected Writings, Vol. 1: 1913–1926*, edited by Marcus Bullock and Michael W. Jennings, 253–263. Cambridge, MA: The Belknap Press of Harvard University Press, 1996.

Bergen, Richard Angelo. "'A Warp of Horror': J. R. R. Tolkien's Sub-creations of Evil." *Mythlore* 36, no. 1 (Fall/Winter 2017): 103–121.

Bissell, Tom and Jeff Alexander. "Unused Audio Commentary by Howard Zinn and Noam Chomsky, Recorded Summer 2002 for *The Fellowship of the Ring* (Platinum Series Extended Edition) DVD, Part On." *McSweeney's* April 22, 2003.

Bob-Waksberg, Raphael. "Macbeth and Macduff Get into an Argument over Semantics." *McSweeney's* April 9, 2010.

Brackmann, Rebecca. "'Dwarves are Not Heroes': Antisemitism and the Dwarves in J. R. R. Tolkien's Writing." *Mythlore* 28, nos. 3/4 (Spring/Summer 2010): 85–106.

Brady, Emily. *The Sublime in Modern Philosophy: Aesthetics, Ethics, and Nature*. Cambridge: Cambridge University Press, 2012.

Briggs, Kate. *This Little Art*. London: Fitzcarraldo Editions, 2017.

Brown, Keisha A. "Blackness in Exile: W.E.B. Du Bois' Role in the Formation of Representations of Blackness as Conceptualized by the Chinese Communist Party (CCP)." *Phylon* 53, no. 2 (Winter 2016): 20–33.

Cai, Xue-Qing 蔡雪青. "'*Hali Pote' xilie liang-an renwu yiming de duibi fenxi* 《哈利波特》系列兩岸人物譯名的對比分析" (Comparative Analysis of Mainland Chinese and Taiwanese Character Name Translations for the Harry Potter Series). National Taiwan University Working Papers in Chinese Language Teaching 臺大華語文教學研究 3 (August 2015): 179–210.

Castle, Terry. "Introduction," in Ann Radcliffe, *The Mysteries of Udolpho*. 1794. Edited by Bonamy Dobrée, vii–xxvi. Oxford: Oxford University Press, 1966.

Chan, Leo Tak-hung. "'Colonization,' Resistance and the Uses of Postcolonial Translation Theory in Twentieth-Century China.'" In *Changing the Terms: Translating in the Postcolonial Era*, edited by Sherry Simon and Paul St-Pierre, 53–70, Ottawa: University of Ottawa Press, 2020.

Chan, Leo Tak-hung. *The Discourse on Foxes and Ghosts: Ji Yun and Eighteenth-Century Literati Storytelling*. Honolulu, HI: University of Hawai'i Press, 1998.

Chandler, Wayne A. and Fry, Carrol L. "Tolkien's Allusive Backstory: Immortality and Belief in the Fantasy Frame." *Mythlore* 35, no. 2 (Spring/Summer 2017): 95–113.

Chen, Yuzhu 陈宇柱 and Lei Qinglan 雷晴岚. "*Cong Sushan Basinaite wenhua fanyi guanjiexi xifang qihuan wenxue xingxiang fanyi yi WuGangyi 'Huobite ren' weili* 从苏珊•巴斯奈特文化翻译观解析 西方奇幻文学形象翻译 以 吴 刚 译 《霍 比 特 人 》为 例" (Using Susan Bassnett's Cultural Translation Perspective to Analyze Western Fantasy Literature Image Translation, Taking Wu Gang's Translation of *The Hobbit* as an Example). *Wenhua Xuekan* 文化学刊 (*Culture Journal*) 7 (July 2020): 87–89.

Cheng, Yinghong. *Discourses of Race and Rising China*. London: Palgrave Macmillan, 2019.

Cheng, Yinghong. "From Campus Racism to Cyber Racism: Discourse of Race and Chinese Nationalism." *China Quarterly* 207 (September 2011): 561–579.

Chisolm, Chad. "Saruman as 'Sophist' or Sophist Foil? Tolkien's Wizards and the Ethics of Persuasion." *Mythlore* 37, no. 2 (Spring/Summer 2019): 89–102.

Chung, Yu-Ling. *Translation and Fantasy Literature in Taiwan: Translators as Cultural Brokers and Social Networkers*. London: Palgrave Macmillan, 2013.

Chung, Yuehtsen Juliette. "Better Science and Better Race?: Social Darwinism and Chinese Eugenics." *Isis* 105, no. 4 (December 2014): 793–802.

Clute, John. "Taproot Texts." In *The Encyclopedia of Fantasy*, edited by John Clute and John Grant, 921–922. New York: St. Martin's Griffin, 1997.

Coleridge, S. T. *Coleridge's Poetry and Prose*, edited by Nicholas Halmi, Paul Magnuson, and Raimonda Modiano. New York: W. W. Norton, 2004.

Colvin, Kathryn. "'Her Enchanted Hair': Rossetti, 'Lady Lilith,' and the Victorian Fascination with Hair as Influences on Tolkien." *Mythlore* 39, no. 1 (Fall/Winter 2020): 133–148.

"Conventions and Abbreviations." *Tolkien Studies* 16 (2019): 5–8.

Coutras, Lisa. *Tolkien's Theology of Beauty: Majesty, Splendor, and Transcendence in Middle-earth*. Palgrave Macmillan, 2016.

Davies, William. "Let's Eat Badly," *London Review of Books* 41, no. 23 (December 5, 2019): 19–22.

Davis, John Francis. *Chinese Novels, Translated from the Originals, to Which are Added Proverbs and Moral Maxims, Collected from Their Classical Books and Other Sources. The Whole Prefaced by Observations on the Language and Literature of China*. London: John Murray, 1822.

de Rosario Martínez, Helios. "*Fairy* and *Elves* in Tolkien and Traditional Literature." *Mythlore* 28, nos. 3/4 (Spring/Summer 2010): 65–84.

Demel, Walter. "How the Chinese Became Yellow: A Contribution to the Early History of Race Theories." In *China in the German Enlightenment*, edited by Bettina Brandt and Daniel Leonhard Purdy, 20–59. Toronto: University of Toronto Press, 2016.

Deng, Jiawan. Interview. Conducted by author, 2017.

Dickerson, Matthew. "Heathenism and Paganism." In *J. R. R. Tolkien Encyclopedia: Scholarship and Critical Assessment*, edited by M. D. C. Drout, 266–267. Abingdon: Routledge, 2007.

Dikötter, Frank. *The Discourse of Race in Modern China*. Stanford, CA: Stanford University Press, 1992.
Dikötter, Frank. "The Racialization of the Globe: Historical Perspectives." In *Racism in the Modern World: Historical Perspectives on Cultural Transfer and Adaptation*, edited by Manfred Berg and Simon Wendt, 20–40. New York: Berghahn Books, 2011.
Dragan, Raymond Anthony. "The Dragon in Early Imperial China." PhD diss., University of Toronto, Toronto, 1993.
Eber, Irene. "Chinese and Jews: Mutual Perceptions in Literary and Related Sources." In *Jews in China: Cultural Conversations, Changing Perceptions*, edited by Kathryn Hellerstein, 223–237. University Park, PA: Penn State University Press, 2020.
Eber, Irene. "Remarks on the Intercultural Nature of Bible Translation." In *Talking Literature: Essays on Chinese and Biblical Writings and Their Interaction*, edited by R. D. Findeisen and M. Slobodník, 63–73. Wiesbaden: Harrassowitz Verlag, 2013.
Eco, Umberto. *Experiences in Translation*, translated by Alastair McEwen. Toronto: University of Toronto Press, 2001.
Eliade, Mircea. *The Quest: History and Meaning in Religion*. Chicago, IL: University of Chicago Press, 1969.
Emig, Rainer. "Adaptation and the Concept of the Original." In *The Routledge Companion to Adaptation*, edited by Cutchins Dennis, Krebs Katja, and Voigts Eckart, 28–39. Abingdon: Routledge, 2018.
Emmerich, Karen. *Literary Translation and the Making of Originals*. London: Bloomsbury, 2017.
Fenollosa, Ernest. *The Chinese Written Character as a Medium for Poetry*. Foreword and Notes by Ezra Pound. New York: Arrow Editions, [1919] 1936.
Ferré, Vincent, Daniel Lauzon, and David Riggs. "Traduire Tolkien en Français: On the Translation of J. R. R. Tolkien's Works into French and their Reception in France." In *Tolkien in Translation*, edited by Thomas Honegger, 45–67. Zollikofen: Walking Tree, 2011.
Fimi, Dimitra. *Tolkien, Race and Cultural History: From Fairies to Hobbits*. London: Palgrave Macmillan, 2009.
Flieger, Verlyn. "The Music and the Task: Fate and Free Will in Middle-earth." *Tolkien Studies* 6 (2009): 151–181.
Fornet-Ponse, Thomas. "'Strange and Free': On Some Aspects of the Nature of Elves and Men." *Tolkien Studies* 7 (2010): 67–89.
Frazier, Robeson Taj. "Making Blackness Serve China: The Image of Afro-Asia in Chinese Political Posters." In *Migrating the Black Body: The African Diaspora and Visual Culture*, edited by Leigh Raiford and Heiki Raphael-Hernandez, 92–113. Seattle, WA: University of Washington Press, 2017.
Gander, Forrest. "The Great Leap: César and the Caesura'. In *In Translation: Translators on their Work and What It Means*, edited by Esther Allen and Susan Bernofsky, 107–116. New York: Columbia University Press, 2013.
Gao, Sifei 高思飞. "*Cong 'Mojie' wenhua fuzaici de fanyi kan yizhe zhutixing zaiqihuanwenxuefanyizhong de zuoyong*从《魔戒》文化负载词的翻译看译者主体性在奇幻文学翻译中的作用" (The Role of Translator's Subjectivity in the Translation of Fantasy Literature from the Perspective of the Translation of Culture-Loaded Words in *The Lord of the Rings*), *Xinxibu* 新西部 (*New West*) 11 (2011): 134–135.
Gitter, Elizabeth G. (1984), "The Power of Women's Hair in the Victorian Imagination." *PMLA* 99, no. 5 (October 1984): 936–954.
Glenn, Evelyn Nakano. "Yearning for Lightness: Transnational Circuits in the Marketing and Consumption of Skin Lighteners." *Gender and Society* 22, no. 3 (June 2008): 281–302.

Gosetti-Ferencei, Jennifer Anna. *The Life of Imagination: Revealing and Making the World*. New York: Columbia University Press, 2018.

Hale, Matthew. "Cosplay: Intertextuality, Public Texts, and the Body Fantastic." *Western Folklore* 73, no. 1 (Winter 2014): 5–37.

Hammond, Wayne G. and Scull, Christina. The Lord of the Rings: *A Reader's Companion*. Boston, MA: Houghton Mifflin, 2005.

Hansen, Valerie. *Changing Gods in Medieval China, 1127–1276*. Princeton, NJ: Princeton University Press 1990.

Hayton, Bill. *The Invention of China*. New Haven, CT: Yale University Press, 2020.

Henry, Eric S. *The Future Conditional: Building an English-Speaking Society in Northeast China*. Ithaca, NY: Cornell University Press, 2021.

Holmes, John R. "'Like Heathen Kings': Religion as Palimpsest in Tolkien's Fiction." In *The Ring and the Cross: Christianity and* The Lord of the Rings, edited by Paul E. Kerry, 119–144. Madison: Fairleigh Dickinson University Press, 2011.

Honegger, Thomas, ed. *Tolkien in Translation*. Zollikofen: Walking Tree, 2011.

Hooker, Mark T. *Tolkien through Russian Eyes*. Zollikofen: Walking Tree, 2003.

Hsu, Ta-Hsiu 許大修. "*Tantao qihuanwenxue de fanyi shoufa yu celüe yi 'Mojie' yu 'Hali Pote' zhongri yiben wei li* 探討奇幻文學的翻譯手法與策略-以《魔戒》與《哈利波特》中日譯本為例" (An Examination of Translation Methods and Strategies for Fantasy Literature Using Chinese and Japanese Translations of *The Lord Of The Rings* and *Harry Potter*). MA diss., Fu Jen Catholic University, Taipei, 2008.

Hutcheon, Linda. *A Theory of Adaptation*. Abingdon: Taylor and Francis Group, 2012.

Jarman, Cody. "The Black Speech: *The Lord of the Rings* as a Modern Linguistic Critique." *Mythlore* 34, no. 2 (Spring/Summer 2016): 153–166.

Jin Yong. *Legends of the Condor Heroes I: A Hero Born*, translated by Anna Holmwood. London: MacLehose Press, 2018.

Jing, Jun. *The Temple of Memories: History, Power, and Morality in a Chinese Village*. Stanford, CA: Stanford University Press, 1997.

Johnson, Brent D. "Éowyn's Grief." *Mythlore* 27, nos. 3/4 (Spring/Summer 2009): 117–127.

Johnson, David T. "Adaptation and Fidelity." In *The Oxford Handbook of Adaptation Studies*, edited by Thomas Leitch, 87–100. Oxford: Oxford University Press, 2017.

Kadiu, Silvia. "Visibility and Ethics: Lawrence Venuti's Foreignizing Approach." In *Reflexive Translation Studies: Translation as Critical Reflection*, edited by Silvia Kadiu, 21–44. London: UCL Press, 2019.

Keats, John. *Jicishixuan* 濟慈詩選 (Selected Poems of Keats), translated by Zha Liangzheng 查良錚. Taipei: Hongfan shudian, 2002.

Kelly, A. Kieth and Michael Livingston. "'A Far Green Country': Tolkien, Paradise, and the End of All Things in Medieval Literature." *Mythlore* 27, nos. 3/4 (Spring/Summer 2009): 83–102.

Kim, Sue. "Beyond Black and White: Race and Postmodernism in *The Lord of the Rings* Films." *Modern Fiction Studies* 50, no. 4 (Winter 2004): 875–907.

Kong, Shuyu. *Consuming Literature: Best Sellers and the Commercialization of Literary Production in Contemporary China*. Stanford, CA: Stanford University Press, 2005.

Lan, Shanshan. "Between Privileges and Precariousness: Remaking Whiteness in China's Teaching English as a Second Language Industry." *American Anthropologist* 124, no. 4 (2021): 1–12.

Lan, Shanshan. *Mapping the New African Diaspora in China: Race and the Cultural Politics of Belonging*. Abingdon: Routledge, 2017.

Lao Tzu. *Tao Te Ching*, translated by D. C. Lau. London: Everyman's Library, 1994.
Le Guin, Ursula K. *The Language of the Night: Essays on Fantasy and Science Fiction*, edited by Susan Woods. New York: Putnam, 1979.
Leibold, James. "More than a Category: Han Supremacism on the Chinese Internet." *China Quarterly* 203 (September 2010): 539–559.
Li Han 李 涵 and Yi Diandian 易点点. "*Liangge 'Mojie' zhongwen yiben zhong zhuanyou mingci fanyi de duibibianxi* 两个《魔戒》中文译本中专有名词翻译的对比辨析" (Comparison of the Translation of Technical Terms in Two Translations of *Mojie*). *Kejiaodaokan* 科教导刊 (October 2010): 217–218.
Li, Hong-man. "Fantasy in Translation: A Study of Two Chinese Versions of *The Lord of the Rings*." *Cross-Cultural Communication* 6, no. 4 (2010): 20–27.
Lin, Kenan. "Translation as a Catalyst for Social Change in China." In *Translation and Power*, edited by Maria Tymoczko and Edwin Gentzler, 160–183. Amherst, MA: University of Massachusetts Press: 2002.
Liu, Wuji 柳无忌 and Zhang Jingtan 张镜潭, eds. *Yingguo Langmanpai shixuan* 英国浪漫派诗选 (Selected Translations from English Romantic Poets). Nanjing: Jiangsu Educational Press, 1992.
Lobdell, Jared. *The World of the Rings: Language, Religion, and Adventure in Tolkien*. Chicago, IL: Open Court, 2004.
MacDonald, George. *A Dish of Orts, Chiefly Papers on the Imagination, and on Shakespere [sic]*. London: Sampson Low Marston & Company, 1893.
Macquarrie, John. *The Scope of Demythologizing: Bultmann and His Critics*. New York: Harper & Brothers, 1960.
Magliocco, Sabina. "'Reconnecting to Everything': Fairies in Contemporary Paganism." In *Fairies, Demons, and Nature Spirits: 'Small Gods' at the Margins of Christendom*, edited by Michael Ostling, 325–347, London: Palgrave Macmillan, 2018.
Mao, Jie 毛洁. "*'Huobiteren' zai zhongguodalu de yijie fenxi* 《霍比特人》在中国大陆的译介分析" (Analysis of the Translations of 'The Hobbit' in Mainland China). *Bulletin of Tonghua Normal University* 41, no. 308 (2020): 86–90.
McBride, Sam. *Tolkien's Cosmology: Divine Beings and Middle-earth*. Kent, OH: Kent State University Press, 2020.
McDougall, Bonnie S. *Translation Zones in Modern China: Authoritarian Command Versus Gift Exchange*. Amherst, NY: Cambria Press, 2011.
McIlwaine, Catherine. *Tolkien: Maker of Middle-earth*. Oxford: The Bodleian Library, 2018.
McRae, John. *Seeing through Zen: Encounter, Transformation, and Genealogy in Chinese Chan Buddhism*. Berkeley, CA: University of California Press, 2003.
Meccarelli, Marco. "Discovering the *Long*: Current Theories and Trends in Research on the Chinese Dragon." *Frontiers of Chinese History* 16, no. 1 (2021): 123–142.
Mendlesohn, Farah and James, Edward. *A Short History of Fantasy*. London: Middlesex University Press, 2009.
Michael, Thomas. "Shamanism Theory and the Early Chinese 'Wu.'" *Journal of the American Academy of Religion* 83, no. 3 (2015): 649–696.
Miéville, China. *Padiduojie chezhan* 帕迪多街車站 (*Perdido Street Station*), translated by Liu Xiaohua 劉曉樺. Taipei: Mouxi Publishers, 2013.
Milburn, Michael. "Coleridge's Definition of Imagination and Tolkien's Definition(s) of Faery." *Tolkien Studies* 7 (2010): 55–66.
Mills, Charles W. "The Wretched of Middle-earth: An Orkish Manifesto". *Southern Journal of Philosophy* 60, no. S1 (2022): 1–31.

Miyazaki, Hayao. *Turning Point: 1997–2008*, translated by Beth Cary and Fredrik L. Schodt. San Francisco, CA: Viz Media, 2008.

Moorcock, Michael. *Wizardry and Wild Romance: A Study of Epic Fantasy*. Austin, TX: MonkeyBrain, 2004.

Moore, Christopher J. *In Other Words: A Language Lover's Guide to the Most Intriguing Words Around the World*. New York: Levenger Press, 2004.

Muling Shengjin 牧靈聖經 (The Bible). Madrid: International Catholic Biblical Society, 1998.

Müller, Gotelind. "Glocalizing 'Race' in China: Concepts and Contingencies at the Turn of the Twentieth Century." In *Racism in the Modern World: Historical Perspectives on Cultural Transfer and Adaptation*, edited by Manfred Berg and Simon Wendt, 237–255. New York: Berghahn Books, 2011.

Ni, Zhange. "*Xiuzhen* (Immortality Cultivation) Fantasy: Science, Religion, and the Novels of Magic/Superstition in Contemporary China." *Religions* 11, no. 1 (2020): 1–24.

Nida, Eugene. "Principles of Correspondence." In *Translation Studies Reader*, edited by Lawrence Venuti, 126–141. Abingdon: Routledge, 2000.

Ostling, Michael. "Introduction: Where's All the Good People Gone?" In *Fairies, Demons, and Nature Spirits: 'Small Gods' at the Margins of Christendom*, edited by Michael Ostling, 1–54. London: Palgrave Macmillan, 2018a.

Ostling, Michael, ed. *Fairies, Demons, and Nature Spirits: 'Small Gods' at the Margins of Christendom*. London: Palgrave Macmillan, 2018b.

Otto, Rudolf. *The Idea of the Holy: An Inquiry into the Non-Rational Factor in the Idea of the Divine and Its Relation to the Rational*, translated by J. W. Harvey. New York: Oxford University Press, [1923] 1958.

Petty, Anne C. "Reflections of Christendom in the Mythpoeic Iconography of Middle-earth". In *Light Beyond All Shadow: Religious Experience in Tolkien's Work*, edited by Paul E. Kerry and Sandra Miesel, 47–67. Vancouver: Fairleigh Dickinson University Press, 2011.

Picton, Oliver. "The Complexities of Complexion: A Cultural Geography of Skin Colour and Beauty Products." *Geography* 98, no. 2 (Summer 2013): 85–92.

Polizzotti, Mark. *Sympathy for the Traitor: A Translation Manifesto*. Cambridge, MA: MIT Press, 2018.

Pratchett, Terry. *Equal Rites*. New York: Signet, 1987.

Purkiss, Diane. *At the Bottom of the Garden: A Dark History of Fairies, Hobgoblins, and Other Troublesome Things*. New York: New York University Press, 2000.

Qi, Shouhua. *Western Literature in China and the Translation of a Nation*. London: Palgrave Macmillan, 2012.

Raw, Laurence. "Aligning Adaptation Studies with Translation Studies." In *The Oxford Handbook of Adaptation Studies*, edited by Thomas Leitch, 494–508. Oxford: Oxford University Press, 2017.

Reith, Gerda. *The Age of Chance: Gambling in Western Culture*. Abingdon: Routledge, 1999.

Reynolds, Patricia. "Funeral Customs in Tolkien's Fiction." *Mythlore* 19, no. 2 (Spring 1993): 45–53.

Rheingold, Howard. *They Have a Word for It: A Lighthearted Lexicon of Untranslatable Words and Phrases*. Louisville, KY: Sarabande Books, 2000.

Roberts, Adam. *The Riddles of the Hobbit*. London: Palgrave Macmillan, 2013.

Romano, Monica. "The Reception of Christianity in China: Terminological Issues in Bible Translation." In *Talking Literature: Essays on Chinese and Biblical Writings and Their Interaction*, edited by Raoul David Findeisen and Martin Slobodník, 85–99. Wiesbaden: Harrassowitz Verlag, 2013.

Ross, James R. "Images of Jews in Contemporary Books, Blogs, and Films." In *The Image of Jews in Contemporary China: A Identity without a People*, edited by James Ross and Song Lihong, 24–36. Boston, MA: Academic Studies Press, 2016.

Rossetti, Christina. *Goblin Market and Other Poems: Xiaoyao moshi* 小妖魔市, translated by Mei Lüjin 枚綠金 (Mélusine Lin). Taipei: Doudian (Comma Books), 2015.

Rowling, J. K. *Harry Potter and the Chamber of Secrets*. New York: Scholastic Press, 1999.

Rowling, J. K. *Harry Potter and the Chamber of Secrets (Hali Pote: Xiaoshi de Mishi* 哈利波特：消失的密室 [Harry Potter: The Disappearing Secret Room]), translated by Peng Qianwen 彭倩文. Taipei: Huangguan Wenhua, 2000.

Ruud, Jay. "The Voice of Saruman: Wizards and Rhetoric in 'The Two Towers.'" *Mythlore* 28, nos. 3/4 (Spring/Summer 2010): 141–153.

Saussy, Haun. "Always Multiple Translation, Or, How the Chinese Language Lost Its Grammar." In *Tokens of Exchange: The Problem of Translation in Global Circulations*, edited by Lydia H. Liu, 107–122. Durham, NC: Duke University Press, 1999.

Sautman, Barry. "Racial Nationalism and China's External Behavior." *World Affairs* 160, no. 2 (Fall 1997): 78–95.

Savelli, Marcantonio. "Translating Tolkien. The Thin Line between Translation and Misrepresentation. An Italian Case-Study." *Journal of Tolkien Research* 11, no. 1 (2020): 1–15.

Schein, Louisa. "The Consumption of Color and the Politics of White Skin in Post-Mao China." *Social Text* 41 (Winter 1994): 141–164.

Schleiermacher, Friedrich. "On the Different Methods of Translating," translated by Susan Bernofsky. In *The Translation Studies Reader*, 2nd edition, edited by Lawrence Venuti, 43–63. New York and London: Routledge, 2021.

Schmidt, Heather. "Chinas Confucius Institutes and the 'Necessary White Body.'" *Canadian Journal of Sociology / Cahiers canadiens de sociologie* 38, no. 4 (2013): 647–668.

Schmiesing, Ann. "Blackness in the Grimms' Fairy Tales." *Marvels & Tales* 30, no. 2 (Fall 2016): 210–233.

Shakespeare, William. *A Mid-Summer Night's Dream. Zhongxiaye zhimeng* 仲夏夜之梦, translated by Zhu Shenghao 朱生豪. Huhan: Hubei Educational Press, 2012.

Shao, Youxue 邵有学. *Zhongguo fanyi sixiang shi* 中国翻译思想史 (New Perspectives on Chinese Intellectual History of Translation). Beijing: Huadong Normal University Press, 2018.

Shih, Shu-Mei. "Race and Revolution: Blackness in China's Long Twentieth Century." *PMLA* 128, no. 1 (January 2013): 156–162.

Shippey, Tom. "'Light-elves, Dark-elves, and Others: Tolkien's Elvish Problem." *Tolkien Studies* 1 (2004): 1–15.

Shippey, Tom. *The Road to Middle-earth: How J. R. R. Tolkien Created a New Mythology*, Revised and Expanded Edition. Boston, MA: Houghton Mifflin, 2003.

Silver, Carole G. *Strange and Secret Peoples: Fairies and Victorian Consciousness*. Oxford: Oxford University Press, 1999.

Sinex, Margaret. "'Tricksy Lights': Literary and Folkloric Elements in Tolkien's Passage of the Dead Marshes." *Tolkien Studies* 2 (2005): 93–112.

Smith, Jonathan Z. "Religion, Religions, Religious." In *Critical Terms for Religious Studies*, edited by Mark C. Taylor, 269–284. Chicago, IL: University of Chicago, 1998.

Smith, Melissa. "At Home and Abroad: Éowyn's Two-fold Figuring as War Bride in *The Lord of the Rings*." *Mythlore* 26, nos. 1/2 (Fall/Winter 2007): 161–172.

Song, Lihong. "Reflections on Chinese Jewish Studies: A Comparative Perspective." In *The Image of Jews in Contemporary China: A Identity Without a People*, edited by James Ross and Song Lihong, 206–233. Boston, MA: Academic Studies Press, 2016.

Srinivasan, Amia. "He, She, One, They, Ho, Hus, Hum, Ita." *London Review of Books* (July 2, 2020): 34–39.

Sterling, Grant C. "'The Gift of Death': Tolkien's Philosophy of Mortality." *Mythlore* 21, no. 4 (Winter 1997): 16–18, 38.

Stoker, Bram. *Dracula*. 1897. New York: Bantam Classic Edition, 1981.

Stoker, Bram. *Xixuegui zhiwen* 吸血鬼之吻 (The Kiss of the Vampire) (*Dracula*), translated by Ye Anhei 夜暗黑. Taipei: Xinchaoshe wenhu, 2013.

Stoker, Bram. *Zhuojiule bojue* 卓九勒伯爵 (Count Dracula) (*Dracula*), translated by Liu Tiehu 劉鐵虎. Taipei: Dakuai wenhua, 2007.

Stopfel, Susanne. "Traitors and Translators: Three German Versions of 'The Lord of the Rings.'" *Mallorn: The Journal of the Tolkien Society*, 43 (July 2005): 11–14.

Strassberg, Richard E. *A Chinese Bestiary: Strange Creatures from the Guideways through Mountains and Seas*. Berkeley, CA: University of California Press, 2002.

Tally, Robert T., Jr. "Let Us Now Praise Famous Orcs: Simple Humanity in Tolkien's Inhuman Creatures." *Mythlore* 29, nos. 1/2 (Fall/Winter 2010): 17–28.

Tan, Teri. "Publishing in Taiwan 2011: Mixing Originals, Translations, Print, and Digital to Create a Thriving Marketplace." *Publishers Weekly*, September 9, 2011.

Teo, Stephen. *Chinese Martial Arts Cinema*. Edinburgh: Edinburgh University Press, 2009.

Tolkien, J. R. R. *The Children of Húrin*, edited by Christopher Tolkien. New York: Houghton Mifflin, 2007.

Tolkien, J. R. R. *The Fellowship of the Rings*. New York: Houghton Mifflin, 1954.

Tolkien, J. R. R. *The Hobbit: Or There and Back Again*. 1937. Boston, MA: Houghton Mifflin, 2001.

Tolkien, J. R. R. *The Return of the King*. New York: Houghton Mifflin, 1955.

Tolkien, J. R. R. *The Silmarillion*, edited by Christopher Tolkien. New York: Ballentine Books, 1977.

Tolkien, J. R. R. *The Two Towers*. New York: Houghton Mifflin, 1954.

Tolkien, J. R. R. *Tolkien on Fairy-stories: Expanded Edition, with Commentary and Notes*, edited by Verlyn Flieger and Douglas A. Anderson. London: HarperCollins, 2008.

Tolkien, J. R. R. *Unfinished Tales of Númenor and Middle-earth*, edited by Christopher Tolkien. New York: Houghton Mifflin, 1980.

Turner, Allan. "Translation and Criticism: The Stylistic Mirror." *Yearbook of English Studies* 36, no. 1 (2006): 168–176.

Venuti, Lawrence. *Contra Instrumentalism: A Translation Polemic*. Lincoln, NE: University of Nebraska Press, 2019.

Venuti, Lawrence. "Local Contingencies: Translation and National Identities." In *Nation, Language, and the Ethics of Translation*, edited by Sandra Bermann and Michael Wood, 177–202. Princeton, NJ: Princeton University Press, 2005.

Venuti, Lawrence. "The Translator's Invisibility." *Criticism* 28, no. 2 (Spring 1986): 179–212.

Vink, Renée. "'Jewish' Dwarves: Tolkien and Anti-Semitic Stereotyping." *Tolkien Studies* 10 (2013): 123–145.

Wang, Jin 王瑾. "Jiyu gongneng duideng lilun de 'Mojie' zhongwen yiben diming fanyi duibi yanjiu 基于功能对等理论的《魔戒》中文译本地名翻译对比研究" (A Comparative Study of Chinese Translation of Local Names of the *Lord of the Rings*, Based on Functional Equidistant Theory). *Wenhua xuekan* 文化学刊 (*Culture Journal*) 01 (2020): 178–181.

Wang, Xiulu. *Bridging the Political and the Personal: Literary Translation in Contemporary China*. Bern: Peter Lang, 2016.

Weinberger, Eliot. *Nineteen Ways of Looking at Wang Wei*. Mount Kisco, NY: Moyer Bell, 1987.

Wen Yixin 文意昕. "Yingzhong wenxue xinci fanyi zhong de yihua celüe—yixiaoshuo 'Mojie' weili 英中文学新词翻译中的异化策略—以小说《魔戒》为例" (Foreignization Tactics in the Translation of Neologisms in English and Chinese Literature—Taking the Novel *Mojie* as an Example). *Dangdai waiyu yanjiu* 当代外语研究 (*Contemporary Foreign Language Studies*) 6 (December 2021): 144–152.

White, Richard J. "Germanic *Fate* and *Doom* in J. R. R. Tolkien's *The Silmarillion*." *Mythlore* 29, nos. 1/2 (Fall/Winter 2010): 115–129.

Whitt, Richard J. "Germanic *Fate* and *Doom* in J. R. R. Tolkien's *The Silmarillion*." *Mythlore* 29, nos. 1/2 (Fall/Winter 2010): 115–129.

Williamson, Jamie. *The Evolution of Modern Fantasy: From Antiquarianism to the Ballantine Adult Fantasy Series*. London: Palgrave Macmillan, 2015.

Wittgenstein, Ludwig. *Culture and Value*, edited by G. H. von Wright, translated by Peter Winch. Chicago, IL: University of Chicago, 1980.

Wittgenstein, Ludwig. *Philosophical Investigations*, 2nd edition, translated by G. E. M. Anscombe. Oxford: Blackwell, 1958.

Wu, Cheng'en 吳承恩. *A Mission to Heaven* (*Xiyouji* 西遊記), translated by Timothy Richards. Shanghai: Shanghai Christian Literature Association, 1913.

Wu, Cheng'en. 吳承恩. *Monkey: A Folk-Tale of China* (*Xiyouji* 西遊記), translated by Arthur Waley. New York: Allen and Unwin, 1943.

Wu, Cheng'en. 吳承恩. *The Journey to the West* (*Xiyouji* 西遊記), translated by Anthony Yu. Chicago, IL: University of Chicago Press, 1977–1983.

Wu, Fuhui. *A Cultural History of Modern Chinese Literature*, translated by Rui Ma. Cambridge: Cambridge University Press, 2020.

Yeats, William Butler. *Weicong zhong de feng: yeci shixuan* 葦叢中的風：葉慈詩選 [Wind in the Reeds: Selected Poems of Yeats], *Selected Poems of William Butler Yeats*, translated by Fu Hao 傅浩. Taipei: Shulin publishing company, 2000.

Zhou Xun. "Perceiving Jews in Modern China." In *The Image of Jews in Contemporary China: A Identity without a People*, edited by James Ross and Song Lihong, 5–23. Boston, MA: Academic Studies Press, 2016.

Zhu, Xueheng 朱學恆. *About Geek: There is No Turning Back!* 一入宅門深似海！*Yiru zhaimen shensihai!* (Once You Enter the Way of the Geek, There is No Turning Back!). Taipei: Gaiya wenhua 蓋亞文化, 2012.

Zhu, Xueheng 朱學恆. *The Power of Dream: We Don't Live Twice!* 夢想無懼! *Mengxiang wuju* (Dream without Fear). Taipei: Gaiya wenhua 蓋亞文化, 2015.

Zhu, Xueheng 朱學恆. *Xinde shijie meiyoushen* 新的世界沒有神 (The New World Has No Gods). Taipei: Gaiya wenhua 蓋亞文化, 2009.

Index

adaptation 23, 32, 162
adventures 41, 47–50, 52, 147
Africa, Africans 86, 88, 91, 92
afterlife 95, 100–115, 123, 124
Ainulindalë 157, 158
Ainur 113, 115, 156–158
Alas 61, 127, 153
allegory 10, 11, 65
Aman, Western Undying lands, Blessed Realm 71, 79, 96, 100, 106, 109, 113, 114, 116, 118, 120–123, 156
ambiguity 31, 37, 38, 61, 66, 67, 70, 77, 80, 81, 84, 97, 117, 125, 127, 148, 153, 161
American Literary Translators Association 17
anachronisms 15, 39, 40, 62, 63, 67, 73, 87
ancestry 56, 59, 60, 61, 67, 81, 90, 92, 96, 103–105, 107, 108, 112
Andersen, Hans Christian 113
angels 63–65, 67, 68, 120
animism 69, 70, 84, 113, 123
Aragorn 34, 43, 44, 48, 58, 63, 81, 84, 87, 89, 93, 104–106, 116, 119, 134, 136, 146, 154
archaisms 27, 143, 145, 146
Arwen 43, 116, 134, 135

Baidu tieba Tolkien forum 29, 86
baizuo (white lefties) 89
Balin 44, 104
ballads 41, 48, 49, 51, 79, 156
balrogs 9, 37, 101, 119, 120, 149
bane 21, 61, 135, 155
Barrie, J. M., Peter Pan 8, 40, 41, 52, 69, 78
believing, belief, disbelief 3–11, 42, 47, 52, 55, 58, 61, 67, 69, 85, 100, 101, 152, 157
Benjamin, Walter 14
Beren and Lúthien 79, 104, 107, 113, 124, 134, 135

Bible 5–11, 20, 63, 123, 133, 156, 158
Bilbo 15, 44, 45, 49, 50, 71, 96, 107, 118, 127, 128, 130, 138, 140, 141, 143, 144, 147, 151
black (color) 51, 65, 92, 93, 96, 97, 101, 110, 134, 143
black people 86–93, 96, 98
Black Speech 138, 149, 150
Blessed Realm, *see* Aman
blood 56, 59, 87, 91, 92, 111, 112, 114
blue mulberry 21, 74
bogey-stories 41, 46, 47, 56
bold font 19, 144
book covers 25, 26, 32, 43
Boromir 21, 44, 46, 74, 87, 97, 98, 105, 130, 134, 136, 146, 153
Brackmann, Rebecca 98
Briggs, Kate 4, 12, 16
Bronowski, Jacob 80
Buddha 36, 66, 100, 118
buddhism 6, 15, 35, 36, 42, 47, 57, 60, 65, 68, 70, 77, 89, 95, 100, 106, 107, 114, 117, 118, 120, 123, 124, 129, 130, 132, 154, 156, 158
Bultmann, Rudolf 7

Campbell, Joseph 13
capitalization 19, 26, 61, 67, 73, 80, 82, 101, 120, 135, 139, 141, 142, 155
Carrock 142
Carroll, Lewis 8
Catholicism 11, 58, 61
Celeborn 21, 74, 96, 103, 121
chance 125, 126, 131, 132, 137
chengyu 20, 21, 34–36, 50, 76, 119, 140, 147
children, children's literature 5, 8, 10, 25, 40–42, 45, 46, 69
Children of Húrin, The 30
Chinese language, compared to English 17–23
chuanqi 44, 45

chuanshuo, legends 7, 42, 44, 47, 49–52
Cirth 139, 143
class 7, 46, 86, 144, 151, 152, 162
coffins, biers 57, 105
cognitive possessiveness, intellectual greed, familiarity 14, 15, 23, 24, 160
Coleridge, S. T. 3, 4, 15
colloquial speech 145, 146
Confucius, Confucianism 23, 64, 65, 68, 78, 85
conjugation of verbs 19, 51, 134, 144, 145, 148
conjurer 37, 63–65, 75, 152
Cottingley fairy photographs 8, 69
count nouns 20, 26, 59, 101, 132
creation
    sub-creation 15, 17, 72, 148, 149, 156, 157, 159
    of the universe 6, 11, 60, 98, 113, 156–159
Crown (Huangguan) publishing co. 32
Cultural Revolution 31, 87
curses 102, 110, 111, 130, 149, 152–155

Daodejing 76, 87
Daoism 43, 61, 68, 75, 77–79, 107, 120, 123, 155, 158, 159
darkness 20, 45, 57, 62, 71, 86, 88, 92–94, 97, 101, 106, 111, 115, 119, 121, 153
death 20, 70, 71, 78, 79, 81, 84, 116–119, 123, 131, 135, 136, 146, 153, 154
    as journey 105, 106, 114
    scenes 81, 105, 109, 116
    sentence 51, 130, 133, 134, 154
    as sleep 103, 104
    views of 100, 101, 102, 112
demythologizing 7
Denethor 62, 63, 67, 105, 135, 136
Deng, Jiawan (Joy Teng) 9, 11, 15, 19, 20, 25, 28–33, 37, 38, 41, 45, 56, 70, 83, 84, 137, 145, 146
devilry 56, 57
Dickens, Charles 14, 31, 41
divinity, gods, God, deities 5–7, 10, 17, 52, 55, 57–61, 66, 67, 74, 89, 96, 107, 117, 125, 129, 132, 133, 135, 149, 156, 158, 159, 161
    Chinese 60, 61
    geek god 29

pantheons 55, 60, 61, 67
Polytheism 60, 67
small gods 67, 69, 84, 85, 108, 122
terminology 59, 60, 61, 70, 158
domestication 13, 23, 27, 31
doom 6, 49, 81, 109, 113, 126, 132–137, 147, 154
Doom of Men 117
Dracula 37
Dragon-con 3, 8–10
dragons 5, 15, 34, 40, 45, 55, 66, 82, 101, 154
dreams 35, 41, 44, 47, 51, 52, 77, 85, 121, 136, 147
Du, Yunci 30
Dúnedain, dúnadan 113, 117, 141
Dunsany, Lord 47
dwarves 36, 44, 47, 48, 80, 98, 99, 107, 113, 117, 138, 141, 142, 149, 153, 154

eagles 11, 120, 138
Eärnur 83, 84
East 45, 86–89, 93, 99, 109
Easterlings 87, 88, 93
Eco, Umberto 3, 84
Eldar 71, 72, 122
Eliade, Mircea 17, 18
Elrond 80, 104, 116, 118, 129, 131, 132
elves 8, 47, 48, 51, 52, 57, 58, 61, 63, 65, 66–80, 84, 85, 88, 89, 92, 94, 95, 98, 102, 104, 105, 107, 108, 113–116, 118, 120–124, 133, 137, 146, 149, 150, 155, 156
    afterlife of 105, 107, 113–115, 118, 120, 121
    high elves 70
    immortality of 76, 77, 89, 105, 113, 114, 118
    languages 71–73, 138, 155
    and magic 74, 75, 77
    wood-elves 70, 71
Enemy, the 75, 88, 94, 142
English language, compared to Chinese, *see* Chinese language, compared to English
ents 47, 48, 94, 107, 113, 136, 144, 145
Éomer 44, 47, 48, 51, 52, 61, 69, 74, 80, 81, 96, 154
Éowyn 81–84, 98, 103, 162

eucatastrophe, happy ending 6, 48, 49, 50, 51, 122, 125, 135
evil 9, 34, 36–38, 43, 47, 56, 57, 65, 75, 86, 88, 92, 93–95, 106, 109, 116, 122, 125, 127, 128, 130, 142, 147–151, 155
exile 73, 75
express train 15
eyes, 37, 57, 74, 85, 123, 147, 152
   black 93
   blue 86
   signs of age in, 21, 74, 160
   "slanted" 95, 96

Faerie 4, 5, 71, 78, 156
fairies 78, 79, 84
Fairy Queen 78
fairy-stories 5, 6, 10, 13, 19, 30, 40, 44, 46, 113, 121, 159
fairy-wife 56
faith 3, 4, 6, 8, 10, 11, 12, 63, 157
Fans for Christ 8, 9
fantasy 3–6, 8–15, 27, 28, 37, 39–45, 51, 52, 55, 66, 67, 73, 87, 121, 156
   Chinese terminology, 42–45, 73
   definitions 8, 13, 39, 40, 41
   fear of 5
Faramir 44, 62, 82, 84, 97, 133, 154
fate 21, 49, 50, 114, 115, 117, 124, 125–128, 130–137, 147
   Chinese terminology 21, 126, 127
fathers 58, 59, 81, 100, 103, 104, 107, 136, 146
Fenollosa, Ernest 17, 18, 22
fidelity (in translation) 13–15, 18, 23, 31, 161
filial piety, unfiliality 57, 81
folklore 8, 42, 47, 55, 58, 102, 122
footprints, footsteps 48, 135, 136, 146, 147
foreignisms, foreignization 14, 15, 23, 24, 27, 30, 72, 138, 145
fortune-telling, divination, prophecy 21, 44, 69, 81–83, 125, 126, 131, 136, 149, 154
Frazer, James George 13
Frodo 21, 28, 30, 33, 41, 48–52, 77, 81, 92–94, 111, 118, 120–123, 125, 127, 128, 130, 131, 133–138, 141, 153, 154, 156, 157, 159

Frost, Robert 17, 18
fu (tally, talisman) 155
fundamentalism 7–12
funerals 57, 63, 87, 98, 100, 104–107

Gaiman, Neil 140
gaisi ("damn it") 127, 130, 153
Galadriel 3, 4, 20, 21, 36, 44, 51, 65, 66, 68, 69, 74, 75, 96, 97, 106, 121–123, 125, 135, 139, 140, 160
Gandalf 15, 20, 23, 34, 43, 44, 48, 58, 62–67, 80, 81, 83, 92, 93, 97, 101, 102, 104, 109, 118, 119, 124, 127–131, 134, 135, 139–145, 147, 149–151, 154–156, 160
gender 56, 57, 78, 80–84, 97, 98, 103, 111, 152
genre 5, 9, 10, 13, 35, 37–47, 49, 51, 52, 57, 125
ghosts 36, 42, 44, 47, 55–57, 67, 70, 95, 102, 105, 107–111, 154
   wight 56, 57, 110, 111, 154
   wraith 57, 82, 11–112, 136
Gimli 43, 44, 94, 98, 109, 118
Glaurung 154
Glóin 117
Glorfindel 81–84, 96, 125
goblins 37, 46, 47, 56, 67, 94, 95, 113, 140, 144
God, *see* divinity.
Goldberry 66, 79
Gollum 21, 34, 36, 92, 93, 102, 111, 130, 133, 134, 144, 153, 154
Gondor 35, 80, 83, 133, 136
grace 6, 118
Great Journey 73
Grey Havens 118
Grima Wormtongue 64, 65, 109, 124
Grimm, Brothers 44, 46
Grishnákh 147, 150
Grond 101, 102
Gu Long 43
guai (weird") 35, 36, 42, 44–46, 55–57, 65, 92, 110, 150
gui ("ghost") 35–37, 47, 55–57, 67, 70, 102, 108–111, 140

hair 17, 74, 82, 86, 90, 93, 97, 110, 117
Han (ethnonym) 63, 88, 90, 91, 96

Harry Potter 9, 32, 41, 64, 78
heathenism, paganism 59, 62, 63, 67, 69, 85, 116, 160, 161
heaven 36, 61, 64, 66, 67, 76, 79, 103, 113, 116–120, 123, 126–129, 132, 137, 158, 161
hell, *diyu* 36, 51, 57, 67, 100–102, 107, 112, 113, 115, 116, 160
Helm's Deep 98, 108
hobbits 18, 28, 44, 46, 48, 52, 56, 58, 64, 66, 75, 77, 79–82, 85, 95, 102, 105, 107, 110, 117, 137, 139, 141, 142, 144, 149
Hobbit, The 11, 15, 31, 36–38, 44–46, 89, 130, 138, 147
   films 30, 33, 34, 89
   Wu translation 31
   Yilin edition 25, 26, 32, 35
   Zhu translation 28, 29
Hongloumeng 35, 47
horses 58, 59, 76, 96, 109, 147
Huanzhulouzhu 43
humans, 4, 7, 9, 10, 40, 44, 55, 56, 60–62, 64, 66–68, 69, 70, 72, 73, 78–84, 88, 90, 93–95, 102, 104, 105, 107, 108, 111–118, 120, 123, 124, 137, 155, 162
   renlei ("human") 80, 82–84, 88, 93, 117
Hume, David 7
hundun (primordial chaos) 158, 159
Hunt for Gollum, The 34
Húrin 102
hybridity 91, 118

Ilúvatar 37, 58, 60, 95, 98, 113, 114, 116, 117, 128, 157, 158, 160
imagination 3, 4, 6, 8, 13–15, 23, 40, 42, 67, 71–73, 157, 161, 162
immortality 5, 37, 43, 45, 69, 76, 78, 79, 105, 113, 114, 116, 120
incommensurability, untranslatability 16, 17
internal publishing, white cover books 31
ISBN numbers 30, 32
Isengard 26, 29, 30, 108, 136
Isildur 21, 44, 125, 145, 146, 150, 154
Istari, wizards 37, 40, 57, 63–68, 84, 92, 97, 111
italics 19, 140

Jesus 3, 5, 9, 11, 58, 65, 101, 110
Jews 98, 99
jianghu 43, 64
Jiangsu People's Publishing House 32
Jin Yong 43, 44

karma 43, 44, 77, 95, 125, 127, 129–132, 137, 148, 160
Keats, John 161
Khuzdul (language) 98, 138, 141, 143, 149

Lang, Andrew 8
legends, *see chuanshuo*
Legolas 43, 44, 76, 79, 85, 87, 94, 98, 108, 153, 154
Le Guin, Ursula K. 5, 11, 16
Lewis, C. S. 10, 11
Liang, Shiqiu 78
Liang, Yusheng 43
lifespans 89, 126, 127
lineages 40, 52, 59, 72, 87, 90, 96, 104
Linjing (Linking) Publishing 28, 32
long defeat 121, 122
Lord of the Rings, The, 5, 11, 20, 26, 32, 36, 38, 39, 41, 43, 46, 49, 80, 89, 118, 125, 138, 160
   book and chapter titles 26, 35, 36
   Deng translation 28–30
   films 9, 25, 27
   Yilin edition 26
   Zhu translation 28, 29
Lothlórien 14, 48, 75, 76, 103, 106, 122
luck 21, 117, 125–127, 129, 131, 133, 135–137
Lúthien, *see* Beren and Lúthien
Lu Xun 35

Macbeth 50, 125
MacDonald, George 6, 15, 159
Macquarrie, John 7
magic 4, 6, 8–10, 12, 14, 15, 26, 36–38, 43, 45, 51, 52, 56, 57, 63, 64–66, 69, 74–79, 82, 84, 107–109, 118, 122, 126, 131, 135, 137, 140, 148, 149, 151–157
Maiar 63, 64, 66
man/men, *see* humans
Manchu, Qing dynasty 42, 87, 90, 91, 108

Mandos, Halls of 100, 103, 106, 107, 112–118, 123, 124, 161
mantra 156
Manwë 114
Mao, Zedong 32, 87, 91
Mara 36
marvels 5, 41, 42, 47, 48, 52, 67
Marxism 25
May 4th Movement 19, 32
medievalism 15, 44, 51, 58, 89, 137
memorate 42
Merry 30, 43, 46, 58, 81–83, 94
Miéville, China 37, 89
miracles 4, 6–9, 12, 16, 42, 44
Miyazaki, Hayao 86
mo ("magic/demonic") 36–38, 45, 55–57, 75, 116, 135, 140
    mofa, moshu (magic) 36–38, 43, 45, 64, 65, 75, 76, 140
    mogui (monster) 35, 36, 37, 57
    mojie (magic ring) 9, 26, 30, 33, 36, 37
monsters 17, 35–37, 44, 46, 52, 55–58, 65, 69
Mooreeffoc 14, 23
Mordor 26, 30, 56, 57, 75, 87, 93, 96, 131, 137, 150, 155
Morgoth, Melkor 36, 37, 58, 62, 94, 101, 102
Moria 101, 104, 117, 138, 143
Morwen 64
Mount Doom 21, 137

necromancer 57, 64, 65
New York World Trade Center 27
Nine springs, Yellow springs 107, 126
ninnyhammer 152, 153
Northern Theory of Courage 84
numbskull 152
Númenor 21, 62, 89, 120

oaths, oathbreakers 44, 59, 107, 129, 149, 154
old wives' tales 41, 46, 47
omens 137, 149
On Fairy-stories (essay) 5, 6, 10, 13, 19, 30, 72, 113, 121, 159
One Ring, the 9, 11, 21, 26, 28, 33, 36–38, 55, 57, 61, 65, 111, 116, 122, 123, 128, 130, 131, 136, 138, 145, 149, 150, 162

orcs 44, 48, 69, 75, 87, 88, 89, 92–96, 102, 107, 108, 113, 123, 124, 146, 150, 151, 153, 155
    Orc-minded 151
Orome 58, 59, 61, 67
Orthanc 26, 29, 30
Otto, Rudolph. 17

paganism, *see* heathenism
palantir 135
parables 5, 7
passive voice 19, 49, 119, 127–132, 134, 137
Peach Blossom Spring 76, 120
Pelennor Fields 81
Penglai 76, 120, 123
picture scroll 157, 159
Pippin 30, 43, 46, 48, 80–82, 93, 94, 134, 145
pity 130
poetry 21, 26, 30, 72, 145, 146, 149
    as "lost in translation" 17, 18, 24
    poetic faith 3
poison 43, 64, 89, 92, 148, 151, 154
prayer 58, 60
preta 95
pretending. 3, 4, 14, 25, 58, 84, 160
pronouns 46, 93, 119, 158
Protestant Reformation 69
proverbs 146
Pu, Songling 44
Puck 69, 78
punctuation 20
Pure land (*jingtu*) 100, 117, 118, 120, 123, 161

Quendi 71–73, 97

race 70, 72, 79, 80, 81, 84, 86–99, 113, 120, 127
    as "color" 90
    race-mute culture 87
    and science 89, 90
    zhongzu 72, 90
racism 23, 86, 87, 90–92, 95, 96, 98
Radagast 63, 97, 141
Rangers 43, 141
Red Book of Westmarch 58, 138, 160
redemption, salvation 11, 93, 95, 113, 160

religion 3, 4, 7, 8, 9, 10, 17, 18, 40, 42, 55, 61, 62, 63, 67, 69, 84, 85, 152
   Chinese 60, 66, 67, 104, 108, 115, 116, 123, 127, 129, 130, 160, 161
   and fantasy 4, 5, 6, 51, 66
   Sui generis 17, 18
   in Tolkien's works 58
   and translation 4
religious studies 5, 17, 18, 40
Richard, Timothy 78
Rings of Power, The 92
Roberts, Adam 10, 162
Rohan 47, 48
romance (genre) 35, 40, 41, 88
Romantics, Romanticism 3, 6, 18, 44
Rossetti, Christina 37
runes 139, 140, 155

Sador 108
Saeros 115, 133
Samwise Gamgee 30, 41, 48–52, 58, 75, 76, 84, 93, 96, 118, 129, 131, 133, 147, 149, 152–154, 160
Sanguo Yanyi (Romance of the Three Kingdoms) 35, 88
Saruman 57, 63, 92, 96, 109, 136, 140, 144, 150–152
Sauron 9, 21, 28, 58, 62, 88, 92, 101, 111, 121, 122, 147, 149
Schleiermacher, Friedrich. 3, 17
science 6–10, 29, 35, 39, 52, 69, 85, 90
science fiction 3, 6, 8, 40–42, 51, 52, 67
scripture, as genre 9–12
secondary world 49, 149
seduction 44, 56, 116, 149, 151
self-censorship 87
shadows 3, 35, 36, 57, 65, 92, 109, 116, 134
Shagrat 93
Shakespeare, William 41, 69, 78, 50, 125
Shangdi 60, 61, 129, 137
Shanghai People's Press 30–32
Shanhaijing 120
shen (god/soul) 17, 35, 47, 56, 57, 59–61, 64, 66, 67, 70, 74, 78, 79, 119, 135, 158
Shi, Zhongge (Ecthelion) 30, 72, 155
Shippey, Tom 27, 44, 59, 62, 113, 133, 142
Shire 51, 75, 121, 139, 141, 160
shrouds 108, 109

Shuihuzhuan (The Water Margin) 35, 43
Silmarillion, The 11, 26, 32, 35, 36, 38, 45, 58, 61, 80, 107, 113–115, 117, 133, 159
   Deng translations 29
   Yilin translation 26, 101
silmarils 51, 115
Sindar, Sindarin 71, 72, 101, 138, 139, 141
skepticism 4, 8, 10, 40, 46, 47, 52, 85, 95
skin 17, 99
   black 86, 93
   lightening 96
   sallow 86
   white 96, 97
   yellow 86, 95, 96
Smaug 66, 98
smell 11, 112, 121
Smith, J. Z. 40
songs, singing 41, 42, 48, 49, 51, 73, 77, 79, 82, 87, 110, 111, 121, 136, 145, 149, 154, 156, 157, 159
sorcery, sorcerer 36, 56, 57, 65, 69, 92
souls, 5, 17, 65, 79, 100, 103, 106, 107, 109–111, 114, 123, 124
   Chinese terms, 55, 57, 60, 70
   lack of, 79, 95, 113, 98
soup, cauldron of soup 13, 14, 45, 158, 159, 161
Southrons 88, 94, 153
spells, incantations 4, 10, 14, 37, 57, 77, 111, 149, 151, 152, 154–157, 159
Spinoza, Baruch 7
stars 21, 58, 61, 71, 74, 96, 97, 110, 135, 136, 138
subject, grammatical 19, 81, 104, 127–129, 134, 137, 144
subordinate clauses 19, 104
subtitles 33, 34, 161
superstition, *mixin* 7, 42, 46, 157
swarthy men 93
syntax 19, 145

Taiwan 9, 19, 26, 28–33, 35, 38, 41, 43, 45, 51, 90
Teiglin 108
Teng, Joy, *see* Deng, Jiawan
the (definite article) 19, 120, 140–142, 148
theatrical metaphor 48, 51

Théoden 47, 58, 59, 64, 81, 82, 100, 103, 104, 122, 125, 134, 147
TheOneRing.net. xi, 86
thinning 7, 118
Thorin 44, 107, 131, 155
Thror 117
tian (heaven) 61, 64, 66, 79, 117, 119, 120, 123, 129, 132
  Laotian 61, 127, 129
  tianming 126, 127, 132
  Tianzhu 60, 61
time 9, 21, 40, 47, 48, 74, 78, 107, 114, 119, 122, 123, 126, 128, 146, 158, 160
  experience of 76, 77, 85
titles
  of books and chapters 9, 26, 30, 33–38, 47, 125, 140
  of people 61, 82–84, 141, 142
Tolkien, J. R. R. 4–6, 9–15, 18, 19, 23, 26, 27, 34, 37, 38, 40, 41, 44–49, 55, 62, 64, 66, 69–75, 79–82, 84–90, 93–95, 97, 99, 101, 110, 111, 113, 116, 118, 121–123, 125–127, 136–139, 142, 145, 146, 148, 149–152, 155, 156, 159, 160
  as "translator" 58, 138, 143, 160
Tom Bombadil 66, 105, 110, 121, 145, 147
tombs, graves 104, 105, 107–111, 117
tonghua, children's literature 5, 8, 10, 25, 40–42, 45, 46, 69
transfiguration 65
translation 3, 4, 11, 12–20, 22–25, 27–34, 37, 38, 41, 58, 61, 64, 70–72, 78, 79, 81, 84, 90, 137, 138, 143, 145, 148–150, 160, 161
  back-translation xii, 20–24, 59, 77
  formal and dynamic 23
  hierarchy of original and translation 13, 14, 16, 148, 160
  as transference of semantic content 14, 18, 119, 133, 137
  of Western fiction into Chinese 31, 32, 70
transmigration, rebirth 70, 95, 100, 112, 107, 114–116, 119, 123, 124
Treebeard 48, 94, 142, 144, 145
trolls 56, 57, 67, 79, 94, 113, 129, 144
truth, true vs factual 3, 5, 6–10, 12, 16, 23, 27, 34, 159

Tuor 19, 58, 127
Túrin 102, 115, 131, 133, 154

Udun 101
Ugluk 150, 153
Ulmo 58, 66
Utumno 101, 102

Valar 58–63, 65, 66, 79, 88, 96, 98, 109, 113–115, 118, 120
Valarin 138
Valhalla 100, 103, 104
Varda Elentári 61
verbs, conjugation 19, 21, 51, 128, 129, 134, 144, 145, 148
Vink, Renée 98
visions 3, 4, 14, 51, 52, 74, 77, 85, 113, 120, 121, 123, 125, 156, 157

waizhuan (unofficial history) 34
Waley, Arthur 78
wandering 43, 44, 56, 64, 67, 73, 75, 85, 105, 119, 157
Wang, Wei 17, 18
wargs 57, 65, 138, 146, 151
Weinberger, Eliot 17
Wenjing Publishing 29, 30, 32, 145
Westron 138, 141, 143, 150
whiteness 91, 96, 97
wight, see ghosts
willing suspension of disbelief 3–5, 10, 11, 47, 85, 152
witch-king 65, 81–84, 102, 111, 135
witches, witchcraft 27, 36, 37, 56, 63–65, 68, 111, 154
Wittgenstein, Ludwig 11, 14, 15, 21
wizards 40, 57, 63, 66, 67, 68, 97
  Chinese terms 37, 63, 64, 65, 84, 92, 111
word-order 19, 104
wraiths, *see* ghosts.
writing as elven craft 4, 14, 156
wulin ("forest" of martial artists) 43
wupo (witchwife) 64

xia ("knight-errant") 35, 37, 42–45, 154, 161
xian (sylph) 37, 43, 45, 56, 66, 70, 71, 73, 78, 79, 116, 120, 124
xianxia (genre) 43, 45

Xiwangmu (Queen Mother of the West) 76, 120
Xiyouji, Journey to the West 35, 36, 42, 52, 78
xuanhuan (fantasy genre) 45

Yahweh 58, 61, 116, 160
yao (category of monster) 37, 46, 47, 55–57, 65, 67, 78, 92, 110
Yavanna 58
Yeats, William Butler 37, 78
yellow earth 42, 105, 117
Yellow Emperor 90, 96
yellow skin (racial category) 86, 90, 95, 96
yeman ("wild") 72, 63
yes and no 77, 78
yestreday 143
yijiaotu ("heretic") 62, 63
Yilin Press 25, 26, 28, 30, 31, 32
yuan (fated relationship) 127, 132

zhiguai (genre category) 42, 44, 45, 57
zhihuanwang ("lord of the rings") 33, 34, 36
Zhu, Xueheng xii, 20, 25, 26, 28–32, 35

www.ingramcontent.com/pod-product-compliance
Lightning Source LLC
Chambersburg PA
CBHW052120300426
44116CB00010B/1747